THE THEORY AND PRACTICE OF
STATUTORY INTERPRETATION

FRANK B. CROSS

The Theory and Practice of Statutory Interpretation

STANFORD LAW BOOKS

AN IMPRINT OF STANFORD UNIVERSITY PRESS

STANFORD, CALIFORNIA 2009

Stanford University Press
Stanford, California

Printed in the United States of America on acid-free, archival-quality paper

Library of Congress Cataloging-in-Publication Data

Cross, Frank B.
   The theory and practice of statutory interpretation / Frank B. Cross.
     p. cm.
   Includes bibliographical references and index.
   ISBN 978-0-8047-5912-0 (cloth : alk. paper)
   ISBN 978-0-8047-8523-5 (pbk. : alk. paper)
   1. Law—United States—Interpretation and construction.   2. Judicial process—United States.   3. Jurisprudence—United States.   I. Title.
   KF425.C76 2009
   347.73'12—dc22   2008022514

Typeset by Westchester Book Group in 10/14 Janson

Contents

Preface   vii

1. The Goal of Statutory Interpretation   1
2. Textualism and Statutory Interpretation   24
3. Legislative History and Statutory Interpretation   58
4. The Canons of Statutory Interpretation   85
5. Pragmatism and Dynamic Statutory Interpretation   102
6. The Justices and Their Practice of
    Statutory Interpretation   134
7. Ideology and the Practice of Statutory Interpretation   159
8. Statutory Interpretation in the Lower Federal Courts   180

Notes   201
Index   225

Preface

While the most controversial judicial decisions typically involve interpretation of the U.S. Constitution, statutory interpretation is more practically significant. Statutory commands dominate the work of the federal courts today. The thousands of statutes governing our nation are rife with ambiguities. This book examines how the courts should interpret those statutes in the presence of these uncertainties. To the conventional theoretical analysis of these questions, I add empirical research on the practice of different theories of statutory interpretation.

The significance, and difficulty, of statutory interpretation is commonly illustrated by a chestnut of a hypothetical. Suppose a legislative body passes a law banning "vehicles in public parks," in the wake of an auto accident. While the core meaning of this law is pretty clear—private citizens should not drive their cars or trucks through public parks—its periphery can be quite murky. While the law may be phrased in absolute language ("no" vehicles), should it be interpreted to make illegal an ambulance or fire truck responding to an emergency within the park? Other disputes may arise over the definition of "vehicle." Should snowmobiles be prohibited? Bicycles? Baby strollers? Wheelchairs? There is no simple and obvious answer to any of these questions, which is why rules or standards of statutory interpretation are essential.

The difficulties attendant to statutory interpretation are not limited to creative law school hypothetical problems. Congress passed a law imposing a five-year mandatory prison term on a person who "uses or carries a firearm during and in relation to a drug trafficking crime." The core of the statute seems fairly clear, but numerous disputes have arisen on its periphery. In one case that reached the U.S. Supreme Court, a person transported marijuana for illegal sale in his truck and had a handgun locked in the truck's glove compartment. A bare majority of the Court held that the mandatory sentence applied, because the defendant was carrying a firearm in connection with a drug crime.[1] Four justices dissented from the ruling, though, and urged that the statute meant that the firearm be borne "in such a manner as to be ready for use as a weapon," before the mandatory sentence should be applied.[2] In another case, a defendant offered to trade his firearm to an agent posing as a dealer, in exchange for cocaine. A majority of the court again applied the statute, finding that bartering a gun was using a gun, but again multiple justices dissented from the majority's statutory interpretation.[3] Plainly, reasonable-minded justices may disagree over the proper interpretation of this criminal statute.

The presence of such persistent disagreement over statutory meaning is troublesome. If the meaning of statutes, especially criminal statutes, is indeterminate, the very rule of law is called into question. The law seems to be merely a function of the predilections of particular judges, whose decisions may be unpredictable. Legal scholars have struggled for decades to bring some systematic structure to statutory interpretation, but this effort has largely failed. This book does not purport to solve this longstanding problem, but it does attempt to shed light on the facts that must underlie any solution.

Judges in the United States were historically accustomed to employing the common law, which is judge-made and hence easily judge-interpreted, or even judge-changed. As statutory law has grown in importance, judges have struggled somewhat to find the proper interpretive approach. The judiciary obviously feels less free to alter the law created by the elected legislature. Consequently, judges require different theories when resolving statutory disputes than they do for their conventional common law decisions. Unfortunately, the courts have struggled with the process of creating a coherent system for their interpretation of statutes. On this background, I present a review of the theoretical disputes and empirical evidence that informs the discussion.

The first chapter provides an overarching construct for judicial statutory interpretation. While judges have the constitutional authority to interpret statutes, this authority is best viewed as that of an agent of the legislature. The legislative authority itself is constitutionally dedicated to Congress, and statutory interpretation derives from that authority. The court should follow congressional clarity and, in the presence of ambiguity or gaps in the law, adopt the decision that Congress would prefer. However, this latter position is often misunderstood. It may be that Congress would prefer to leave the courts with discretion to "do what is best," rather than prefer a specific outcome. Because Congress cannot anticipate all possible future circumstances, it cannot possibly have substantive preferences for all such outcomes. This delegation theory does not resolve all statutory interpretation disputes, because Congress has not been clear about its interpretive preferences. Understanding the delegation, though, informs the understanding of statutory interpretation. Theories of interpretation must be held up against the delegation construct.

The next four chapters analyze the leading methods and theories of statutory interpretation—textualism, legislative intent, interpretive canons, and pragmatism. Here I review the extensively discussed theoretical arguments underlying each approach. In the process, I dismiss claims that a theory, such as textualism, is constitutionally compelled. Judges have legally authorized choice in interpretation, and the issue is what choice should be made. Central to the analysis, and to this book, is the concern that judges will be willful and outcome oriented in their decisions. This means that they choose the result they prefer and then manipulate the legal materials to support that result. Some theories, especially legislative intent and pragmatism, have been criticized as unduly amenable to this sort of willful judging.

Chapter 6 examines the practice of the Supreme Court justices in over one hundred cases decided during the recent Rehnquist Court. This is commonly considered the age of textualism, but the Court still uses legislative history and other sources with frequency. Although individual justices show different preferences, pluralism plainly prevails at the Court, with the justices using different interpretive methods in different cases. Nor does there appear to be a great conflict between different approaches. This finding might be a sign of effective legal analysis, adapting the interpretive tools to the facts, but it alternatively might be viewed as evidence of dishonesty, adapting legal standards however necessary to reach the justices' preferred ends.

The latter possibility is tested in Chapter 7. Political scientists have conclusively established that the justices are sometimes influenced in their votes by their ideologies. One might think that the invocation of the statute's "plain meaning" could be exempt from this effect, but the data show that this standard is applied in a very ideological fashion. While no theory escapes ideological influence, it was pragmatism that appeared most neutral in its application. The research also finds that use of legislative intent and pragmatism tend to produce more liberal outcomes, regardless of the ideological preferences of the particular justice.

The final chapter briefly considers lower court statutory interpretation. While lower courts must obey Supreme Court directions, the Supreme Court has given no clear orders on the appropriate method of statutory interpretation. A study of recent history reveals that legislative history use in the circuit courts has declined dramatically (much more than at the Supreme Court level), while textualism and pragmatism have boomed. I considered the precedential effect of the Supreme Court opinions studied in the prior two chapters and found that reliance on textualism produced far more citations than for other theories, though pragmatic interpretation also had more citations. The greatest statistical effect of textualism, though, was found in negative citations, which distinguish or decline to apply the Supreme Court's holding. This casts some doubt on the clarity and value of textualist interpretive methods.

The book is ambitiously titled the theory and practice of statutory interpretation because both are important to addressing disputes over statutory interpretation. In typical social scientific study, one begins with a theory and then tests it against practice. The statutory interpretation debate has been consumed with competing theories, with relatively little examination of how those theories operate in practice. Yet the latter examination is crucial in order to evaluate the theories. My research shows that at least some presumptions of the theoreticians appear to be wrong. No theory is exempt from the risk of ideological willful judging, and pragmatism is the theory that was associated with the least outcome orientation.

THE THEORY AND PRACTICE OF
STATUTORY INTERPRETATION

CHAPTER I

The Goal of Statutory Interpretation

The goal of statutory interpretation should be central to understanding its theory and practice. Unfortunately, there is no consensus about the proper goal of this interpretive enterprise, either politically or legally. Fortunately, consensus is unnecessary for purposes of this book. However, it remains important to understand the goal of statutory interpretation in order to evaluate the different theories set forth in the book. Practices and consequences cannot be appreciated in the abstract, especially given the concern about unconstrained willful ideological discretion of the judiciary. Consequently, this chapter sets forth, relatively briefly, the theories about the appropriate purpose of judicial interpretation of statutes.

The judicial power, including that of statutory interpretation, derives from the Constitution. The Constitution, however, does not provide much guidance on the relevant question. It simply "leaves statutory interpretation to be resolved by the 'judicial power' without specifying how that interpretation should be conducted."[1] No provision "sets out explicit instructions to

1

judges about the limits of interpretive flexibility."[2] The Constitution leaves us with only the broad principle that statutory interpretation should be a "judicial" exercise, which leaves considerable discretion about the proper nature of judging the application of statutes in individual cases. Various leading scholars have claimed that their proposed interpretive method is constitutionally inspired, or even required, but they have reached this same conclusion in support of different approaches. While some substantive interpretive canons, discussed in Chapter 4, have an apparent constitutional provenance, there is no accepted general thesis of constitutionally directed statutory interpretation.

Historically, the dispute over the goal of statutory interpretation has largely been drawn between those who believe that judges should hew closely to their assessment of what the legislature intended, based upon all available evidence of that intent, and those who think that the purpose is simply to give effect to the statutory language adopted by the legislature and eschew consideration of extrinsic evidence about the legislature's intent. This dispute is closely bound up with the interpretive theories of each school, and it will be explicated further in succeeding chapters. Those who believe that the purpose of the process is to discern intent commonly argue for consideration of legislative history, while those who would limit interpretation to language are of the textualist school. A third purpose has also emerged, which contends that interpretation should be guided by a concern for the best policy consequences under the circumstances. This is generally considered the pragmatic approach to interpretation, which uses its own discretionary standards.

The debate over the proper purpose of statutory interpretation has lasted for many decades. The Supreme Court has cycled among different purposes at different times. While one approach or another has gained ascendancy for a time, it has eventually lost this position. None of the theories have knocked out competing theories. For most of our history, the different theories have coexisted. This book does not purport to resolve the proper theoretical basis for statutory interpretation, but it is important to understand these theories, as their application is examined and evaluated.

This introductory chapter first sets forth the overall theoretical construct for statutory interpretation disputes. The interpretive role of courts should be seen, I contend, as an exercise of power delegated by the legislature. The courts should view themselves as agents who do the bidding of Congress in their interpretations of congressional statutes. Next, I review the major interpretive theories and how they may fit within this delegation scheme. Finally, I summarize the overriding issue of faithless judicial ideological decision making, which pervades the debate over interpretive methods and is discussed throughout the book.

Statutory Interpretation as Delegated Power

Before examining the competing purposes for statutory interpretation, it is important to address its context. Congress passes statutes but does not apply them to individual cases; the judiciary is in charge of that task in our constitutional model. In statutory interpretation cases, judges are applying the legislation passed by Congress. Consequently, judges are often viewed as fiduciaries, or agents, of the legislature. Thus, "[m]ost academic theories of statutory interpretation, and perhaps all judicial ones, see judges as agents of Congress."[3] This is the theory of legislative supremacy in the statutory sphere.

Legally, judges are not true delegatees but have their own independent constitutional interpretive authority that is not derivative of the legislature. The Constitution invests the judicial power in the judiciary, and this serves as its authority to interpret statutes when deciding cases. However, this declaration begs the question of what the "judicial power" means. The judicial power is not that of arbitrary decision making nor that of legislating. The delegation theory suggests that viewing themselves as legislative agents when interpreting statutes is the proper understanding of how judicial power should be exercised.

In this schema, the legislature is the principal and the courts are its agent, analogous to private agency relationships. A corporation, for example, relies on individual officers and employees to carry out its business. The law recognizes the corporation as a principal and the officers as its agents, who are delegated authority to advance the interests of the corporate principal. Because the corporation and its directors are unable themselves to make every day-to-day managerial decision to carry out their broad business policies, they provide this authority to others through delegation. This delegation may provide more or less discretion to an agent. The agent may have broad authority to take action, as in the case of a legal power of attorney, or quite limited authority to take only a given action or actions below a certain monetary threshold. Moreover, there is some residuum of authority that cannot be delegated to officers but must be reserved for the board of directors, under corporate law.

Analogously, the legislature is like a board of directors that sets national policy but delegates its implementation. The executive branch is somewhat like the officers of the corporation, in its actions applying the law. The federal judiciary has a separate constitutional authority, but its ability to exercise that authority is often governed by the legislature, which has some jurisdictional control and, more significantly, adopts the laws that the judiciary is to interpret. The legislature lacks the resources to control the case-by-case interpretation and application of those laws, and this is the judicial power delegated to the judiciary by statutes.

William Eskridge has argued that legislation by its very nature "delegates policy-making authority to agencies and courts."[4] A major article by Matthew Stephenson examines the delegation issue in an elaborate form.[5] He reviews the evidence of delegation and specifically analyzes why legislatures delegate some questions to courts but others to agencies of the executive branch and notes that courts exhibit more stability over time and more ideological heterogeneity across issues. Of course, courts have the authority to review agency actions, so any delegation to agencies ultimately transfers some authority to the courts. Indeed, Congress uses courts to monitor and control abuses of its delegation to agencies though legislation such as the Administrative Procedures Act.

The delegation context has been extensively explored in the context of administrative agencies. One major theoretical construct is based on the assumption that constituents care less about the details of policy than about their effectiveness.[6] Legislators will delegate more authority to bureaucrats, on this theory, when they believe that bureaucratic expertise will yield better policy outcomes. Congress "often lacks the knowledge it needs to obtain desired policy outcomes."[7] Because Congress has such a broad agenda and legislative action is so costly, it is difficult for the legislature to monitor and modify its statutes in light of their practical effect in particular applications. Agencies, though, have a better ability to perform this ongoing function.

Although ideologically the agency will not align perfectly with the legislature, the common interest in successful policy outcomes may overcome any such differences.[8]

Epstein and O'Halloran's classic work on such agency delegation notes that a reason "that bureaucracies are created in the first place is to implement policies in areas where Congress has neither the time nor the expertise to micromanage policy decisions."[9] They hypothesize that legislators will delegate more where a policy area is complex and informationally intensive. Epstein and O'Halloran then constructed a quantitative index for the extent of statutory delegation to federal agencies. They analyzed the extent of degrees of discretion in different statutes over time and found that the magnitude of discretionary delegation to agencies varied slightly with the executive branch's political alignment and that greater delegation existed in complex areas.

As Stephenson notes, the decision to delegate to courts parallels that of agency delegation, though his theory is not complete. Some have theorized that delegation to courts is riskier for Congress than delegation to agencies, because judicial independence gives the legislature less control over judicial decisions. In some ways, delegation to courts may be less risky, though, because the judiciary contains many different judges with many different ideological preferences, in contrast to an executive branch largely under the control of a single president. Moreover, judicial decisions are made on a case-by-case basis rather than a top-down determination by a national agency in the form of a rule. The advantages of this process are discussed in Chapter 5. In any event, this book is not about the delegation choice of agencies versus courts. It is about the legislative decision to delegate decision-making discretion to courts by using more ambiguous statutory language or leaving gaps in the statute to be filled by judicial application. The next section describes the distinct types of legislative delegation.

Types of Delegation

The legislative delegation to courts takes two distinct forms. The first might be called "background delegation." No matter how precisely Congress may attempt to draft, it is humanly impossible to foresee every future circumstance.

H. L. A. Hart suggested that hard cases arose from the legislature's "inability to anticipate" future circumstances.[10] Judge Posner has noted that the realities of the legislative process make it unrealistic for Congress to consider "fully the potential application of their words to novel settings."[11] James Madison himself wrote that "[a]ll new laws, though penned with the greatest technical skill and passed on the fullest and most mature deliberation, are considered as more or less obscure and equivocal."[12] Some cases will arise that fall through the cracks, or interstices, of the statutory language. Statutes remain on the books indefinitely while society changes around them. They will constantly be applied to new circumstances which may not even have existed at the time of their passage. With these new circumstances not being clearly governed by the statutory language, the court must nevertheless somehow interpret the language to rule on the case. The delegation construct means that the court should do so with an eye to what the legislature might have intended for the case, had it known of those circumstances.

The second form might be called "direct delegation." This involves the legislature affirmatively delegating decision-making authority to the courts. In this case, the legislature purposely leaves issues unresolved in the statutory language, issues that must be settled by courts applying that language to particular disputes. Such direct delegation may arise for a variety of reasons. It may be that Congress could not reach agreement on precise language and, rather than abandon the legislation in toto, chose to leave the statutory lacuna.[13] The Supreme Court recently concluded that in passing the 1991 Civil Rights Act, the members of Congress simply "agreed to disagree about whether and to what extent the Act applies to preenactment conduct."[14] Hence, they left the issue unresolved for the courts to settle. Alternatively, it may be that Congress thought that government policy reflected in statute could be better made by the case-by-case development of law than by setting a "one size fits all" uniform national statutory rule. Cynics might suggest that such broad direct delegation reflects "lack of will: Congress may recognize a potentially divisive issue but decide to finesse the issue with ambiguous or incomplete language."[15] Some consider this an inappropriate form of delegation, an attempt to escape accountability for legislative determinations. In this event, greater interpretive discretion suits the ends of Congress. Yet another reason might be the enlistment of court power in monitoring the actions of the executive branch.

An obvious example of such direct delegation is found in the 1980 adoption of the Comprehensive Environmental Response Compensation and Liability Act (CERCLA), the federal Superfund statute. This law, of great economic and environmental importance, was hastily adopted by Congress and contained many unresolved gaps in application. One plain example of delegation was the question of the joint and several liabilities of CERCLA defendants. The original bill provided for such liability, but the provision was deleted from the final bill. The deletion was not accompanied by an alternative standard, though, and Congress openly left the resolution of the liability apportionment question to the courts that would apply the law. Another gap in CERCLA involved the standards for causation that would govern liability under the statute, which the Congress did not directly define. The same was true of many important contested issues such as the liability of parent and successor corporations under the act. Indeed, CERCLA's legislative history indicates that Congress intended to have some issues about the scope of liability determined under common law principles, the application of which was explicitly endorsed in the legislative history of the Superfund Amendments and Reauthorization Act (SARA), which amended CERCLA. CERCLA provides an example of substantial direct delegation of decision-making authority to courts.

This process of legislative delegation to the courts was closely studied in the context of federal labor law.[16] This study analyzes direct delegation and how "legislators sometimes deliberately include ambiguous language in statutes that allows judges to make policy choices as they resolve interpretive controversies about the meaning of the ambiguous language."[17] Examination of labor laws, such as the Wagner Act, Clayton Act, and Erdman Act, revealed that legislators carefully avoided creating precise rules but delegated many controversial decisions to the courts, even though Congress foresaw those controversies. Not entirely pleased with the courts' resolution of those issues, the legislature later adopted clearer linguistic requirements in the Norris-LaGuardia Act to limit the courts' choices. The history demonstrated how the legislature titrated judicial discretion based on the circumstances of the legislation it addressed.

A more recent study of the Private Securities Litigation Reform Act also illustrated direct delegation.[18] In attempting to tighten judicial standards for securities fraud actions, Congress focused on requirements for plaintiffs pleading the *scienter* standard for liability. Congress resolved that plaintiffs be forced to plead facts demonstrating a "strong inference" of *scienter* but said little about precisely what this meant. The study of the act's passage demonstrated that the record was replete with contradictory positions on the meaning of the standard and ultimately ducked the issue, leaving it to the courts to flesh out the statutory standard with meaning.

The statute books are replete with examples of broad delegation to agencies and courts. Consider the authority of the Federal Communications Commission to grant licenses in the "public convenience, interest, or necessity" without elaboration on the interpretation of those very broad words. The legislature sometimes uses simply the "public interest" as its governing rule. Professor Richard Pierce estimates that nearly all the congressional delegations to agencies are statutes with broad goals and broadly delegated discretion.[19]

While most of the public controversy is about direct delegation, background delegation may be the even more significant issue. The courts decide thousands of statutory cases every year, and many more are settled in anticipation of court action. Innumerable circumstances involve statutory application in the shadow of the law that never results in a case filing. When the statute is clear, there is little reason to litigate, expending attorneys' fees in pursuit of a foregone conclusion. It is precisely the disputes where the law is unclear that result in litigation. Each dispute that produces a legal case involves unique facts and, with hundreds of millions of Americans, a wide range of factual settings will arise. Moreover, those factual settings will inevitably change over time as society changes. This inevitably means that even the most precisely crafted statute cannot anticipate and linguistically resolve all the disputes that arise under the act.

A crucial question for the judiciary regards *what* is being delegated. By their nature, courts adjudicate disputes and in the process must apply statutes. To apply a statute, a court must interpret its meaning in the context of a particular case or controversy. While this interpretation of statutory language may be simple, that is not typically the case. Sometimes the statutory language simply does not resolve the dispute. Just as with private delegation, the courts have certain authority to interpret, authority which might be exceeded by an erroneous interpretation. A court may exceed its authority by creating statutory provisions not included in the act's language or misuse its authority through self-dealing, such as giving a meaning to a law contrary to that of the legislature, because it is preferred by the ruling judge.

The legitimate nature of this delegation and consequent judicial application is hotly debated. Some dispute the magnitude of the role of courts in statutory interpretation and contend that the legislature has illegitimately delegated legislative power to the judiciary when it engages in direct delegation. This argument typically reduces to a semantic debate over the meaning of "legislative" and "interpretation," however. Everyone agrees that courts can interpret but not write legislation. At its most extreme level, the delegation theory seems objectionable—Congress could not simply pass a bill that did no more than direct the courts to criminalize objectionable behavior. But Congress has not, and presumably would not, choose to delegate such untrammeled authority to the separate branch of the judiciary. The dispute is over the scope of the meaning of interpretation as opposed to legislation, and I join this debate in greater detail in subsequent chapters.

It is in this context of delegation that disputes over statutory interpretation must be analyzed, but delegation does not resolve the dispute. When Congress delegates, it may intend that courts use evidence of its underlying legislative intent in application or it may have preferred that courts used the principles of textualism and the long-established canons of interpretation. Alternatively, the legislature may have contemplated a broader delegation for courts to use pragmatic policy concerns in their interpretation, akin to the common law, which is judge-made. Congress has made no formal declaration of the proper interpretive method, though. This absence may well reflect a delegation of the proper interpretive method to the judiciary as well or reveal a pluralist preference, that judges use the method best suited to the circumstances of the cases that they decide. Congress is perfectly capable of giving interpretive instruction for particular statutes or more generally but does not do so, preferring to delegate the interpretive question to the judiciary. This leaves open the question of what method judges *should* use in their case-by-case statutory interpretations. A grant of interpretive discretion to the courts does not mean that it is unbounded or cannot be improperly exercised by deciding courts.

Legislative Intent

Those devoted to legislative intent believe that the judges should be the faithful fiduciaries of the enacting legislature and adhere to what that legislature "meant." They believe that judges should adjudicate cases and reach the outcomes that the legislature would have chosen, had it foreseen the specific facts of the case before the court. In the early days of our republic, Chief Justice Marshall embraced this theory, announcing that it is "the duty of the court to effect the intention of the legislature."[20] At that time, though, statutes were relatively few and did not make up the bulk of the Court's docket. The question of the purpose behind statutory interpretation has evolved considerably since that time. However, for the first two centuries of our nation's jurisprudence, the intentionalist goal of statutory interpretation generally ruled.[21]

Some have referred to this intentionalist approach to interpretation as "imaginative reconstruction."[22] It attempts to reconstruct what an earlier legislature would have thought of the facts presented in the contemporary adjudication. The renowned circuit court judge Learned Hand, explained the process as telling a judge to "try to think his way as best he can into the minds of the enacting legislators and imagine how they would have wanted the statute applied to the case at bar."[23] Legislative history and intentionalism has been cited as a tool for addressing background delegation as a measure of discerning "what the words can be made to bear, in making sense in light of the unforeseen."[24] The General Accounting Office (GAO), itself a branch of Congress, has declared that the "goal of statutory construction is simply stated: to determine and give effect to the intent of the enacting legislature."[25]

The foundational criticism of focusing on legislative intent is the claim that no such intent even exists, sometimes called the "social choice" critique. The GAO has itself conceded that the concept of legislative intent "is in many cases a fiction."[26] It goes on to note that tools for statutory interpretation in pursuit of such intent serve "the essential purpose of providing a common basis for problem-solving."[27] The GAO suggests that in the absence of a perfect approach for statutory construction, the accepted methods of seeking intent work in practice. This argument is explored further in Chapter 2.

Another basis for criticizing legislative intent as the polestar of statutory interpretation is its indeterminacy. Critics question the ability of courts to identify and implement a legislative intent, assuming that it exists. William Eskridge suggests that the actual intent of the legislature is "unknowable."[28] Of course, "knowability" is not a binary concept. One can approach an understanding of legislative intent with greater or lesser reliability. One oft-expressed concern is that parties may manipulate the apparent legislative intent to favor positions not chosen by Congress, and it is essential that courts be able to discern such action.

It might superficially seem that the legislative intent approach is most faithful to delegation because it envisions the courts as the agent of the legislature. This is not necessarily the case. No one has demonstrated that the legislature *wants* the courts to rely on legislative intent. The delegating legislature might well prefer that the courts limit their consideration to the text of the statute or expand their consideration to the policy consequences of their decisions. A principal, in its own self-interest, may wish to constrain or free an agent's discretion, and it merely begs the question to presume that the principal wants the agent to follow its own view of the principal's intent, rather than using some other standard. Conceivably, the legislature might clear up this problem by adopting a statute that directs the courts' interpretive discretion. Some have proposed just this answer, but Congress has adopted no such statute and there are some questions about the constitutionality of its doing so.

"Rule of Law" Statutory Text

The primary opponents of focus on legislative intent argue for the "rule of law," by which they mean the text of the statute itself. The "words of the statute, and not the intent of the drafters, are the 'law.' "[29] Some adherents to this view reject "the faithful agent model and instead adopt a model of courts as autonomous interpreters who seek answers to questions of statutory meaning through application of the ordinary reader perspective, supplemented by various judge-made rules of interpretation."[30] Others, though, argue that textualist interpretation is the best means of being a faithful agent of Congress. Professor Manning calls the approach a superior "basis for implementing legislative supremacy."[31]

A foundation of the "rule of law" statutory language approach is constitutional. John Manning argues that the "semantic integrity" of a statute must take precedence over giving it "coherence."[32] This, he argues is implicit in legislative supremacy and the constitutional procedures for legislating. Textualists have also raised other reasons why their interpretive theory is constitutionally compelled under the rule of law, and I will address these in Chapter 2.

However, the exclusive focus on statutory language proves both too much and too little. It proves too little in the sense that no one disagrees that text should be of central importance when interpreting statutes. In this sense, it proves only the obvious. It proves too much in the sense that it may not help resolve the truly difficult interpretive issues. These are cases in which the statutory text provides no obvious answer, as evident from the examples of statutory delegation discussed above. While textualists have various techniques for extracting meaning from ambiguous words, the theory that the rule of law commands those techniques, as opposed to others, is not obvious. Textualists typically do not claim that their methodology is perfect but only that it is comparably preferable, but this too requires proof.

Declaring that giving effect to the "rule of law" should be the primary purpose of statutory interpretation is not meaningless. There are cases where an interpreting court has seemingly disregarded apparently clear text in favor of a contrary intentionalist approach, but these cases are few. The focus on statutory language has importance in these cases but does not address the great bulk of statutory interpretation questions. While a purely theoretical case has been made for the statutory text purpose, its main justification is a more consequentialist one involving the constraint of the judiciary, discussed below and throughout this book.

The "rule of law" statutory language purpose might seem inconsistent with the delegation context, in its disregard of the principal's underlying intent (though there remains the possibility that this *was* the interpretive intent of the legislature). But for devotees this is unproblematic in any event. Our principal, the legislature, is not all powerful in the American system and is bound by the Constitution. Consequently, it is not free to delegate any interpretive standard that it might choose. The bicameralism/presentment argument contends that the legislature may delegate no interpretive rule other than the "rule of law" one. The true principal, in this vision, is the Constitution itself. In addition, a rational legislative principal might prefer this standard for delegation to the judiciary, believing that it best fulfills its purposes.

Reliance on text, rather than searching for intent, might be a surer guide to that intent.

Pragmatic Policy

A third purpose for statutory interpretation is the pragmatic or "best policy" standard, which has been analogized to practical reason. The approach is said to rely on a "less structured problem-solving process involving common sense, respect for precedent, and a sense for society's needs.[33] This approach views the judiciary as a partner with the legislature in the nation's governance, capable of making independent determinations of sound outcomes or even correcting the flaws of the legislative process. Pragmatism may come in varying strengths, from assuming the power to declare old laws null and void to claiming a more modest power to adapt legal language to the circumstances of cases in a way that makes the most sense to the judiciary.

Justice Holmes, often regarded as a pragmatist, famously rejected the stronger interpretive tenets of pragmatism, declaring, "if my fellow citizens want to go to Hell I will help them."[34] For the modern pragmatist, this conclusion is not self-evident. Perhaps judges should play a role in protecting the citizenry from going to hell. Pragmatism is generally informed by statutory text or legislative history. Pragmatism does not ignore the text or statutory background, an ignoring that might itself be unpragmatic, but adds an additional consideration. Many pragmatists place great importance on statutory text, especially insofar as it may direct the compliance decisions of the private parties who appear in court. However, neither text nor evidence of legislative intent is considered a dispositive source of information. A pragmatist will look further, to the societal consequences of different interpretations, before choosing one. This is something like the approach of the common law, where courts ask the question: "What is the best legal policy choice?"[35] Courts do not openly ask this question in connection with statutory interpretation, but pragmatists suggest that perhaps they should do so more often. In this view, the courts are inevitably "supplemental lawmakers" as they apply and flesh out statutory language, and pragmatism simply recognizes this reality.[36]

Employing judges as pragmatic partners in governance has some theoretical benefits. A legislating body can at best create general rules, based on the inevitably limited information at the time it acts. Judge Posner has observed that a "statute necessarily is drafted in advance of, and with imperfect appreciation for the problems that will be encountered in, its application."[37] Courts are presented with a variety of circumstances applying the statute, including the unforeseen. It is judges who directly witness how the law works in practice and where it may fail to work. As the course of litigation proceeds, judges accumulate additional knowledge about a law's functioning. They are in an institutional position that enables them to adapt the law to differing case facts and, at least in theory, optimize its effects.

Advocates of pragmatic statutory interpretation cite a number of other advantages of the judiciary, which are discussed in more detail in Chapter 5. Central to the theory is the judicial exercise of pragmatic or "practical wisdom" in applying the statute to the facts of the case before the judge. Facially, the theory seems to grant much greater decision-making discretion to the judge. This seems to involve a transfer of legal power from the legislature to the judiciary.

Pragmatism seems most removed from the delegation context of statutory interpretation, because it assumes considerable policy-making discretion for the courts. One might reasonably be skeptical of agents who assume great discretion to depart from the apparent directions of their principal. Pragmatists often present their theory as more of a partnership of institutions, rather than an agency relationship. This has been expressed vividly in a nautical metaphor of the process:

> Congress builds a ship and charts its initial course, but the ship's ports-of-call, safe harbors and ultimate destination may be a product of the ship's captain, the weather, and other factors not identified at the time the ship sets sail. This model understands a statute as an on-going process (a voyage) in which both the shipbuilder and subsequent navigators play a role. The dimensions and structure of the craft determine where it is capable of going, but the current course is set primarily by the crew on board.[38]

Likening Congress to a shipbuilder may give too little credit to Congress, which may be more like the ship's owner, who may determine its destination.

The nautical metaphor is still illuminating, though, because a ship's owner will choose to delegate considerable discretion to its crew, with respect to the path to the destination. When weather conditions make the mission unduly dangerous, a wise captain would even delegate the authority to the crew to abandon the mission to the destination. Professor Vermeule has thus noted that "[s]ensible legislators might have a higher-order preference that judges be not only faithful agents but also intelligent ones, updating primary legislative instructions over time to accomplish legislative purposes."[39]

A classic example of this may be found in the Sherman Act, which was essentially a grant "of authority to the federal courts to make common law" of antitrust.[40] The statutory text of the law is quite abbreviated and has been called "essentially devoid of content."[41] As such, it appears to be a broad delegation of discretionary authority to the judiciary. In the statute "Congress in effect delegated most of its lawmaking power to the judicial branch."[42] In applying the law's vague language, judges have typically evaluated a number of policy concerns, with the most recent a heavy emphasis on economic theory. This plainly seems to be the creation of a lawmaking partnership with the judiciary.

Even the conventional partnership concept of pragmatism is not inconsistent with an agency structure of statutory interpretation, however. Partners are legal agents of one another. It is certainly plausible that a legislature might wish to grant broad discretion to its agents, or partners. Legislation, at its best, is not a combat between ideological opponents but instead a sincere search for the best governing rules for our society. A conscious legislature might easily understand that it cannot foresee all future developments affected by its statute and might therefore wish to grant a trusted judicial agent the discretion to adapt its commands to the circumstances of an adjudication. If so, pragmatism fits neatly within the delegation context. Martin Redish distinguishes statutory interpretation asking "what did the legislature intend?" from common law asking "what is the best policy choice?"[43] This distinction artificially presumes that the legislature did not intend for courts to rely on the best policy choice when interpreting statutes.

The plausibility of such delegation of discretion is evidenced by the analogous law of contracts. Parties draft contract text, much as a legislature might draft statutory text. In the course of so doing, they have a choice between very specific clear rules to be applied by a court and vaguer standards that provide considerable room for a court's discretionary judgment. Both are used, and broad delegation of discretion through standards is common.[44] Contracts typically contain "missing provisions and ambiguous clauses" because of the difficulty of anticipating the future, negotiation costs, and "thinking costs."[45] Legislation shows a similar pattern of differential delegation of discretion for similar reasons.[46] Moreover, contracts often delegate their resolution to arbitrators who need not even follow the law in resolving disputes and whose decisions are unappealable. This is a plain indication that the efficient decision may be delegation of decision making to a *post facto* neutral third party with the discretion to choose the most suitable outcome of the particular dispute.

Pragmatism is subject to its own criticisms, however. Not least of these is the concern that freeing judges to make policy would contravene their role as agents and render them principals, making choices best left to the legislature. Ample research demonstrates that judges are predisposed to their own ideological inclinations about proper outcomes and render decisions accordingly. In addition, there is a developed argument that judges are ill-suited to effectively make the necessary pragmatic decisions. Once again, we are left with uncertainty about the precise authority they have been legislatively delegated.

Preference Elicitation

Another theory of interpretation bears at least brief mention. Einer Elhauge has argued that statutory interpretation should be designed so as to elicit the true preferences of the legislature.[47] The theory clearly respects legislative supremacy and is a form of the Court's forward delegation to future legislators. He argues that courts should decide cases in the manner preferred by the contemporaneous legislature or in a manner best able to elicit the preferences of the contemporaneous legislature via statutory modification. The theory is a dynamic one in its concern for contemporary rather than enacting legislatures.

This preference elicitation theory has not been explicitly embraced by the Court or by most of the commentators. However, Professor Elhauge has argued that the approach in fact can explain the outcome of a number of Supreme Court decisions. These opinions are all justified on other grounds, though, and I will not treat the theory with the same significance as those traditional methods on which the Court has more explicitly relied. The theory does provide a good complement with dynamic, pragmatic approaches and it will be considered in that context.

Interpretive Pluralism

It is not theoretically necessary for judges to adopt a single uniform theory of interpretation and apply it universally. Rather, a judge may embrace all the available tools as theoretically legitimate and selectively employ those that are best suited for the particular case. Justice Holmes thus declared that "every question of construction is unique, and an argument that would prevail in one case may be inadequate in another."[48] Evidence of such appropriate pluralism may be found in an earlier study showing that the justices used legislative history at very differential rates for different statutes being analyzed.[49] Thus, sometimes a judge may privilege the text and associated materials, while in other cases the judge might find that legislative history or pragmatic considerations call for a departure from the apparent textual meaning. Such pluralism is a form of judicial self-delegation that authorizes judicial discretion in interpretive method. This delegation may conform to legislative delegation, as a survey of congressional staffers found that no monolithic theory reflected the legislative process.[50]

Pluralism recognizes that different approaches may be best suited to different types of statutory authorizations. Professors Eskridge and Ferejohn have thus argued that Congress occasionally passes "superstatutes" to achieve broad purposes. Such statutes, they argue, are meant to be applied pragmatically, to "generate a dynamic common law implementing its great principle and adapting the statute to meet the challenges posed to that principle by a complex society."[51] If these statutes are suited to pragmatic interpretation, other statutes with better defined, technical requirements might call for another approach, though, such as textualism.

While a great deal has been written on the rise and fall of various theories over time, pluralism predominates in practice, at least in recent history. Few judges limit themselves to a single interpretive tool, and many do not even strongly privilege one approach. Some, such as Justice Scalia, are adamant in their criticism of reliance upon legislative history but still occasionally supplement textualism with more dynamic pragmatic concerns or purposivism. Chapter 6 provides some evidence of this effect on the Rehnquist Court.

Pluralism may be criticized for its unpredictability. Nicholas Rosenkranz argued that "[a]s theories and judges have multiplied, it has become ever more difficult to predict which judge will apply which theory to which case."[52] He adds that the "interpretive status quo is cacophonous."[53] This situation has been lamented as something of a judicial power grab, undermining legislative supremacy. How is Congress to effect its preferences through legislation when it has no idea how its words will be interpreted in future cases? In the delegation context, though, this does not follow. Perhaps Congress wants the courts to adapt its statutes through pluralist interpretation. Rosenkranz suggests that Congress dictate the interpretive standards to be used by courts, but the fact that it has not seriously attempted to do so suggests that the federal legislature is happy with the purportedly cacophonous status quo. Moreover, pluralism in practice is not anarchic. Judges generally have a "familiar framework for analysis and a stable set of concepts and tools that they use in explaining their statutory interpretation decisions."[54]

Pluralism is not strictly an interpretive theory parallel to the others discussed above. Reliance on pluralist alternatives conveys considerable discretion to judges, in reliance on their ability to discern the best interpretive method for particular cases. Yet I will discuss how the relative use of different methods has fluctuated considerably over time. There is no reason to believe that the facts of the underlying cases varied systematically over time in a manner that would justify these shifts. Perhaps the greatest concern over pluralism is the degree of discretion it accords to judges and the fear that they will use this authority to advance their own goals at the expense of those of the legislature.

The delegation construct does not clearly resolve the dispute over methods of statutory interpretation. Assuming that the goal is to have the courts be agents of the legislature, the obvious reconciliation of the different interpretive methodologies would be to ascertain the approach the legislature wanted the courts to use. If the goal is the judicial exercise of power in a manner preferred by the legislature, it is important to know what manner is preferred. The fact that the legislature has not generally attempted to dictate interpretive practices or complained much of judicial interpretation indicates that the prevailing pluralist methods of the judiciary do not badly violate the agency relationship. The legislative principal appears relatively satisfied.

While the national legislature has not addressed the interpretive questions, some state legislatures have done so. Minnesota, for example, has declared by law that the "object of all interpretation and construction of laws is to ascertain and effectuate the intention of the legislature." The state law first directs that clear textual language is primary. However, if the words are not explicitly clear, the law directs consideration of a laundry list of pluralist guides. These include the "contemporaneous legislative history." Courts are also directed to consider the pragmatic question of the "consequences of a particular interpretation." Minnesota, at least, consciously makes a broad delegation of interpretive discretion to its judiciary.

There are some occasional indications of legislative dissatisfaction with judicial interpretations, in the context of legislative overrides. Occasionally, judges interpret a statute in a given way, and Congress promptly responds by amending the statute to compel a different interpretation. This is at least a hint of a judicial error in the first instance, but not necessarily evidence of any judicial faithlessness in interpretation. The judicial decision may instead be a simple error, analogous to mismanagement rather than fraud.

However, much of the debate over interpretive methodologies involves assertions of willful action tantamount to fraud. The discussion often involves a mistrust of the judges making case-by-case interpretive decisions. Commentators fear that judges will manipulate given theories to reach results compatible with their own ideological policy preferences, rather than acting as honest legislative agents. Expunging all judicial preferences from decision making is surely a fool's errand, but its role may be moderated. It seems probable that the legislature prefers its own preferences, expressed in the statute, to those of the presiding judges. Hence, a crucial issue in the debate is the degree to which the theories cabin this judicial discretion.

The Key Issue: Ideological Judicial Decision Making

While much ink has been spilt on the theoretical underpinnings of statutory interpretation, a great deal of the debate largely comes down to a nontheoretical matter—the discretion accorded by the theories to the interpreting

courts. The debate centers on the amount of discretion accorded the interpreting courts and about which theories best constrain or free the courts to
exercise the optimal amount of discretion. The concern for judicial discretion is animated centrally by a concern over ideological, extralegal judicial
decision making, where judges impose their wills on the litigating parties, in
disregard of the law written by Congress. In the presence of ideological decision making, there is a fear that courts will overrule legislative preferences
and resolve disputes that were not authentically delegated to them by Congress. This concern is generally expressed by textualists, but it hovers over
the entire dispute.

The issue of concern for ideological decision making is a legitimate one.
When a judge is granted decision-making discretion, he or she may be inclined to reach his or her preferred ideological outcome. If a statute is conservative, a liberal judge may have a dislike for the statute itself. In this
circumstance, an ideological liberal judge might disregard the statute and do
what he or she deems "best" in the case. Such an action goes beyond proper
judging and transforms the judge into a legislator, or worse. Within our
agency context, there is generally little reason to believe that Congress would
choose to empower judges to apply their personal ideologies, and the Constitution implicitly rejects such a broad judicial exercise of power as well.

Concern over ideological judicial decision making is not new. Critics
have long lamented "willful" judicial decision making according to the
judges' preferences rather than the materials of the law. Judicial activism is a
common lament, often voiced in constitutional adjudication but likewise
relevant to statutory interpretation. Claims of activism essentially maintain
that unelected judges are privileging their preferences over those of the enacting legislature and acting as faithless agents.

Political scientists have conducted considerable research that supports
the concern for ideological judicial decision making. The best known and
most comprehensive of these studies has been performed at the Supreme
Court level.[55] This research has shown a very significant association between ideology and judicial votes. Segal and Spaeth's seminal investigation
of ideological, or attitudinal, voting at the Supreme Court broke down the
accuracy of their predictions in various issue areas and found that the ideological model did not predict outcomes in numerous statutory areas (including antitrust, bankruptcy, ERISA, intellectual property, areas of regulation,

and taxation).[56] Even the extensive and persuasive studies of ideological decision making at the Supreme Court have not shown that ideology exclusively drives decision making, as they have a considerable residual of decisions unexplained by the theory. While different ideologies apparently explain the majority of differences among the votes of justices, they predict only a minority of the overall votes of the justices. Studies of ideological decision making have generally focused on constitutional matters, but there is no reason to question that the influence also extends to statutory cases.

The finding of empirical regularities, characterized as ideological judging, do not necessarily yield any reliable conclusions about the internal thought processes or intentions of the justices. If there is ideological judging, it need not be the product of conscious manipulation but may demonstrate only the more innocent practice of subconscious motivated reasoning.[57] Regardless of whether the bias is a conscious or subconscious one, most agree that the ideological effect should be restrained. Fundamental to the notion of the rule of law is the fact that it is the law, and not the personality of the interpreter, that should dictate outcomes. The key issue therefore is what legal principles may best restrain ideological decision making, and one need not attribute affirmative dishonesty to the judiciary.

For some, such as the devotees of critical legal studies, any attempt to constrain judicial ideology is hopeless. The empirical evidence does not support such a strong claim, however. Such research has found that the establishment of a significant precedent has an effect on subsequent outcomes.[58] Other empirical analyses have found that procedural legal rules have an important effect on outcomes, over and above judicial ideological preferences.[59]

Plainly, the law matters in statutory interpretation. This includes both the law of the underlying statute and the law that governs a court's interpretive methodology. Nonetheless, the ideological preferences of the deciding judge are also relevant to judicial outcomes. So are other factors that are facially illegitimate. Lawrence Baum has persuasively made the case that judges are influenced by the reaction of their various audiences to their decisions.[60]

The constraint of judicial ideology is thus a central one for statutory interpretation. Maximum constraint is not necessarily preferable. Some argue that ideological judicial decision making is a legitimate function of the courts, as coequal partners in governance.[61] The legislature itself may use judicial ideology to frame its desired statutory policies. The congressional delegation of judicial discretion in the interpretation of labor legislation was explained in part by the anticipated ideological proclivities of the judiciary at the time (which was accurately perceived as being pro-employer in such matters).[62]

Some constraint on judicial ideology, though, seems appropriate and constitutionally required. The legislature could not lawfully adopt a law saying nothing more than: "the judiciary shall make the policy decisions it deems appropriate in the area of labor law." Thus, two of the crucial questions of statutory interpretation are: (1) how much discretion is appropriately left to the courts, given the ideological influences on judicial decision making; and (2) which interpretive methodologies are most effective in so limiting judicial discretion. The latter question will frame the discussion of much of this book.

The Importance of Empirics

Commentators have long debated the proper method of statutory interpretation. Much of this analysis is purely theoretical, rather than descriptive, but even the theoretical analyses rely on factual claims. Thus, some textualists argue that alternative interpretive methodologies, particularly reliance on legislative history in pursuit of legislative intent, are prone to abuse by judges seeking to advance their own personal preferences. Advocates of contrary philosophies have of course claimed the converse. In addition, some argue that particular justices are reliable followers of particular methods, which lead to particular types of results.

Unfortunately, the descriptive claims underlying the theoretical analyses are woefully underevidenced. Those who claim that particular theories result in more ideological decision making have made no effort to study or prove this claimed effect. While political scientists have conducted hundreds of empirical studies on judicial decision making, they have focused overwhelmingly on constitutional cases and largely ignored the consequences of legal interpretative theories. Most of the empirical research by legal scholars in the area has addressed the frequency with which particular theories have been used over time, not their relative validity, though more useful quantitative analyses have recently begun to emerge.

Adrian Vermeule suggests that the key question is "will a formalist or non-formalist judiciary, in one or another domain, produce more mistakes and injustices?"[63] As he recognizes, this framing is difficult to capture rigorously. One man's injustice may be another's justice. Professor Vermeule further argues that "courts must choose interpretive doctrines on largely empirical grounds, under conditions of severe empirical uncertainty."[64] This situation may explain the rather ad hoc practice of pluralist statutory interpretation. Yet some empirical evidence is available to be analyzed. We may not be able to empirically quantify justice or mistakenness, but it is possible to find some rough proxies for judicial error that inform the discussion.

One cannot design an empirical test to directly measure the degree to which judges are relatively faithful agents. It is possible to test the degree to which judges consistently pursue their own preferences, though. I assume that a legislature, *ceteris paribus*, would prefer legal methodologies that induce judges to vote against their own preferences more often, constraining them with the legislature's own preferences. Similarly, I presume that a legislature would prefer approaches that conduce to judicial consensus and induce different judges to agree on the correct answer. Such consensus is more likely to produce correct answers and, equally important, will reduce uncertainty about the meaning of statutes, which should also be a legislative objective.

A major purpose of this book is to undertake an empirical analysis of interpretive decisions in the Rehnquist Court, and to a lesser degree lower courts, with a focus on the interaction of judicial ideology and interpretive method. Because the debate over proper interpretive methods has a substantial theoretical component that is empirically irresolvable, this analysis cannot determine the correct method. I do hope to inform the discussion, though, and demonstrate that certain key arguments for particular methods are sound or unsound.

CHAPTER 2

Textualism and Statutory Interpretation

The simplest and most straightforward approach to statutory interpretation is to decide based on the text of the statute passed by Congress. This theory is presented as simply applying the law and does not necessarily rely on any delegation theory. However, it is grounded in the fundamental principle that judges should give effect to what the legislature actually promulgates in statutory text and not go beyond those words with judicial discretion, which is fundamental to the agency concept. John Manning, a leading modern proponent of textualism, proclaims that the theory is most consistent with a "faithful agent" theory of judicial statutory interpretation.[1] Textualist theory directly addresses the delegation issue in the sense of arguing that some delegations are illegitimate, an argument discussed below.

Textualism "does not admit of a simple definition, but in practice is associated with the basic proposition that judges must seek and abide by the public meaning of the enacted text, understood in context."[2] The concept is often oversimplified, but textualists do not utterly disregard the context and background of a statute's words, as if they were sent from space. Modern textualists understand that words are but marks on a page that must be contextually animated. Textualism might best be conceived as simply placing limits on the sort of extrinsic evidence relevant to interpretation and its relative significance.

Textualism may be supported on several distinct theoretical legs. The justification for textualism, though, is not entirely abstract. Rather, textualism is also defended by comparison to alternative interpretive approaches, in particular the use of materials of legislative history. Modern textualism essentially rests on a "common core of rejecting legislative history."[3] Consequently, much of this chapter (and the next on legislative history) will consist of a comparison of those two approaches to statutory interpretation. The advocate of textualism, or any theory, need not demonstrate its perfection in the abstract. Instead, the defender of a theory needs show only that it is superior to the alternative grounds available for interpreting statutes. Consequently, the analysis is a comparative one. The defense of textualism typically centers on what it is not—reliance on legislative history, so this contrast shall be a focus of the chapter. In most cases, the theoretical defenses of textualism are comparably applicable to other theories, such as pragmatism.

The Meaning of Textualism

The classical textualist approach to statutory interpretation takes the words of the text and attempts to discern their "plain meaning," though textualists will use certain supplementary tools that are discussed below. Textualism seeks a reasonable and objective measure of the meaning of statutory language and makes no attempt to discern any underlying intent of the adopting legislature. In philosophy, this distinction has been expressed as intentional versus extensional meaning, with the former referring to the meaning of the speaker and the latter referring to the meaning of the words themselves. This approach does not necessarily reject the relevance of speaker intent, though, but may assume that such intent is best found in the text, rather than in any underlying legislative materials. Under this approach, judges look first at the "plain meaning" of a text for the resolution of the case before them.

The immediate objection to textualism is that statutory language may not have any plain meaning. A school of legal thought known as critical legal theory arose to argue that all texts were radically unclear. Even the apparent plain meaning of a text could be deconstructed to mean something very different. In this view, meaning is entirely controlled by the interpreter, not the author of the text. Although the radical version of critical legal theory has not taken hold, it contained a grain of truth. Gadamer's classic work on hermeneutics observed that each interpreter brings his own history to the understanding of text, so that meaning may vary to different interpreters and in different contexts.[4] This is not so radical and, as Hart and Sacks observed in a legal context, language is a social institution, and its "successful functioning depends upon commonly accepted responses to particular verbal symbols used in particular kinds of contexts."[5] This understanding is discussed further later in the chapter.

Thus, one need not go to the largely discredited extreme of critical legal theory to recognize that some texts may be semantically ambiguous. The meaning of statutory language may be murky, and it may even be ungrammatical. Even when the text appears clear on its face, its application to a case may be unclear. In the elegant words of Justice Oliver Wendell Holmes: "A word is not a crystal, transparent and unchanged, it is the skin of a living thought and may vary greatly in color and content according to the circumstances and the time in which it is used."[6] A text may be consistent with a number of meanings, which requires the textualist to create decision rules for these circumstances. The classic law school hypothetical for statutory interpretation involves a simple municipal law banning "vehicles" in a public park, sparked by an accident in which a child was struck by a car. The professor then asks whether the ban extends to bicycles, or skateboards, or ambulances on an emergency mission, or wheelchairs, or motorized scooters needed by the disabled. The text by itself does not resolve this question. While the question is merely hypothetical, it is a plausible problem. And very similar problems may in fact arise. If an 1875 legislature adopted a statute regulating "vehicles," does it extend to automobiles or other vehicles not even extant at the time?

Textualists are not so simplistic in orientation to dispute this fact, and they attend to the statutory context, such as the circumstances of an act's passage. Justice Scalia has distinguished his textualism from strict constructionism, emphasizing the need to consider the context in which a statute was passed.[7] Justices "are happy to use the public context in which Congress acted as a guide to the meaning of statutory language."[8] The theory would consider the meaning of the word vehicle at the time of passage. Textualists might even consider the purpose of the statute. Judge Easterbrook addressed this sort of issue when resolving whether an exemption in a statute for "mowers" applied to equipment called a haybine that did not exist at the time of the statute's enactment. He wrote that: "A statutory word of description does not designate a particular item (e.g., 'a Massey-Ferguson Mower, Model GY-2589, manufactured in 1935, serial number 3875808') but a class of things that share some important feature."[9] He held that a haybine was a "mower" based on the statute's structure and function but, ironically, lamented the lack of informing legislative history.

The context considered by textualists may sometimes be quite broad. For the problematic case of antitrust laws with little illuminating text, for example, Justice Scalia has maintained that the Sherman Act's textual term "restraint of trade" refers not to "a particular list of agreements, but to particular economic consequences, which may be produced by quite different sorts of agreements in varying times and circumstances."[10] While perfectly plausible, this reduces the text to a purposive or pragmatic evaluation that undermines the essential claim of textualism. One must wonder why all texts should not be read in this manner, though textualists obviously treat this application as a rare one.

Textualist interpretation must give meaning to statutory words and tends to rely heavily on dictionary definitions of what those words mean. Some time ago, Learned Hand criticized this approach, suggesting that "one of the surest indexes of a mature and developed jurisprudence [is] not to make a fortress out of the dictionary." This was recognized in a famous case deciding whether the tomato was a fruit or a vegetable for the purpose of determining its tariff rate.[11] Per dictionaries, the tomato is technically a fruit, but the court noted that tomatoes are considered vegetables "in the common language of the people" and so held. Yet the strength of dictionaries is their ability to define words in common language, and such departures obviously add significant indeterminacy to their usage by courts. Justice Scalia has specifically objected to reliance on *Webster's* dictionary as being too colloquial to be relied upon for proper usage in statutory interpretation.[12] It is not at all clear how textualists would resolve whether a common or technical definition should be applied to a given statute, without some reference to intentionalism.

Moreover, dictionaries themselves often do not resolve a word's meaning. Different dictionaries often have somewhat different definitions for the same word, and dictionaries of different contexts, such as technical dictionaries, may produce very different definitions. The typical dictionary offers a series of possible definitions for each word. While these definitions are typically prioritized, there is no obvious reason to presume that a congressional use of a word necessarily adopts the "first" definition found in a dictionary. The "second" definition is often a commonly used one. Thus, the dictionary resource allows a measure of judicial discretion in its application. Moreover, some dictionaries are not expressions of the actual contemporary meaning of words but instead the authors' prescription of what words *should* mean, making them an uncertain textual guide.[13] Even political considerations have "made their way into dictionaries," especially in the past.[14]

Some have claimed that the use of dictionaries gives undue range to judicial manipulation of meaning. The practice called "dictionary shopping" is one where the interpreting judge considers numerous dictionary definitions in order to find the one that best suits his or her desires for a given outcome of the case.[15] The Court cited around 120 different dictionaries in the 1997–1998 term alone. Yet the justices offered "little explanation or methodology for their choices" of which dictionary to use in a particular opinion.[16] On occasion, the Court's majority and dissent have used different dictionaries for their different statutory interpretations.[17]

Still another problem for textualism arises in the not uncommon presence of statutory silence. Sometimes, silence may be read as a textualist command that the statute does not apply, but this is not always the case. Suppose that a statute clearly creates a private right of action for its enforcement but is silent on the criteria for the exercise of such a right. Should liability be strict, based on negligence, or based on intent? Is liability joint and several? Is there a right to contribution? How is a textualist judge to resolve such silences?

The textualist might claim that such instances of ambiguity are rare. Indeed, even a critic of pure textualism has noted that the "vast majority of legal texts have plain meanings in the vast majority of cases."[18] Yet this claim does not truly benefit the textualist interpreter. Such clear language generally does not yield litigation, precisely *because* its meaning is clear to the affected parties. Cases arise at the margin, where the meaning of language is unclear, and it is these cases with which judges must grapple. It is the hard cases that require interpretive guidance, not the easy ones. Moreover, the prevalence of this type of statutory ambiguity may be understated, as discussed in Chapter 1. CERCLA, an enormously important statute both environmentally and economically, was very hastily passed and is notoriously replete with uncertainties and even apparent contradictions. Likewise, the Securities Exchange Act, which established the federal law against securities fraud, leaves many application questions unanswered. Professor Brudney contends that "[f]ederal legislation often includes language that is inconclusive on some important matter of public policy."[19]

If the text seems unclear, textualist judges may consider the statute as a whole, or perhaps other statutes using similar language, to interpret the textual meaning. As Justice Scalia has explained, statutory interpretation "is a holistic endeavor" and a provision that "may seem ambiguous in isolation is often clarified by the remainder of the statutory scheme—because the same terminology is used elsewhere in a context that makes its meaning clear, or because only one of the permissible meanings produces a substantive effect that is compatible with the rest of the law."[20] The latter language represents a considerable departure from textualism, though, and sounds of purposivism, which is something of an antipode to textualism.

Textualists have sought to avoid such purposivism through alternative decision rules. For example, textualists generally do not broadly object to the use of interpretive canons (discussed in more detail in Chapter 4). While given textualists may find particular canons objectionable, they do not object to consideration of the canons in the abstract. Indeed, many textualists actively embrace the reliance on such canons of linguistic interpretation, if not on the substantive canons that favor a particular interpretive end. Many textualists, including Scalia, recognize the relevance of some sense of legislative intent when interpreting ambiguous texts, but distinguish objective textual evidence of intent from more subjective consideration of external sources of such intent. Some call this "objectified" intent, as "the intent that a reasonable person would gather from the text of the law, placed alongside the remainder of the *corpus juris*."[21] The focus is on what a reasonable reader would believe the intent of the statute to be, not on what the author of the statute meant. In this concept of "intent," there is no real concern for the true subjective intent of the legislature or its subjective purpose for the statute; the only concern is for whatever intent can be logically inferred from the language of the statutory text.

The textualist does not necessarily care if his or her methodology accurately captures the true purpose of the legislature, to the extent such a true purpose exists. The textualist judge is interpreting a statute, not an intent. If that interpretation is contrary to the wishes of the legislature, it should pass a new statute containing clearer text that resolves the matter as it wishes. The remainder of this section will consider the textualists' theoretical arguments against legislative history and similar extrinsic aids to interpretation, to which textualism is typically opposed, but these theoretical arguments often apply to other interpretive theories, such as pragmatism or dynamic statutory interpretation as well.

The Public Choice Rejection of Legislative Intent

One key theoretical argument for textualism is the absence of a viable alternative—that the effort to discern legislative intent behind a statute is a meaningless or incoherent one. Each legislative branch is itself a collective body, and a statute typically requires the combined assent of two collective bodies and the president of the United States. While an individual may have an intent behind his or her actions, the ability to find a common intent for a collective body is much more difficult, if it is possible at all. The shorthand for this argument has become: "Congress is a they, not an it." The famous political scientist, Kenneth Shepsle, said that "[l]egislative intent is an internally inconsistent, self-contradictory expression."[22]

In the legal literature, this criticism of legislative intent is most closely associated with Judge Frank Easterbrook. Judge Easterbrook has various criticisms of legislative history reliance, but the public choice critique is prominent among them. He maintains that it is "impossible for a court—even one that knows each legislators' complete table of preferences—to say what the whole body would have done with a proposal it did not consider in fact."[23] The attribution of intent to a collective entity is not unknown to the law, however. For example, a collective entity such as a corporation is chargeable with common law or securities fraud, though such a violation requires an attribution of *scienter* to the corporation itself. The interpretation of business contracts commonly requires an assessment of the intent of the contracting parties, which are collective entities. I am aware of no textualists that oppose these practices. However, the ability to do so in other contexts does not necessarily demonstrate the viability or wisdom of doing so in the context of statutory interpretation.

The public choice hypotheses about the decision making of groups, such as legislatures, have been the subject of much explication and study by social scientists. The Nobel laureate Kenneth Arrow demonstrated mathematically that a group's decision is not necessarily a stable one with a clear meaning but rather may rest upon a coincidence of circumstances.[24] After making several plausible presumptions about democratic group decision making, Arrow's theorem explained how there is no single policy decision that a majority will prefer over all other policy decisions. Arrow's argument is often associated with predictions of democratic cycling among different policies and it fundamentally claims that any given democratic policy choice is an arbitrary one, not intrinsically the preferences of a majority.

The theory of Arrow, though, does not appear to correspond to practice. Projections of majoritarian cycling are at odds "with our empirical knowledge of legislatures."[25] Defenders of the theory argue that the absence of cycling can be attributed to various legislative institutions and procedures that interfere with perfect democratic choice. There are other reasons, though, why Arrow's theorem may not conform to practice. It depends on a random assignment of preferences with the assumption that all are equally likely. In fact, random distribution of preferences is less likely than interdependent preferences. The "distribution of citizen or representative preferences over policies is usually not divergent enough . . . to produce inconsistent collective preferences."[26]

The projected arbitrariness of the theorem collapses entirely if an issue is unidimensional, and preferences are single-peaked. This situation arises when voter preferences are based on a single standard, such as a liberal versus conservative scale, without a second dimension balanced against that value. The arbitrariness and cycling concerns do not exist in such an arrangement of preferences.[27] In general, about 70% agreement on an underlying dimension is sufficient to make the paradox "rare."[28] Such single-peaked preferences generally characterize congressional voting. An elaborate study found that for every single Congress since the founding, a single dimension could explain nearly 70% and typically around 85% of the representatives' voting patterns.[29] The Arrow theorem itself is silent about the frequency of inconsistent patterns of preferences and does not establish the meaninglessness of legislative intent.[30]

Even if the public choice Arrow's theorem argument were true, it would not entirely support textualism. By its nature, it suggests the choice of legislative words was arbitrary. As discussed below, textualists maintain that the text demonstrates the "objective" intent of the legislature. But if a collective group cannot have an intent, it cannot very well have an objective intent. If text does not reflect legislative intention, why privilege text? A textualist might fall back to the position that, absent coherent legislative intent, the text is the only alternative. But this is obviously wrong, because one could just as easily say, absent coherent legislative intent, courts should refer to the published materials of legislative history or pragmatic judicial policy making. Those materials may not reflect the true intent of the legislature, but neither does the text, according to Arrovian theory. Objectified intent of the text is no more coherent than the objectified intent of legislative history.

A somewhat more limited and refined approach to this theory does not argue that statutes lack any collective intent but maintains that such intent can best be found in the text.[31] In this view, the text represents a delicate compromise between legislative objectives; attempts to extrapolate the "spirit" of a law may upset this balance. This refinement, though, collapses the collective intent to the reliability critique of reliance on extrinsic sources, such as legislative intent. It is best analyzed in the context of that criticism, which is discussed in the chapter on legislative history.

There is some irony to the fact that it is textualists who make the public choice criticism of legislation. This criticism fundamentally calls into question the legislative process itself, yet it is the textualists who proclaim devotion to the constitutional legislative process and who tend to dismiss judicial authority. In other contexts, conservatives commonly associated with textualism have embraced a preference for common law over statutory law for similar public choice reasons. Perhaps for this reason, Justice Scalia does not embrace the public choice criticism but argues instead that textualism better approximates the legislature's collective intent. Rather than supporting textualism, the public choice theory is actually most supportive of a pragmatic approach to statutory interpretation, discussed in Chapter 5, where judges are less worshipful of precise congressional determinations.

The Constitutional Argument for Textualism

The constitutional argument for textualism is grounded in the Constitution's requirements for passing a law of the United States. These requirements include bicameralism (the need for statutes to pass both the House and the Senate) and presentment (the need for statutes to be presented to and signed by the president, or have his or her veto overridden by legislative supermajority vote). Judge Easterbrook explained that textualists "are worried that the gauntlet that the Constitution requires bills to run before they become law will be bypassed if judges give heed not just to the enactment itself but to what individual members of Congress said about it."[32] This is illustrated by a now classic colloquy in which Senator Armstrong objected:

> I only wish the record to reflect that this is not statutory language. It is not before us. If there were matter within this report which was disagreed to by the Senator from Colorado or even by a majority of all Senators, there would be no way to change the report. I could not offer an amendment tonight to amend the committee report.[33]

This frustration captures the constitutional problem of legislative history, though it does not truly address the delegation issue; Senator Armstrong was not precluded from proposing a statutory amendment that counteracted the committee report, either explicitly or implicitly.

The constitutional argument addresses a basic problem with textualism under an agency theory, the presumption that the text is a careful reflection of the legislature's action. In his classic article, Max Radin argued that to "say that the legislature is 'presumed' to have selected its phraseology with meticulous care as to every word is in direct contradiction to known facts."[34] One cannot assume that legislators are aware of the techniques of textualist interpretation, including technical grammatical rules or interpretive canons or dictionaries.[35] Legislators may be unfamiliar with the content of the text of the bill itself.

Justice Scalia has argued that it is "simply incompatible with democratic government, or indeed, even with fair government, to have the meaning of a law determined by what the lawgiver meant, rather than by what the law-maker promulgated."[36] Yet this assumes the answer to the question of "what the lawmaker promulgated." Others, such as John Manning, have responded to this concern and argued against consideration of legislative history, on the grounds that it represents unconstitutional self-delegation as a source of "what the lawmaker promulgated."

The constitutional argument for requiring strict textualism ultimately fails because it proves too much. The basic claim of this argument is that the text, and only the text, has passed through the constitutional procedures for enactment, so the text alone has constitutional authority. Textualists argue that consideration of materials of legislative history, such as a committee re-port or a floor statement of an individual legislator, improperly elevate such comments to the status of law themselves, though the statements have not been passed by both houses of Congress or signed by the president. They sometimes argue that members of Congress, or even staffers, insert legisla-tive history into the record that is contrary to the intent of the full body, in order to manipulate its meaning.

The fundamental shortcoming of this constitutional argument is its con-fusion of law with interpretation. No school of statutory interpretation re-jects the statutory text as the fundamental source of law. The only true dispute among the schools of interpretation is how that text should be inter-preted. Advocates of legislative history believe that those materials are helpful when interpreting the text. They don't claim that the materials of legislative history *are law*, just that they are helpful information for interpretation of the meaning of the law. Textualists reject these materials but inevitably must rely on some source for interpretation of the law's textual language, such as a dictionary or perhaps the canons of construction. Yet those interpretive materials likewise fail the constitutional test. Dictionaries are not adopted bicamerally and neither are they presidentially signed. A judicial deference to "legislative history is . . . no more problematic (on delegation grounds) than incorporation of any other exogenous texts, such as dictionaries. . . ."[37] Hence, the straightforward application of the constitutional argument would invalidate the consultation of dictionaries or any outside aids to interpretation. Words do not interpret themselves, though, and an external source of some sort is fundamental to the very act of interpreting, which courts must do.

The textualist answer to this criticism is that some external materials are presumed by the legislators; that Congress writes text on a background of word meaning such as that found in dictionaries. Perhaps this is so, but the response also begs the question. One might just as easily argue that reliance on legislative history is presumed by the legislators; that Congress writes text on a background of its committee reports and other sources of legislative history. Thus, the constitutional argument is a circular one that relies on the textualists' unsupported descriptive assumption that Congress means for dictionaries but not legislative history to be used in interpretation. Such an assumption requires evidence, which is lacking. Indeed, it seems more likely to presume that Congress intends that legislative history be used as an interpretive aid. Otherwise, why would legislators spare the resources necessary to create it? Justice Stevens has argued that this self-delegation is a matter of fact, writing that "Representatives and Senators may appropriately rely on the views of the committee members in casting their votes," such that the "intent of those involved in the drafting process is properly regarded as the intent of the entire Congress."[38] This is supported by congressional rules that explicitly provide the terms of the self-delegation to the legislature's committee system.[39]

For Manning, even if Congress intends the use of legislative history to be employed in judicial interpretation, it is a matter of unconstitutional self-delegation. But this argument runs afoul of the same theoretical flaw. Manning's perfectly plausible argument against the legislature delegating authority to a subset of the legislature would apply with equal or greater weight to the legislature delegating authority to Merriam-Webster or Random House, who write the dictionaries, or to the courts who create the interpretive canons or to professors of linguistics who set out the rules of grammar. The Constitution authorizes no delegations to private dictionaries or to grammarians. The point is that no language can be entirely self-contained. By its nature it requires something external for interpretation, and there is no reason why that external thing could not be a subset of the Congress. Moreover, it is not a true delegation if the adoption of the final statute is viewed as an independent ratification of that legislative history. Such a ratification would make the underlying history an appropriate interpretive tool.

Defenders of use of legislative history contend that the statutory history should be considered incorporated by reference into the statutory text itself. Manning responds that such incorporation is legitimate but should be explicit and not implied. He acknowledges that Congress may legitimately define extrinsic sources in the text of a statute as a source of law.[40] However, he believes that any implicit delegation is too easy, so legislative history should not override the "clear import of the adopted text."[41] This is surely plausible but provides only very weak grounds for textualism. When the text has such a "clear import," it is extremely rare for courts to ignore that. The vast majority of cases involve textual ambiguities, in which event the legislative history may better reflect the legislative compromise than would resort to a dictionary definition. Precisely the same requirement for explicit statutory reference could be made to judicial use of dictionaries as interpretive aids or reference to other statutes by analogy or any of the other extrinsic interpretive sources on which textualists rely. Justice Scalia "sometimes seems to go out of his way to consult any and all extrastatutory texts, provided they are not legislative history."[42] Textualists employ an *a priori* presumption that some extrinsic sources require no textual validation, but without independent justification.

A second major shortcoming of the argument against self-delegation is its failure to reflect the reality of congressional self-governance. This practice will be discussed further in Chapter 3, and the reality is that Congress constantly self-delegates authority to its subbodies, including the content of the text itself. The modern legislature could not function without such self-delegation. The words of a statute itself are largely or entirely the product of self-delegation to congressional committees. In practice, "only certain small groups of legislators have positions of great control over the content of legislation," including the legislative text itself.[43] Use of legislative history is but a very mild form of this self-delegation. The constitutional argument thus proves far too much—it would invalidate virtually all legislation passed in recent decades if applied with the theory embraced by textualists. But it need not be so applied, because self-delegation of legislative history is justified on the same grounds as self-delegation of statutory text, through the subsequent ratification of a majority of the whole body.

One might argue that delegation to legislative committees disempowers the president, because he must sign or reject the statutory text and has no direct control over the committee reports. But this argument is unpersuasive, because it also proves too much. A president may veto a bill, because of an awareness that the textual language is likely to be given a certain judicial interpretation due to committee interpretive guidance. If the president disapproves of that interpretation, he or she must simply decide whether that committee report is a "poison pill" that warrants a veto. This is the same analysis that a president must undertake when facing a bill with an unappealing amendment or rider contained in the statutory text. Even a president that signs a bill is not powerless, though. Presidents commonly use "signing statements" that explicate a view of the proper interpretation of a statute, which are somewhat like legislative history and may be consulted by the interpreting courts.[44]

Textualists abandon the constitutional argument when they recognize the need to correct scriveners' errors in statutes. It was the erroneous statute that underwent the constitutional presentment. Many of the textualists making the constitutional argument also nod when it comes to the issue of executive interpretation of statutes. In the renowned *Chevron* decision,[45] the Supreme Court declared that it would defer to an administrative agency's interpretation of its statute, at least when the text could be considered silent or ambiguous. The court would override the agency where the text is clearly contrary, but textualism suggests that answers can be found in the text, which makes it always clear. Thomas Merrill notes that the "textualist judge treats questions of interpretation like a puzzle to which it is assumed there is one right answer."[46] If there is one right answer, there's no need for a *Chevron* deference doctrine; the agency either got it right or it did not.

Judge Easterbrook is quite open about the basis for this deference. He argues that when the text provides no clear answer to its interpretation, "a court should not put one there on the basis of legislative reports . . ." but should "go to some other source of rules, including administrative agencies. . . ."[47] He suggests this essentially because these extratextual judgments are political ones, and agencies are suited for political judgments, while courts are not,[48] and because the administering agency yields but a single interpretation.[49] These are plausible pragmatic policy arguments but entirely irrelevant to the bicameralism/presentment argument that is used to dejustify judicial nontextual interpretation. There may be some arguments for preferring administrative agency interpretations to those of congressional committees, but the Constitution is not among them. The Constitution does not even recognize the existence of much of the administrative state, much less grant it legal power to define statutory meaning. Judge Easterbrook and other textualists would apparently defer to an agency that relied upon legislative history to interpret a statute, but not to the legislative history itself. Of course, he presents no constitutional reason why such "laundering" of legislative history is not illegitimate extralegislative legislating.

Adrian Vermeule has provided a different justification for textualism in the context of *Chevron* deference. He argues that agencies are *better* at interpreting the law and hence seeks to constrain judicial review that would overturn such interpretations, through textualism.[50] He complains that judges override proper agency interpretations. This is a narrow defense of textualism, though, as a vast number of judicial interpretations do not involve any agency interpretation and require judicial interpretation in the first instance. Moreover, Vermeule assumes without evidence that textualism is indeed a more restraining methodology for judges, an assumption that lies at the heart of the contested interpretive terrain. Professor Eskridge argues that textualism would have the opposite effect and produce more overrides of agency interpretation.[51]

Professor Manning attempts to draw a methodologically relevant theoretical distinction between the legislature's delegation of interpretive authority to executive agencies and to its own bodies, but the distinction fails. He notes that when "Congress enacts a vague statute and leaves it to an agency or court to fill in the details, it consciously cedes potentially significant policymaking discretion to a different branch of government," which provides a "built-in structural incentive for Congress itself to specify important federal statutory policy."[52] In contrast, he suggests that delegating such authority to the legislature's own judicial agents lacks this same incentive. He specifically fears that Congress may use the legislative history to cut deals with special interests, deals for which Congress may escape accountability because the deals are not found in the statutory text.

Manning's distinction fails at several levels. It relies upon an arbitrary and unsupported assumption that legislatures purposefully cede discretionary interpretive authority to agencies but not to courts. Such delegation is sometimes, but not always, explicit in statutory text. The argument ignores the fact that legislatures have the same "built-in structural incentive" when delegating to courts that they have when delegating to agencies. It relies on the factual premise that Congress is inhibited from cutting deals with special interests in the text itself, belied by the numerous examples in tax law, appropriations law, and elsewhere in which Congress has textually provided "pork" to special interests. Manning's distinction also assumes, without proving or even evidencing, that legislatures can escape accountability for special interest deals found in legislative history rather than text or supplied by administrative agencies.

The distinction also begs several crucial questions, rather than dealing with them. First, Manning presumes that Congress escapes accountability by relying on committee reports rather than text, but this is nowhere demonstrated. If the materials of legislative history have practical importance, one would expect that a rational observer would hold Congress accountable for them as well, and Manning's concern is misplaced. If this system breaks down, one might expect the same to be true of text. After all, today's legislation is of enormous length and great detail, and the imperfect outside observer is unlikely to ascribe full accountability for small details of the statute that benefit special interests.

The distinction also relies on an entirely unproven assumption that delegation to subbodies of the legislature facilitates irresponsible special interest deals, while delegation to administrative agencies does not. Administrative agencies are plainly subject to some degree of special interest influence. While the traditional "regulatory capture" theory of agencies no longer prevails, there is little doubt that the statutorily regulated bodies have ample ongoing opportunity to influence the interpreting agencies. While the Agriculture Committee of the House may have a particular interest in farm interests, so may the U.S. Department of Agriculture. Surely the delegation of authority to another branch evades accountability more than to a congressional committee. Moreover, the administrative agencies may be strongly influenced in their actions by the congressional oversight committees, whose influence Manning disdains.[53]

Congress is delegating no actual authority to its committees through legislative history, because those committees wield no adjudicative power. The existing cases that proscribe self-delegation involve actual decision-making power by a legislative subordinate. By contrast, in statutory interpretation Congress is delegating authority to the courts who possess adjudicative power (and sometimes to administrative agencies) but not to any legislative subbody. The legislative history is only of interpretive significance if the courts accord it significance. Consequently, the rejection of the use of legislative history is not denying power to delegate to congressional bodies, it is merely *limiting* the delegation of power to the courts. The constitutional question is not whether legislative committees have authority, it is whether courts should have authority to rely on those committees for interpretive assistance, or not, in the discretion of those courts. Yet textualists have not made the constitutional argument why the delegation to courts should be limited in this very targeted way.

Manning himself ultimately recognizes this fact. Despite his extensive writings against the use of legislative history, he suggests that courts may choose to consult legislative history "that supplies an objective, unmanufactured history of a statute's context."[54] His objection is only when legislative history is deemed "authoritative," with the power to "control" court interpretation. But this objection is largely to a straw man argument. Judges are never controlled by legislative history; they simply choose to employ it when they find it helpful to discerning the proper interpretation of statutory text. The case is not against the use of legislative history; it is against the misuse of legislative history. Ultimately, the case is not a constitutional one but rests on a mistrust of courts, which is addressed in the textualism versus pluralism section below.

The Rule of Law Argument for Textualism

Textualism takes as its lodestar the straightforward understanding of a statutory text in the way that an ordinary person would have read it at the time of enactment. It maintains that "citizens ought to be able to read the statute books and know their rights and duties."[55] This traces one of the most fundamental underpinnings of the rule of law. The interpretive approach is thus associated with "ruleness."[56] Justice Jackson invoked this argument when he objected that the acceptance of "legislative debates to modify statutory provisions is to make the law inaccessible to a large part of the country."[57] It is arguably much more costly, and perhaps impossible, for a citizen to fully comprehend the legislative history underlying a statute

While the rule of law is much lauded, its meaning is seldom explored. Various commentators have fleshed out its meaning as grounded in multiple criteria. In Lon Fuller's classic discussion of the concept, he emphasized features such as: that laws must be publicly known, must be disclosed in advance of their application, and must be clear in meaning.[58] Such requirements seem compatible with textualism and its reliance on public statutory text. The text of the law is available to all those who may be charged with its violation.

The exaltation of law *qua* law can easily become the triumph of formalism over substance. The thesis worships even those laws that are dysfunctional. There is a traditional critical aphorism: *Vocabula manent, res fugiunt*, or "the words remain after the thing has vanished." This has been invoked by Bacon and others as a caution not to raise the importance of words over what they are to represent. It is the things that are important, and a rigid textualism risks apotheosizing the words of the statute at the expense of its rationale. Nevertheless, the textualist may claim that the rule of law requires this outcome.

However, the rule of law case for textualism can be disputed, as illustrated through the theory's reliance on dictionaries. Typically, the textualist would use a dictionary from the time period in which the law was passed. Yet the reader of the statute is likely to view it through the lens of the word's contemporary meaning. Word meanings change over time, and the textualist focus on the reader, from the rule of law perspective, would mean that the statutes likewise changed over time, which would conflict with the textualist focus on the constitutional procedures of valid legislation. The escape hatch from this conundrum, expecting statutory readers to consult old dictionary meanings, hardly seems distinguishable from expecting them to consult materials of legislative history.

Even if one bought into the strongest rule of law value, the realism of the rule of law case for textualism might itself be questioned. It assumes that individual readers can readily know the textual requirements of a statute but not so easily discern the legislative history underlying the law. In today's world, "the most widely used kinds of legislative history are now no less available to the citizenry than the statutory texts they purport to explain."[59] One suspects that in most cases, the typical citizen is unfamiliar with the details of *either* the text or the legislative history. Those most interested in the application of the statute, conversely, are likely familiar with both.

Indeed, the rule of law argument might even cut against textualism. The ordinary citizen can hardly be expected to know the details of the many statutes that govern them but might realistically have some idea of the broad intent underlying those statutes. The notion that citizens "read the statute books" is clearly a fiction, and the world would be terribly inefficient if ordinary citizens spent a great deal of time doing so. Consequently, an intentionalist approach to interpretation might better conform to the rule of law values at issue. Americans are much more aware of the intent of the civil rights laws to prohibit certain discrimination than they are aware of the particularities of the text of that legislation. While citizens have the theoretical ability to discover that text, it certainly adds costs to the functioning of the legal system to expect them to do so for the extraordinarily large body of statutory law governing contemporary America. The citizenry plausibly has a much better sense of broad legislative intent underlying a statute than of its textual details. Judge Posner thus suggests that a rather vague legal standard, such as negligence, better informs citizens about the rule of law than would "a network of precise but technical, nonintuitive rules covering the same ground."[60]

The "rule of law" argument also has broad implications that arguably prove too much. The common law is judicially constructed from individual cases that often contain relatively little "ruleness." It is largely made up of standards, readily distinguishable on the facts of particular cases. Perhaps for this reason, Justice Scalia has been critical of common law approaches. Yet this very common law is historically associated closely with the rule of law.

The rule of law argument for textualism also largely presumes its conclusion. It presumes that textualism is more determinate than alternative interpretive approaches and accurately reflects the textual meanings perceived by the citizens who read the statute books. Yet critics of the approach maintain that textualism is itself manipulated by willful judges to create meanings other than those of the citizen reader. Consequently, the rule of law argument, while presented as purely theoretical, in effect may collapse into the claim that textualism best constrains judges' ideologies, a claim discussed below and studied in Chapter 7.

The rule of law argument seems to have some persuasive weight but only when raised against a caricature of the contrary hypotheses. The argument for consideration of legislative history does not call for the disregard of clear text on which Americans might rely, it calls only for the utilization of ancillary materials of legislative history, when that text is ambiguous. The very presence of such ambiguity is itself contrary to the strict rule of law argument, yet it is the circumstance at issue in most statutory interpretation decisions. Moreover, the rule of law argument applies as well to other interpretive methods that even textualists embrace. The citizen cannot know for certain which provisions will judicially be found to be absurd or even be expected to know all the canons of interpretation and how they would be applied to a particular text.

The Incentives for Legislator Argument

A less common argument for textualism involves its purported value in reforming the legislative process. In this claim, courts' insistence on adherence to text will cause legislators to write statutory language more carefully and clearly. The typical statutory interpretation problem involves an ambiguity in language or a gap in the statutory text. Advocates of textualism suggest that legislatures will write the text more precisely if that is the sole source of judicial interpretation.

This argument presumes that legislators could realistically produce more determinate text if only they tried harder or had greater incentive. As discussed above, language is inherently indeterminate at some level, so perfect linguistic precision is impossible. Obviously, this is impossible in the case of background delegation for unforeseen circumstances. Undoubtedly, greater clarity in statutory text is at least sometimes possible, though the "amount" of greater precision is certainly debatable. More fundamentally, it may be unrealistic to assume that a collective body such as Congress will be able to agree on more precise language.

As Judge Easterbrook and others argue in connection with their criticism of legislative intent, legislation is typically a matter of compromise. It is the "need to compromise conflicting interests" that "render the final legislative product vague."[61] Statutory ambiguity is not due to incentive problems that may be cured with new interpretive rules. Some ambiguity is inevitable in language, producing background delegation, and other statutory ambiguity might be ascribed to the inability of a legislative majority to agree on a precise policy. The vagueness is the product of compromise, and no method of judicial statutory interpretation can eliminate this need of legislators to compromise.

Abner Mikva, with experience in all three branches of government, has explained the compromise process and the difficulty of determining statutory text. He notes that:

> Those 535 people [in the U.S. Congress] are going to find it difficult to agree on an agenda, let alone on the words to describe whatever consensus they reach. The consensus that is reached to get a bill passed in the first place is a tenuous and confused one. Is it any wonder that the words they do finally choose tend to have diffuse and ambiguous meanings?[62]

However judges might wish to discipline the legislative process, they are confronted with the impossible task of herding cats. There is no reason, logical or empirical, to believe that standards of judicial statutory interpretation purportedly demanding textual precision would have the effect of actually yielding such textual precision.

The difficulty may be even greater than portrayed in the above discussion—Congress may actively frustrate judicial efforts to improve the legislative drafting process. Grundfest and Pritchard take note of the point made by textualists in the context of the public choice argument, that compromise is necessary for legislation.[63] Ambiguity is an essential tool of such compromise, and strict judicial interpretive doctrines can ruin the ability of legislatures to make statutes ambiguous. The legislature hence engages in an "arms race" with the judiciary, creating obscurity despite the best judicial efforts to resolve ambiguity. In such cases, the judiciary cannot force the legislature to draft more clearly, whatever its efforts. Textualists argue that the text is central to the legislative compromise and that courts must give it effect in order to enable compromise, but this makes the unevidenced assumption that the legislature *wants* some precise meaning in its compromise rather than delegating future applications to judicial discretion. Judicial discretionary judgment would not upset the legislative balance if that *was* the legislative balance.

Even when the intentional ambiguity hypothesis does not apply, there is no reason to think that textualism would make Congress better drafters of statutes. Under the present system, Congress has an incentive to draft a statute as clearly as reasonably possible, because unclear language simply gives judges greater leeway to depart from the statute and impose their own rules. That situation is equally true, regardless of whether the judges use textualism. When legislators use imprecise language, they may have a good reason for doing so. The most obvious such reason is the legislature's inability to foresee all the possible consequences of its enactment and corresponding desire to enable some flexibility in its future application.

Textualists could resist the legislature's grant of such flexibility through ambiguity. But this resistance has nothing to do with the quality of legislative drafting. Apparently imprecise statutory drafting may be exactly what the legislature intended, as it meant to delegate case-by-case interpretation of the statute to future courts. The issue therefore is not one of "better" legislative drafting but one where courts dictate a certain limited type of legislative drafting, in order to limit delegation to courts. Thus, the argument for better legislative drafting essentially collapses into the constitutional argument about the appropriate role of courts.

The whole legislative drafting argument is even a little demeaning. It involves the judicial agents telling the legislative principals how to fulfill their responsibilities and objectives. The very textualists who exalt the legislature constitutionally seem to think that it needs help from another branch in improving its drafting, despite the fact that statutory language may be closely scrutinized by interest groups, the press, and interested legislators. A rational legislature has no reason to be pointlessly sloppy in its drafting (save for time constraints that cannot be altered by any interpretive theory). Ultimately, the dispute cannot be over the quality of the legislative product; the true dispute is over the quality of the judicial interpretive product.

Textualism vs. Pluralism

The case for textualism is not limited to claims that it is theoretically the *best* approach to statutory interpretation. Rather, many of the theory's devotees argue for the virtue of a single, relatively determinate approach, rather than a variety of possibilities. This variety was the "conventional approach to statutory interpretation," which "involved an eclectic mix of reliance on text, canons of interpretation, legislative history, purpose, and public policy."[64] In this approach, judges could pick or choose the interpretive material they deployed in statutory interpretation on a case-by-case basis. Justice White argued for the ability to consider plural interpretive tools on the grounds that "common sense suggests that inquiry benefits from reviewing additional information rather than ignoring it."[65] Much earlier, Justice Marshall made the same point, writing that when "the mind labours to discern the design of the legislature, it seizes every thing from which aid can be derived."[66] This is the traditional approach; that when such evidence is available and the text implies an unreasonable, if not absurd, result, justices should consult such evidence.[67]

This pluralist approach is one of great judicial discretion. A judge could, in his or her judgment, rely on statutory text in one case, legislative history in the next, and perhaps rely on some broad invocation of legislative purpose or pragmatic consideration in the following decision. Pluralism is a system that grants great deference to judges, believing them able to best choose the rules to govern any individual dispute. Awarding such great deference to judges is not unique to this area but is found throughout American law, interspersed with more rigid rules of decision. For some, this pluralism might simply be considered a form of "ordinary judging" of the sort that courts generally undertake in making legal decisions.[68] The textualists plainly disapproved of such broad discretion, though, for various reasons.

Judicial pluralism seems to add a level of indeterminacy to decisions. Even if each and every arbiter were judging in good faith, trying only to reach the soundest outcome, different judges may weigh the balance of interpretation differently. Indeed, judges have different levels of capability, and some better judges will reach a different decision than will those of less analytical deftness. The private party trying to discern the meaning of a statute gets more guidance from a rigid rule than from a pluralist doctrine of judicial discretion. The relative unpredictability of interpretive pluralism was a mark against the theory for textualists, who sought a more determinate standard to guide private parties.

The greatest concern of the textualists, though, may not be the indeterminacy *per se* but the fact that judicial discretion enables ideological decision making, rather than judgment by law. A judge that interprets statutory language is making a fundamentally political decision, akin to that of the legislature that adopted the statutory language. Ample empirical evidence demonstrates that judges will yield to the temptation to render decisions compatible with their personal ideology, be it liberal or conservative. Pluralism, according to Scalia, simply gives judges another tool to be ideological and can only augment the problem.[69] This is the response to Justice White—that the consideration of "additional information" only empowers the judiciary to do wrong.

Textualism vs. Ideological Decision Making

While textualism has been justified on a variety of purely theoretical grounds, as summarized above, the concern for ideological decision making may form the core of the case for textualism.[70] The theory of the argument is that text is relatively determinate, while other interpretive tools are more malleable and, consequently, more vulnerable to manipulation in pursuit of a judicial ideological end. Textualism is commonly associated with judicial restraint. For many textualists, it is this constraint on willful judicial ideological decision making that best justifies the practice. The theoretical, constitutional arguments are secondary to the effect of the practice, which advocates profess makes law more determinate and less ideological.

This concern may well lie at the root of the case for textualism. Most textualists realize that texts can be ambiguous and fail to determine the proper result in a case of statutory interpretation. Interpretation is necessary, but textualists seek to minimize the *amount* of judicial interpretation, if interpretative discretion can be said to be quantifiable. It is difficult to draw lines between permissible interpretation and interpretation that goes too far and contravenes the text. For example, some have argued from interpretation of "cruel and unusual punishment" that capital punishment is unconstitutional. A textualist, observing that the Constitution mentions capital punishment as an available penalty, would find such interpretivism impermissible. Alternative interpretive theories, such as purposivism, could unduly enable such expansive interpretivism. A textualist may recognize the limitations of his or her theory but find it preferable to alternatives that enable overinterpretivism.

And the danger of allowing judges an expansive field of interpretivism is the degree to which it empowers them to act as "superlegislators" and impose their own ideological preferences on society, overriding those of the elected legislature and its statutory text.

The threshold presumption of this argument, that judicial ideological decision making is inappropriate, is widely accepted. Such ideological consideration seems incompatible with the very nature of judging according to law. It implies that different judges would produce different outcomes, even if every other consideration was held constant. Such differences seem contrary to the very nature of the rule of law. This challenge to the rule of law in turn seems to threaten the very legal enterprise, which produces the calls for the control of judicial ideological decision making.

The presence of judicial ideology is not so horrendous as often presented. The law is filled with vague directives, like "reasonableness" or "due process." There can be no neutral evaluation of what such terms require. So long as laws are vague and judges must fill in the legal gaps, judicial values, including ideology, will be a basis for decision making. Some have aggressively argued for the propriety of such judicial ideology, as a check on the other branches of government.[71] If all the branches are engaged in a fundamentally political enterprise of national governance, and the formally coequal branches are meant to check one another's power, there is nothing intrinsically objectionable to an ideological judiciary counteracting the contemporary ideology of the legislature and executive. Indeed, such discretionary ideology might be valuable in counteracting a sudden popular ideological demand, tempering it with a longer-range perspective. A commonly held vision of the appointed federal judiciary is that the judges reflect the past ideological preferences of the past presidents and Congress who appointed them. If these judges apply their ideology to decision making, they are functionally acting as a brake on the immediate preferences of the elected branches, slowing the rapidity of change. This effect is at least arguably a positive one that produces stability in the political system and more reflective, long-run decision making.

Terri Jennings Peretti has made an affirmative case for such ideological judicial decision making. She stresses that the Court is connected with democracy via appointment and other factors and that the Constitution assigns it a role compatible with at least some ideological decision making.

The Court "possesses the capacity for serving as a particularly profitable redundancy in the policymaking process, by invoking interests and values overlooked in other branches and by being sensitive to unintended or harmful policy consequences in individual cases."[72]

Judge Posner argues that such judicial "legislation" is an inevitability, regardless of its relative desirability:

> Playing by the rules is also consistent with judges' often voting their policy preferences and personal convictions. For in our system the line between law and policy, the judging game and the legislating game, is blurred. Many cases cannot be decided by reasoning from conventional legal materials. Such cases require the judge to exercise a legislative judgment, although a more confined one than 'real' legislators are authorized to exercise.[73]

Posner is using the relatively cavalier notion of legislating, though he later qualifies it by the "confined" context of judging. Critics of judges often refer to their policy-making judgment as "legislating." This is a misnomer, because such actions do not go through the legislative process, nor do they show up in the statute books, nor are they treated by subsequent decisions as legislation, rather than as precedent. The claims of "judicial legislation" are a misleading red herring; the real dispute is over the extent of appropriate judicial policymaking through interpretation. It is still too simplistic to declaim all judicial policymaking, though, because every interpretive decision makes government policy. The real dispute is over the extent of discretion to allow the judiciary and the consequent scope of the policymaking to be permissible. Because such policymaking is generally grounded in judicial ideologies, it is often criticized.

Even if one theoretically approves or accepts some level of ideological decision making, it does not follow that judicial ideology should be unlimited in its exercise. The traditional rule of law without undue ideological influence has significant societal benefits, and a judiciary that utterly disregarded the law would be harmful. Hence, the criticism of willful judging survives to a degree. The presence of *some* ideological decision making is surely unavoidable and even desirable. The extent of such ideology, though, might be properly constrained.

Assuming that some reduction of ideological decision making is valuable, the next issue is whether textualism has this effect. At its most simplistic level, this argument for textualism rests on a false premise—that internal analysis of a text can itself clearly resolve disputes. Philosophers have long addressed the ambiguity of language, in the study of hermeneutics. Among the foremost of these is Hanz-Georg Gadamer, who urged that a text is variable among different interpreters of the text and in different contexts of interpretation. Per Gadamer, this is an inevitable feature of language. An interpreter need not consciously impose their background beliefs on text, because it is an inevitability. In the legal context, Felix Frankfurter declared that "[a]nything that is written may present a problem of meaning," due to "the very nature of words" themselves.[74] Reliance on text alone therefore does not guarantee determinacy or expunge the possibility of individual judicial ideology as determinative of judicial outcomes.

As noted above, radical critics of law have seized upon this linguistic indeterminacy to argue that the law can have no meaning, but this is excessive. The linguistic indeterminacy is bounded. When debating the meaning of the word "blue," some might include a color such as turquoise, while others would disagree, demonstrating indeterminacy. Few if any would classify an orange color as blue, however. One can dispute whether a tiger is a "cat," but no one would place a dachshund within that definition. Thus, the meaning of language "is not radically indeterminate; instead, meaning is public-fixed by public behavior, beliefs, and understandings."[75] At least within a given language community, words carry some informative meaning. While language may never convey a precise meaning, it may nevertheless have a fuzzy meaning, with greater or lesser levels of precision, depending upon the words chosen.

Most textualists acknowledge the inevitable indeterminacy of textual language. Judge Easterbrook, for example, urges: "Let us not pretend that texts answer every question . . . we must admit that there are gaps in statutes, as in the law in general."[76] For textualists, though, such gaps are not pervasive and can be addressed without turning to legislative history. Professor Manning notes that in contrast to the "plain meaning" approach, "modern textualists do not believe that it is possible to infer meaning from 'within the four corners' of the statute," but must look at the body of law and other contextual considerations.[77]

The textualists admit of techniques that go beyond simple linguistic analysis of text. They accept the consideration of statutes in their broader context. For example, they adhere to a principle that words should be interpreted as to have independent meaning and not serve as mere "surplusage." If a given interpretation of statutory language would render it redundant of other statutory provisions, that interpretation is disfavored. Courts presume that the legislature is not redundant but uses additional words to convey additional meaning. Textualists typically also suggest that a statute must be read as a whole, so the meaning of words may be discerned from their use elsewhere in the statute, sometimes called the "whole act" rule. Words' meanings are determined by their context in the statutory syntax.[78]

While the whole act rule has some obvious appeal, it may not accurately reflect legislative intent. Numerous statutes have seen progressive amendments over the years that may not be perfectly coherent. A later Congress may not have intended the linguistic meaning in its amendment that the original Congress used for a particular word.[79] Moreover, reading the statute as a whole may allow considerable discretion that undermines the purported constraint of textualism as an interpretive method.

A classic application of textualism arises in the interpretation of given statutory terms. Not infrequently, a particular word is used multiple times in different places in a single statute. Some decisions have held that the word may be given a different meaning in different statutory contexts, but a recent Supreme Court decision held that the same statutory word cannot be given "different meanings in different cases."[80] This is the adoption of what has been called the "unitary principle" in contrast to a "polymorphic principle."[81] Textualists have also considered the greater body of legislation. If Congress leaves a word undefined in a statute, they may consider its definition and use in prior statutes. These principles help assign meaning to otherwise unclear language, but they also empower judicial discretion in consideration of other statutes.

The supplemental principles acknowledged by textualists may not resolve statutory ambiguity. In one recent decision of the Court, Justice Thomas conceded that the whole act rule apparently conflicted with the principle that a term should be given a consistent meaning across statutes.[82] There are numerous cases where both the majority opinion and the dissent have invoked the whole act rule as supporting opposite resolutions of those cases.[83]

Moreover, these supplemental contextual interpretive principles may range far afield. In one opinion, Justice Scalia found that the meaning of the text was "by no means clear" but gave it the "only reading that comports with the statutory purpose."[84]

Central to textualism is the plain meaning rule, and this standard would facially seem to be a constraining one. There is little doubt that words in context may have a "plain meaning" that is easily discerned. It is easy to say that orange is not blue. Unfortunately, those easy cases are not the ones likely to come before the courts. Thus, "statutory language is rarely plain on a point disputable enough to reach the level of judicial review."[85] The easy cases are usually settled, as parties have no reason to expend the costs of litigation when the outcome is relatively certain. This principle has become known as the "Priest/Klein hypothesis," for its original authors.[86] While the hypothesis is not perfectly reliable, empirical evidence confirms its rough accuracy.[87] Consequently, it is the "turquoise" cases that come before the court. Courts don't need a plain meaning rule to resolve the "orange" cases, which seldom appear and are easily disposed of at lower levels of the federal judiciary. Interpretive theory is important for the more difficult "turquoise" cases, where plain meaning doesn't determine the answer. Indeed, one criticism of textualism is that it takes cases where textual meaning or context is not plain and pretends as if it were. Judges have attributed a plain meaning to statutory language that "was nearly universally believed to have a contrary meaning for many decades."[88] Thus, plain meaning may not indeed be plain but may be yet another tool of judicial discretion. This effect is empirically examined in Chapter 7.

If textualism is itself indeterminate, the practice would enable the same willful judicial ideological decision making as other interpretive practices, and restraint of judicial ideology would not justify textualism. Textualists can offer two responses. First, they may maintain that textualism is relatively less indeterminate than other interpretive methods and hence will offer relatively greater constraint on judicial ideology. Second, they may contend that the existence of indeterminacy within one single prevailing method must inevitably be less than the level of indeterminacy when judges may pick and choose among interpretive methods in a pluralist system. Because all disputants recognize that textualism is at least *a* legitimate interpretive consideration, the amount of indeterminacy within textualism is a constant. The ability to supplement textualism, in a judge's discretion, with a variety of alternative approaches can only increase ideological discretion. Consequently, a shift to textualism as an exclusive interpretive method would relatively reduce this discretion.

Enhancing the constraint imposed on the judiciary by statutes may be considered the key project of the theories of statutory interpretation. For some, textualism is the answer to this project, providing greater predictability and objectivity in statutory interpretation. They may suggest that reliance on the "ordinary meaning" of text can enable diverse ideologies to reach a consensus.[89] This standard limits the available materials of legitimate interpretation and hence might remove the tools necessary for a judge to be ideological. Moreover, even if textualism itself were not more determinate than any given alternative method, the limitation to a single methodology might be constraining. The choice of methods, in a pluralist approach, gives the willful judge a greater body of materials from which to find an approach that better suits their ideological proclivities.

Ultimately, the ideological discretion argument is an empirical one. While there is a theoretical reason to believe that textualism could reduce discretion, there is also theoretical reasoning to the contrary. Such theories require actual empirical testing for proof. If judges were utterly ideological, no legal interpretive rule could constrain them. Insofar as the critique is based on a premise of judicial infidelity to neutral law, it is a little inconsistent to believe that any rule of neutral law would be constraining. Daniel Farber conducted a small case-study comparison of the decisions of Judge Easterbrook (a committed textualist) and Judge Posner (who criticizes textualism and embraces pragmatism).[90] He found that their theoretical differences transferred into only a very marginal difference in their judicial outcomes and commonly produced agreement. Judge Easterbrook is a conservative who, on balance, renders conservative judicial decisions. While it would be unfair to automatically ascribe his conservative opinions to ideological bias, his record does not provide evidence that textualism constrains judicial ideological discretion.

Assuming that judges are only somewhat ideological and also concern themselves with the proper use of the law, certain interpretive methods may constrain to a degree, but it is not intuitively obvious which methods will be most constraining. One assessment of judicial interpretation of consumer protection laws concluded that "textualism proved to be an extremely flexible method of justifying virtually any decision the court desired."[91] There are colorable arguments why legislative history may constrain better than textualism, arguments which will be discussed in the next chapter. Empirical analysis is necessary to resolve the dispute.

Textualism as Ideology

As discussed above, a leading case for textualism is the claim that the process can constrain the ideological preferences of particular judges. Typically, this claim presumes that a statutory dispute has a *right* answer, which may be conservative or liberal. Textualism strives to find that right answer, regardless of its ideological direction and the ideological preferences of the judges. In this vision, textualism constrains both liberal and conservative ideological inclinations.

While this constraining effect is frequently invoked, it is unproved. As noted above, texts can be ambiguous, and ideologues can read their own preferences into the words, including the use of dictionary shopping. Moreover, textualists use various contextual tools to analyze the meaning of statutes and these also may be subject to textual manipulation. Some have suggested that the true case for textualism, though, is the instillation of a conservative bias that has the effect of producing a pattern of more conservative decisions. In this view the ideological effect of textualism is intrinsically conservative, so that its choice as an interpretive method may reflect judicial ideology.

One aspect of textualism may be to limit the domain of statutes. Rather than use legislative history or other extrinsic aids to define the scope of a statute's coverage, textualism would consider only the text. This could have the fundamental effect of constraining the legislature. Congress must make clear the extent of its authorization in the language of the statutory text itself and must employ words that convey the full breadth of its intent. Absent this indication, a textualist might simply argue that the statute is inapplicable. If one makes the assumption that most statutes are liberal in nature, at least antilibertarian, this is a constraint on statutory liberalism. By making the production of statutory requirements more limited and time-consuming, the interpretive theory will limit the production of those requirements. This limitation in turn limits the effect that the legislature has on society generally. Justice Scalia's interpretive method is said to "systematically narrow the domains of statutes."[92]

One of the foremost contemporary judicial textualists, Judge Easterbrook, has candidly discussed this effect of his theory in an early article.[93] He observes that a common threshold question of statutory interpretation is whether the statute in question even applies to the dispute before the court. If the court finds the statute inapplicable, that ends its analysis. His view is openly an antilegislation one, as he acknowledges that he relies upon a presumption against government interference in the free market. Judge Posner notes that political conservatives "who are skeptical about the good faith of legislators, fear the excesses of democracy, think of statutes as unprincipled compromises, and do not want to help legislators achieve their ends . . . tend to favor strict interpretation."[94] Textualism may thus be a strategy to reduce the authority of the federal legislature and the statutes that it adopts. This is confirmed by a study of the legislative process. Professor Brudney has explained how "Congress' use of legislative history enhances its overall product by diminishing burdens on the legislative calendar."[95] If so, judicial reliance on legislative history enables greater statutory output. The greater burden of legislating without influential legislative history could prevent the enactment of even those laws that carry majority support. Of course, this theory depends on the claim that legislation is generally liberal in direction, which may be untrue, given the conservatism of some recent Congresses. A conservative deregulatory statute, for example, would be limited in its scope by the theory.

Superficially, textualism appears to be judicially modest and legislature-respecting, but in reality it may be contrary. Judge Barak suggests that if "we take legislative supremacy seriously, we must take legislative intent into consideration."[96] The legislature may wish to pursue broad societal goals and do so with flexible directions to the courts, consistent with a general intent. Textualism rejects that legislative wish, insisting upon precise directives or nothing. Even if the legislature does not want its language taken literally, textualists insist that is the only alternative. Textualism thereby constrains the legislature, as well as the courts, and basically limits the scope of government in life. This limitation is generally a conservative one, and so textualism might be deemed a structurally conservative doctrine.

There is an apparent association between the ideology of justices and their interpretive methodologies, analyzed later in Chapter 6. The most conservative justices, such as Scalia and Thomas, appear to be the most opposed to use of legislative history, while relatively liberal justices seem to favor the use of that interpretive approach. This suggests at least a possibility that the commitment to interpretive methodologies itself is insincere. For example, use of legislative history may be opposed by Scalia and Thomas simply because it would yield liberal results contrary to the preferences of conservative justices, while it is favored by liberal justices for the contrary effect. A study of judges on the Seventh Circuit has found that the use of the interpretive methodology of originalism is very highly associated with ideological conservatism.[97] While the directionality of this association is indeterminate, it is possible that conservatives prefer originalism (and liberals dislike it) because the method inherently conduces to conservative outcomes.

The above discussion is largely hypothetical. Some legislation is clearly conservative in nature, and sincere textualist interpretation would limit the domain of that legislation as well. In other circumstances, one can imagine a textualist interpretation that could expand the scope of statutory coverage, unlimited by hedging legislative history. If regulatory statutes are considered liberal, as is commonly the case, deregulatory statutes must be conservative. Likewise, many criminal statutes are conservative in direction. As in the case of the debate over individual judicial ideological discretion, the test for textualism's structural ideological effect must be an empirical one.

Conclusion

Some discussions of textualism are frustrating because they resort to the straw man argument: "when the text is clear it should not be overridden by legislative history or purposivism." This position, though, is relatively uncontroversial. While textualists can point to occasions of such overrides, they are uncommon. The "first impulse of even the strongest purposivist is to try to read the statute in light of the accepted semantic import of the text."[98] The courts "almost universally begin their explanation of reasons for their decisions in statutory interpretation cases with the statutory text."[99] Professor Vermeule notes that both textualists and intentionalists "agree that the statutory text is the starting point for interpretation, and both accept the view that courts should not lightly depart from the text."[100]

The typical salient dispute is one where the import of the text is not so clear, and these are the cases for which an interpretive methodology is required. A textualist would scour the methodologies' tools, such as dictionaries, to try to define meaning, while others would seek other forms of evidence of statutory purpose. Textualists can fairly attempt to resolve these apparent ambiguities without extrinsic sources such as legislative history, but that is what must be justified, not the simple claim that clear text should override extrinsic sources.

CHAPTER 3

Legislative History and Statutory Interpretation

The case for the use of legislative history derives from the contention that the polestar for statutory interpretation should be legislative intent. It seems logical then to seek evidence of that intent in legislative materials. Historically, courts pursued legislative intent but not necessarily legislative history. Prior to the twentieth century, judges tended to rely on traditional common law interpretive devices, such as the linguistic canons. After 1900, judges increasingly began to consider materials of legislative history in interpretation, and the consideration came into full bloom in the 1940s and 1950s.[1] For "much of our history," the Supreme Court has proclaimed that the legislative intent is the "touchstone of federal statutory interpretation."[2]

The use of legislative history has come under increased criticism, though, typically by textualists, for reasons discussed in the preceding chapter. Some of these criticisms of legislative history address only a straw man, suggesting that proponents of its use ignore the statutory text. In truth, all methods are devoted to interpreting text; "the real arguments" are over what judges "should interpret and what interpretive attitude they should adopt."[3] Even nontextualists acknowledge that any interpretation must "have an Archimedean foothold in the language of a text" which "sets the boundaries of legal interpretation."[4] Those who would use legislative history do not disregard the text, they seek to illuminate it. But there is a more sophisticated textualist criticism of legislative history, arguing that those who use legislative history inevitably and illegitimately divert too far from the text. After reviewing the basis for judicial reliance on legislative history, this chapter examines those criticisms.

Intentionalism

The basic theoretical case for consideration of legislative history lies in a broader theory about the importance of "intentionalism" in statutory interpretation. Per this theory, the court's objective should be to ascertain the legislature's intent underlying the statute and ideally how the legislature would have intended this particular statutory interpretation case to be decided. The judge basically inquires into the question of how the legislature would have meant for the instant case to be resolved, had it explicitly considered that case. Joseph Raz argues that since the legislature has the lawmaking power, the law must be presumed to be what it intended to enact. The interpretation of such a law would be legitimate only insofar as it reflected that enacted intent. This theoretical basis for statutory interpretation has a long pedigree, as Chief Justice Marshall noted that "[m]ost of the prominent treatises . . . invoke the intent of Congress as an interpretive guide."[5]

   It is unrealistic to expect clear intentionalist instructions for the resolution of each individual dispute that might arise, so advocates of this approach generally seek a broader intent that informs the proper interpretation of statutory text. While the typical intentionalist places great weight on text as evidence of legislative intent, he or she is willing to depart from the textual language if a particular application would seem to contravene such intent. In the words of one Supreme Court opinion, when the implication of textual language seems "an unreasonable one plainly at variance with the policy of the legislation as a whole, this Court has followed that purpose, rather than the literal words."[6]

Intentionalism is basic to the most traditional law unrelated to statutes, such as contract interpretation. When courts are required to interpret a contract, they rely heavily on its language but sometimes must examine the intent of the contracting parties. In this process, they may examine the contract negotiation process. The prevailing view is that a court should consider context, including extrinsic sources, in order to determine the intent of the contracting parties. It is not uncommon for parties to a contract to avoid or limit this intentionalist examination through an integration clause, which precludes the consideration of materials extrinsic to the contract. While the legislature might include a similar term in legislation, it has not done so. Thus, intentionalism generally would imply using resources such as legislative history.

The broader search for general legislative purpose sometimes goes by the term "purposivism." This very general theory is often associated with the seminal work of Hart and Sacks.[7] They contend that every statute is a purposive act of the legislature, of reasonable legislators who are seeking a particular outcome. Each statute should be fitted into the broad legal landscape in order to best effectuate the purpose of the enacting Congress. Rather than focusing on congressional intent with regard to the case at hand, which is likely to be in vain, purposivists strive to best fulfill congressional purposes, on the assumption that the legislature probably had not contemplated the details of the particular case. Justice Frankfurter explained that "the fair interpretation of a statute is often 'the art of proliferating a purpose,' revealed more by the demonstrable forces that produced it than by its precise phrasing."[8] One finds elements of purposivism in many judicial decisions, but on today's Supreme Court it is most commonly associated with Justice Stevens. A clear example of purposivism that is relatively uncontroversial involved the interpretation of the Civil Rights Act. The question was whether "Arabs" could be seen as a distinct "race" for purposes of prohibiting discrimination against that ethnic group. While few dictionaries would consider Arabs a separate race, the Court extended the protection to them based on the general purpose of the statute.[9] As Justice Frankfurter declared in an earlier decision: the question is "not what do ordinary English words mean, but what did Congress mean them to mean."[10]

The case for a particular form of purposivism has been made by Aharon Barak, the president of the Supreme Court of Israel.[11] His approach includes a synthesis of subjective elements, such as author's intent, with objective elements, such as textual evidence.[12] He privileges the text as a source of purpose but is ready to go beyond the text in some circumstances to examine the subjective purposes of the text's authors. Such an examination includes the circumstances surrounding the text's creation and legislative history. Barak distinguishes purposivism from intentionalism by suggesting that the latter philosophy is too limited in its assessment of subjectivity. Nevertheless, the two share in common an effort to discern and give effect to the intentions of the legislature in judicial decision making.

Even when the legislative intent may be discerned, as a theoretical manner, some question the ability of the judiciary to do so. Judges, at least those at levels below the Supreme Court, have a large number of cases to decide, with relatively little time to devote to a particular case. They are unable to investigate the process of statutory enactment in the depth of something like a doctoral dissertation. Hence, they can at best rely on the most obvious cues to intent, which may not be the most reliable indicators of what Congress meant, discussed further below.

The intentionalist approach requires something that may be referred to as "imaginative reconstruction," a term initially coined by Judge Learned Hand.[13] This involves the judge attempting to enter the shoes of the legislators and discern their intent at the time, and how they would have wanted the statute applied to the case before the court. Some have questioned the validity of such reliance on the judicial imagination. Given the intervening years, the process may be difficult. Judge Posner cites the example of a statute selecting jurors from voting rolls passed at a time before women had the right to vote.[14] When women receive the right to vote, should they become eligible to serve on juries? Perhaps the "eligible voter" standard was initially adopted for the express purpose of preventing women from being jurors, in which case allowing service would defeat the authors' purpose. It is difficult to imaginatively reconstruct intent when circumstances have changed so dramatically. Moreover, when a statute involves a legislative deal in compromise, as is frequently the case, but such a deal "is likely to be under the table," a court will have difficulty discerning its content.[15] Discernment of the deal will often be impossible for a later court. Indeed, the presence of a hidden purpose may mean that judicial attempts to discern a purpose will be systematically wrong because they will be denied the information about the true basis for the legislation.

Textualists argue that their preferred procedure will best discern the content of the legislative compromise. They stress that the final form of a statute is a "decision to go so far and no further" and that purposivist approaches are associated with going further. While this analysis is uncertain, it begs the question. The issue is what the final form of the statute is, and means, and that textualism best captures that form. More centrally, the argument fails to address the pervasive background delegation of statutes. As previously noted, the legislative compromise will not have foreseen, much less resolved, novel future applications of the statute. These are the sort of difficult cases most likely to be litigated. If there was no congressional consideration of these facts, the legislative compromise is unhelpful.

Purposivism underdetermines most of the major interpretive disputes, as noted in the Supreme Court decision in *Exxon Corporation v. Hunt*.[16] There, the Court majority interpreting CERCLA acknowledged that "the overall purpose of a statute is a useful referent when trying to decipher ambiguous statutory language" but proceeded to note that CERCLA had competing purposes: balancing the need to clean up hazardous wastes against "the potentially adverse effects of overtaxation on the competitiveness of the American petrochemical industry." Such circumstances are typical. Legislation is by its nature a compromise among competing purposes. In the presence of such a conflict, the generalized statutory purposes do not determine which purpose should prevail in a particular litigated dispute.

Barak recognizes this problem but suggests that it will be limited to "rare cases."[17] This assumption is too facile, because nearly every dispute over legislation involves a battle of conflicting purposes. Legislation is a compromise, and that compromise is between conflicting goals. Every piece of regulatory legislation has this conflict. The Occupational Safety and Health Act has as its central purpose the promotion of occupational safety and health, but it also has the less obvious purpose of limiting that protection. It authorizes not boundless authority to promote occupational safety but only limited authority, qualified by the costs of such protection and other factors. Disputes typically arise on the margin over whether the act directs a particular regulation providing particular protection at particular cost. This is a direct conflict in purpose, and absent direct statutory guidance to resolve the conflict or perhaps legislative history, purposivism does not provide much help. The court has observed that "no legislation pursues its purposes at all costs" so that it "frustrates rather than effectuates legislative intent simplistically to assume that *whatever* furthers the statute's primary objective must be the law."[18]

The shortcomings of purposivism do not entirely demean its consideration, as was recognized by the Supreme Court in *Hunt*. Statutory purposes are often found in the text itself, as many statutes begin with "findings and purposes" sections or preambles that lay out the rationale for their enactment. Still, these general textual provisions seldom help resolve the difficult close questions about legislative compromises. Here, legislative history is a useful guide to the purpose or intent of the legislative drafters. Such statements go to the subjective purpose of the enacting legislature, at least if used with care. While there is little dispute that reliance on intent or purpose of legislative history should not be badly done, the questions are whether it can be well done as a theoretical manner and whether judges can successfully do so in practice.

For textualists, as discussed in Chapter 2, intent is not meaningful unless clearly expressed in statutory language. Judge Easterbrook boldly pronounced: "What any member of Congress thought his words would do is irrelevant. We do not care about his mental processes."[19] The unstated intent of the legislature has not satisfied the bicameralism and presentment requirements for legislation and consequently lacks legal import for the textualists. Intentionalism is central to reliance on legislative history, however. Justice Frankfurter summarized this use, explaining that "the fair interpretation of a statute is often 'the art of proliferating a purpose,' revealed more by the demonstrable forces that produced it than by its precise phrasing."[20]

Intentionalism via legislative history may take two forms. The first is specific. The statutory text may seem ambiguous, with respect to the particular facts presented to the court for resolution. Some item of legislative history, though, may address those facts with specificity and declare how they should be resolved. Reliance on such precise direction gives effect to specific intentionalism. The second is general. While legislative history may not directly address the contested facts of the litigation, it may evince a broader intentionalist theme that, when applied to the facts, directs their resolution. An example of this is Chief Justice Warren's decision interpreting the Celler-Kefauver Amendment in *Brown Shoe*, where he found that "[t]aken as a whole, the legislative history illuminates congressional concern with the protection of *competition*, not *competitors*."[21] He therefore was able to rule that a competitor had no standing to complain of an antitrust violation, without showing harm to consumers through inhibition of competition.

The Tools and Standards of Legislative History

Merely declaring the relevance of legislative history for statutory interpretation does not define the legislative history that is important for this end. A bill's passage finds many opportunities for legislators to comment on the meaning of its terms, in varying circumstances. Moreover, the legislative process involves a series of votes on those words, sometimes rejecting alternative language. This extensive olla of comments and actions provides the overall legislative history. Within this backdrop, one can regularly find congresspersons who take opposing views on numerous controversial questions. Given the presence of contradictory materials in this history, courts have developed guidance to determine the most reliable sources of intent.

The typical rationale for this hierarchy is sometimes "explained by their perceived connection to mental-state intentions."[22] In the context of legislative intentionalism or purposivism, this is certainly debatable. There is no reason to necessarily presume that the intention of the full legislature must correspond to any of the sources of legislative history. The hierarchy makes more sense from a delegation context, which I explain below as I briefly review the hierarchy.

Of the hierarchy of legislative history sources, the content of the report of the conference committee stands at the apex, as the "most authoritative single source."[23] It is the only source that discusses the precise text of the bill that would be voted on and become law without further changes. Moreover, it is the only resource that clearly reflects the input of both houses of Congress. The conference committee is clearly delegated the task of drafting the actual text of the final bill, and its report therefore clearly reflects the position of delegatees. Some justices have explicitly held that the "most authoritative report is a Conference Report acted upon by both Houses and therefore unequivocally representing the will of both Houses as a joint legislative body."[24]

After the conference committee report, the next most reliable sources of legislative history are the reports of the committees that reported the bill out to their respective houses. These committees are commonly the source of the bill's language and a primary object of congressional self-delegation, discussed below. They must be used with some care, however, as the reports discuss the bill reported out of committee, which may not have the same language as the final bill that became law. Judges have displayed "widespread agreement" on the preeminence of such committee reports, which "receive the most citations and the greatest weight" in opinions.[25]

A salient source of legislative history can be found in the record of changes made to a bill prior to its passage, or the changes consciously not made. Suppose that an amendment to a bill is proposed on the floor of Congress and voted down. This aspect of the legislative record provides fairly persuasive evidence that the content of the amendment was not the legislative intent. While this is not conclusive (the amendment might have been rejected as surplusage, for example), a judge should be cautious to adopt a statutory interpretation that tracks that of the rejected amendment. The best explanation of this reasoning is still that of James Landis, who wrote:

> Successive drafts of the same act do not simply succeed each other as isolated phenomena, but the substitution of one for another necessarily involves an element of choice often leaving little doubt as to the reasons governing such a choice. The voting down of an amendment or its acceptance upon the statement of its proponent again may disclose real evidence of intent.[26]

This source of legislative history fits better with the intentionalist approach than others but is also consistent with delegation, though it is more a delegation to the whole body.

Another common source of legislative history is the floor debate on the bill after it has been reported out of committee. Committee reports will not be helpful for amendments made on the floor that postdate the committee report. In such a debate, an advocate of the bill might explain that it was meant to apply in this way, or not apply in that way, in order to persuade other congresspersons to vote for the bill. If effective, this illustrates the delegation procedure. Congress passed the law after learning of its application from a member and based upon that understanding. Alternatively, an opponent of the bill might describe the meaning of the bill in such a way as to discourage other congresspersons from supporting it. This legislative history is generally considered less reliable, because opponents may have an incentive to distort the bill to make it appear unreasonable, in order to gain allies for its rejection. Bills have individual sponsors, and statements by a sponsor interpreting legislation may be entitled to greater weight, as statements that have been called "[a]lmost as important as committee reports."[27]

Another potential source of legislative history is statements in committee hearings on a bill. When a committee is preparing a bill's text, it typically conducts hearings in which interested parties may participate and make arguments about the appropriate congressional action. Committee witnesses may include other members of Congress or representatives of the administration. Such testimony is generally given little weight as legislative history, because there is little reason to believe that the full Congress delegated any authority to witnesses at committee hearings. Indeed, congresspersons often do not even have access to the full content of the hearings at the time they vote on a bill, in contrast to committee reports and floor statements. This undermines its validity under the self-delegation theory.

Another questionable type of legislative history is post-enactment. This arises when a member, or even a committee, of a later Congress comments on the proper interpretation of a statute passed by an earlier and different Congress. Because such statements occurred only after the bill's passage, it is obvious that other members of Congress did not rely on them when voting. In addition, much post-enactment history comes from an entirely different Congress, with different members, and hence may not reflect the views of the enacting Congress. The Court has occasionally relied on post-enactment history, though, when it seems more reliable, such as a later statement by the sponsor of the earlier legislation.[28]

Subsequent legislative action may be considered more compelling in the context of an enactment, rather than a report or comments by legislators. The Supreme Court has held that "[s]ubsequent legislation declaring the intent of an earlier statute is entitled to great weight in statutory construction."[29] Instances of such use are not so common, though, and the theory is more consistent with a dynamic interpretive approach than one reliant on legislative history. There is no reason why a subsequent legislature should provide an authentic depiction of the intent of the enacting legislative history.

Even strong advocates of the general use of legislative history often reject judicial reliance on post-enactment legislative history unless it is in the context of legislative action to amend or renew the earlier legislation. This conclusion makes sense from a delegation perspective. Legislators are much less likely to attend to legislative history that is unrelated to any bill up for their consideration and have no opportunity to ratify (or reject) such legislative history with a vote on such a bill. There is no intrinsic reason for them to make such a delegation, and the agent's statements may simply be an attempt to manipulate the statute.

Legislative History as Delegation

The best conception of legislative history produced by a committee or otherwise is as a delegation of authority by the legislature to inform future courts about the meaning of legislation. This fact is suggested by the very existence of legislative history, such as committee reports. Their primary function presumably is to provide information to interested, voting legislators, but that very fact gives them great relevance for interpreting judges. Jeremy Waldron has criticized use of legislative history given the diversity of interests in the body who dispute and compromise. He concedes that reference to legislative intentions would be appropriate in the case of a bill introduced by a single legislator, which the body adopted out of comity. While he presumes, no doubt correctly, that these particular circumstances are rare, they closely parallel the common internal self-delegation, in which the body defers to the intentions of a committee, as expressed in its report.

Members of Congress have occasionally referred to the judicial interpretation issue, and "the practice of relying on legislative history to discern the meaning of statutes has been endorsed by an array of current and former senators and representatives."[30] Although textualism's rejection of legislative history is typically associated with conservative Republican appointees in the judiciary, Republican legislators have remarked that "legislative history can serve to focus general statutory text, offer meaning when a provision is produced in the course of floor debate, and prevent slippage from agreements reached in Congress."[31] The nature of congressional self-governance, discussed in Chapter 2 and in greater detail below, means that

Congress delegates to committees and other subbodies the authority to make influential decisions about legislation. Logically, Congress would also delegate to those subbodies the authority to explain those decisions to the full body. This is a small and simple extension of the functional delegation.

Under the internal delegation theory, there is no need to undertake the difficult and complex effort of discerning the mental state of Congress. A given piece of legislative history may be important, not because the majority considered the question and mentally concurred but because they delegated a question's resolution to the author of that piece of legislative history. Its existence *is* its importance. This is not a theory of historic intentionalism, though, which tries to capture the legislature's mind. The only intentionalism at issue under the delegation theory is the intent that legislative history be relevant for interpretation.

Justice Breyer has addressed the significance of legislative history in the congressional process, noting that in striking compromises, legislators negotiate about not only the statutory text but also the contents of committee reports and other legislative history sources.[32] A case study of several statutes found that the legislative history represented "an integral part of the shared understanding reached by Congress as a whole."[33] Justice Breyer suggested that a "legislator may vote for technical language that the legislator does not understand (perhaps because of their faith in the drafting process) that it has a proper function."[34] This reflects the important delegation of the full body to the work of congressional committees, including their reports on bills sent to the floor for consideration. Justice Scalia has confronted this argument, but his answer amounts to no more than an assertion that legislators would not so delegate.[35] Many states have adopted legislative standards for statutory interpretation. Forty of the state statutes explicitly authorize judicial inquiry into legislative history, and none of the statutes prohibit it.[36]

I criticized purposivism above for being unable to discern the terms of legislative deals, but this criticism does not apply as strongly to reliance on legislative history, used as a basis to infer purpose or otherwise. If the legislative deal makers know that a future court is likely to rely on legislative history, they will ensure that the legislative history reflects the deal. Doing otherwise would be self-defeating. Of course, there remains the problem of others creating legislative history to disrupt the deal or gain favor for a legislator's position. The resolution of this problem depends on the judiciary's good faith and ability to differentiate reliable from unreliable legislative history.

The Validity of Legislative History

The question of the validity of legislative history goes to whether the declarations of a subset of Congress can ever be said to represent the collective will. They are not the formal product of a decision of the body. Jeremy Waldron argues that a final statute is a compromise that "may in no way reflect the objectives and intentions of those legislators who enacted it together."[37] While used to question reliance on legislative history, or any intentionalist theory, Waldron's claim also suggests that the text does not reflect legislative intent. One could just as easily say that legislative history reflects intent as well as the text, as discussed in the preceding chapter. Under the theory, the only case for textualism is the rigid constitutional one that utterly disregards legislative purpose.

Even if a collective will could be found, the next challenge is to identify what if any legislative history reflects that will. This determination requires some analysis of the organization of Congress. One excellent analysis reviews the practice of congressional governance.[38] It explains how Congress developed its committee structure and other supporting systems in an attempt to "maintain coequal policymaking status with the executive branch."[39] It is important that Congress consciously created its internal governance system, including committees, and specifically empowered them to produce reports on proposed legislation. This evidences a purposeful delegation of authority to the subbodies of the legislature.

Keith Krehbiel argues that congressional committees provide services to the full legislature, including the development of specialized expertise and associated information provision. Each house thus prefers committees that center around the median position for the full body, to serve as "microcosms of their parent chamber."[40] This enables the committee to create a legislative product that takes advantage of their expertise in the subject and that is ideologically compatible with the overall house. Krehbiel demonstrated that the committees in fact appeared to have ideological medians comparable to those of the full body in all but a few cases, though this conclusion has been disputed. When the ideological composition of the overall Congress changes, committee ideological representation clearly responds.[41]

It is surely the case that subordinate bodies are not perfectly representative of the full legislative body. Typically, "legislators tend to self-select into those committees in which their supporters have the greatest stakes."[42] Thus, the Agriculture Committee is likely to be composed primarily of representatives from the farm states. It is the committees who first define the language of bills for a vote, and they therefore have some measure of agenda control. The evidence on the representativeness of subordinate legislative bodies is not conclusive. Other research suggests that committees' function is to provide information to the full body, even when they do not clearly represent the median.[43] Committees are heterogeneous, though, so that legislators not on the committee have a variety of perspectives off which to cue. The analysis found that "committee members were cue-givers to like-minded floor colleagues."[44] The full body's median may cue off a median committee member for the full body, even if he or she is not the committee median. To gain passage of its legislation, therefore, the committee must attend particularly to members closest to the overall median.

Perhaps the greatest legislative delegation to a subbody, beyond the creation of the materials of legislative history, involves "closed rule" votes. This is a procedural restriction that prevents the full body from amending a statute sent to the floor by a committee for a vote of the full chamber. The committee's statutory language is therefore presented on a "take it or leave it" basis. No floor amendments to the bill are allowed under this procedure. The use of such closed rule voting restrictions has increased substantially in more recent Congresses.[45] The theoretical justification for use of such a rule in part involves the full body's deference to the greater expertise of the committee regarding the subject matter of the legislation. Enacting a law under this rule, though, is a much greater delegation of authority to a subbody than any interpretive reliance on legislative history. Under the closed rule, the committee, and only the committee, controls the very text of the statute passed.

The same issue typically arises when the two houses of Congress pass different but parallel bills that have to be reconciled in conference committee. The conference committee is a small subbody of both houses of the legislature which revises both bills to produce compromise legislation. That compromise must be ratified, unamended, by both houses to become law, but it is the conference committee membership, not the full body, that controls the text of the ultimate law, as a product of self-delegation to this select group of representatives. This self-delegation suggests that the most reliable source of legislative history is the report of the conference committee, followed by the report of the committee reporting the bill to the floor, and these are in fact generally regarded as the most reliable.

Another feature of the legislative process is known as "logrolling." This is a practice of trading votes. A legislator who cares less about the subject of a particular bill will vote contrary to his or her preferences in order to gain the vote of a different legislator (who cares more about this bill but less about some other bill that is important to the original legislator). It is possible, given logrolling, that a particular statute was the preference of only a minority of the members of Congress. Yet this in no way dejustifies the legal significance of the statute. Statutes passed due to logrolling have the same legal significance as any other statutes.

Judge Easterbrook has suggested that the presence of logrolling means that it is impossible for the judiciary to discern the intent of the legislature.[46] While this obviously seems true, in the sense of discerning the mind of the pivotal legislator, it does not dejustify legislative history from a delegation context. Legislative history is not useful because it is an intrinsic reflection of legislative intent in the abstract. It is useful because the legislature has delegated explicatory authority to the committee or other source of legislative history.

Legislative history has some functional similarity to logrolling. Individual legislators all have the power to directly create some legislative history on the floor of Congress. Members of the committee have the ability to affect the language of committee reports. Other legislators also have an indirect power to create legislative history by insisting on certain language in a committee report in order to gain their vote, a form of logrolling. All legislative history is somewhat like logrolling, in the sense that the creation of such history takes some time and effort, commodities that are scarce in the busy legislature of today. Those legislators who most care about a bill are the ones who will provide the legislative history for interpretation. While critics might claim that legislative history is illegitimate, because it gives more weight to some legislators than to others, this argument proves far too much. The presence of logrolling makes it clear that the exact same critique applies to the text of the laws passed by the Congress. The creation of legislative history to be considered by the judiciary may well be a form of logrolling. Indeed, a member of Congress might trade his vote on a bill for the creation of a bit of legislative history.

If logrolling were regarded as a "bad thing," this could count as an argument against the use of legislative history. The interpretive use of legislative history materials probably facilitates logrolling. Moreover, if legislators to some degree select into committees on issues where they have greater preference intensity, reliance on materials from those committees may innately reflect logrolling. The same would be true of reliance on sponsors' statements, given that sponsors likely have particular interest in the particular bill they sponsor. Indeed, this may be part of the reason why Congress creates those materials. However, social scientists have not established that logrolling is bad, and there is a credible argument that it is democratically beneficial.[47]

The most common materials of legislative history are the product of a structural congressional decision to create them. Hence, Judge Wald writes that "to disregard committee reports as indicators of congressional understanding . . . is to second-guess Congress' chosen form of organization and delegation of authority, and to doubt its ability to oversee its own constitutional functions effectively."[48] Such a view hardly sounds of legislative supremacy. However, even if a judge defers to the validity of legislative history, as demonstrated by its existence, this does not resolve its significance. For legislative history to be helpful, it must be amenable to reliable interpretation by the courts.

The Reliability of Legislative History

The reliability of legislative history issue goes beyond that of validity and involves the possibility that such materials may be manipulated. Some legislators or even legislative staff may attempt to manipulate the interpretation of a statute by manufacturing legislative history supporting an interpretation that could never receive the assent of the full legislative body. Critics argue that legislative history simply reflects positions that could have been introduced as amendments to the text but were not, presumably because such a more definitive resolution would have been futile, destined for defeat in a full vote.

One branch of the reliability critique argues that legislative history may be manipulated. Thus, "canny legislators or staffers will have an incentive to salt the *Congressional Record* with misleading statements that further their own special agendas."[49] For some legislation, such as the Speedy Trial Act, this scenario apparently played out.[50] If one "assumes that legislators and staffers are on the lookout for opportunities to salt the legislative history, their opponents presumably are aware of this risk and will either prevent misleading language or counter it with their own disavowals or competing bits of misleading history."[51] Of course, the competing legislative history could simply produce confusion. Because judges "operate at some remove from the legislative process," they are claimed to be "pretty bad" at discerning the reliable legislative history from the unreliable.[52]

This criticism of legislative history presumes that courts are unable to distinguish the reliable from the unreliable forms of legislative history. Adrian Vermeule argues that the effort required to learn the complete content of the legislative history is so great that courts are unlikely to accurately reach the correct conclusion.[53] This presumption has not been established, though, and courts have considerable assistance in this project. Private services and Congress itself have published volumes of all the legislative history underlying major statutes that are frequently litigated. Cases are briefed by advocates who can be expected to scour the legislative history for all the references supporting their position, providing the courts with all the necessary information. As one who was once a young associate who had to scour the legislative history of an especially elaborate statute that was just passed, CERCLA, I would testify that the effort is not truly so daunting.

Vermeule further argues that the costs associated with use of legislative history could skew the process, so that more "affluent parties" would gain an advantage.[54] They presumably would be better able to spend the resources to exhaustively explore the available legislative history. This criticism surely proves too much, as affluent litigants have this advantage across the board in litigation, and there is no reason to single out legislative history as a unique source of such advantage to be expunged. The textualist principle that language is to be interpreted in the context of all the other laws of the statute books potentially requires far more research than the study of the legislative history of one given statute.

The cost problem is not unique to legislative history or statutory interpretation; it applies with much greater force to decision making according to precedent, which is a much vaster resource to search than the legislative history of a given statute. I am unaware of anyone who has suggested that the costs of researching precedent somehow dejustify the practice of *stare decisis*. Many textualists are also constitutional originalists, a theory that requires them to assess the even greater body of information on the Founders' intentions. Of course, decisions weigh costs against benefits, so the greater costs of reliance on precedent would be outweighed by its greater benefits, but this simply returns the debate over legislative history to the question of its value, not the costliness of its use.

There are cases where courts have effectively distinguished the reliability of legislative history sources. For example, Senator Helms, in an attempt to drive the interpretation of CERCLA, argued on the floor that the legislation's omission of express joint and several liability reflected a legislative judgment that joint and several liability was rejected by Congress. The courts rejected this as manufactured and manipulated legislative history when interpreting CERCLA, in light of more persuasive contradictory legislative history. Professor Brudney argues that at least some materials of legislative history should be considered "highly reliable."[55]

In theory, any such manipulative attempts might be defeated by broader legislative intent, through more extensive contrary legislative history. But legislative time is scarce, and legislators cannot realistically be expected to screen the full legislative history of a bill. Justice Scalia observes that it is "not certain that even the members of the issuing committees have found the time to read the reports" issued by the committee.[56] Thus, it is argued that the "principle of consent by silence, upon which the theory rests, is fallacious."[57] However, a principal may by delegation consent to abide by documents of which the principal is unaware. Consent by silence is intermittently recognized by the Court when statutes are amended or reenacted. Justice Scalia explained that where there was a judicial interpretation of language of an existing statute, the congressional reenactment of the same language, unamended, is presumed to incorporate and codify the "settled judicial interpretation."[58] This is the same consent by silence, just applied to judicial interpretations rather than legislative history.

The same criticism may be applied to textualism. Indeed, Senator Specter has reported that that members of Congress "are more likely to read a committee report than the bill itself,"[59] not to mention their probability of reviewing all the contemporary dictionary definitions of all the bill's terms. An experienced congressional staffer reported that legislators "who sought written information asked primarily if not exclusively for the report and almost never for the text of the reported bill."[60] Scalia acknowledges that legislators may not have read the statutory language either, but argues that "genuine knowledge is a precondition for the supposed authoritativeness of a committee report, and not a precondition for the authoritativeness of a statute."[61] This is an artificial set of preconditions, though. If the legislature wants the legislative history considered, one simply presumes that the statute incorporates that history, so genuine knowledge is no longer a precondition for authoritativeness of legislative history any more than of statutes.

It is significant that Congress requires "that any committee report filed be made available to all members before the bill is considered on the floor."[62] James Buckley, a federal judge and former Republican Senator, has written that his understanding of the legislation on which he voted was based on "my reading of its language and, where necessary, *on explanations contained in the accompanying report*."[63] Unsurprisingly, he has relied on legislative history on occasion to interpret statutes as a judge of the D.C. Circuit. Thus, the materials of legislative history may be more salient to the congressional approval of a bill than the text itself.

Scalia recognizes the reality of congressional reliance on the work of its subbodies but finds judicial interpretive use unconstitutional, because the Constitution cannot authorize a committee, a mere subset of the full body, to make a law or to "fill in the details" of such a law, but this argument also fails, as a variant of the subdelegation issue addressed in the prior chapter. The answer misstates the issue, as it is not the committee that is creating a law when legislative history is used. The legislative history of a bill only becomes meaningful after the bill is passed. The Committee Report predates the legislation's passage. Hence, if Congress intends the use of legislative history and passes a statute with a given legislative history already existent, you have the full Congress endorsing that legislative history and making its use constitutional by that very act. This is no different from the fact that legislative committees draft statutory language that may be unread by members or even unamendable by the full body, but that language nevertheless becomes constitutional legislation by the vote of the full legislature. Professor Brudney urges that "there is no reason to conclude that committee-drafted legislative history is significantly less imputable to Congress than committee-drafted text."[64]

The principle of consent by silence is therefore not "fallacious." It is fallacious to presume that the full legislative body is informed of the legislative history and affirmatively consented to it (though the same is true of the text). It is not fallacious to presume that the legislature consented to the salience of the legislative history even without knowing its content. This is a standard aspect of a principal/agent relationship. A principal company delegates decision-making authority to an agent, such as an employee, and is bound to have consented to the agent's decisions, regardless of whether the principal is familiar with the content of that decision or not. Such actual knowledge of content is required only when the agent has exceeded his or her authority. The true question is whether the full Congress has delegated this authority to amplify a law's meaning to the sources of legislative history. Some have argued that what "most legislators think they are considering, most of the time, is just a bill's language."[65] This claim begs the question, though, insofar as it is utterly unevidenced and contrary to the congressional sources cited above.

The dispute over the reliability of legislative history largely misses the mark. The history is *ipso facto* reliable if the full Congress endorses its use by passing the bill. This leaves us with the same basic question: does Congress intend for courts to use legislative history in statutory interpretation? I have argued that Congress could easily ban its consideration (or simply not produce legislative history) if Congress did not want such a history to be considered. The contrary position might be defended by noting that Congress could explicitly command the consideration but has not done so.

Given the absence of a clear prohibition on the use of legislative history or command that it be used, the logical conclusion is that Congress intends that its use be left to the discretion of the interpreter of the law—the judiciary. It is precisely this discretion that opponents of legislative history fear, though, for its possible empowerment of willful ideological decision making by judges. Scalia complains that consideration of legislative history "has facilitated rather than deterred decisions that are based upon the courts' policy preferences, rather than neutral principles of law."[66] This important criticism must be addressed by any defender of legislative history and will be addressed below.

There is another stronger reliability critique of legislative history, involving judicial aptitude. As noted above, Adrian Vermeule and others have suggested that the ability to get the correct interpretation of legislative history was costly. While the extent of this effect is debatable, it may be that the legislative history provides limited interpretive aid, even when it is all readily available for scrutiny. Judges may be able to ignore manufactured legislative history, but this still may not give them the interpretive answer required. Legislators speak on the floor for a variety of reasons, not the least of which is pandering to their constituents. Relying on such speeches runs the risk of adopting as policy something the individual legislator did not intend to enact, much less the entire Congress.

Vermeule concludes that "fallible judges are less likely to recapture legislators' intentions successfully by using such documents than by refusing to use them."[67] This is a plausible criticism, though not one that is conclusively proved. Unfortunately, the thesis is an extremely difficult one to test, because there is no objective standard of legislative intention against which the judges' decisions may be measured. One can measure the effect of judicial ideology, which provides some test of the accuracy of judicial interpretations, so such a test (provided below) offers at least a remote evaluation of the claim.

The above discussion of the committee structure of Congress indicates how committee reports seem to be relatively reliable sources of legislative intent, at least for unamended provisions of a bill. Sophisticated analyses of congressional decision making complicate the search for legislative intent, however. It is not enough for a bill to have majority support in Congress, as the legislative system requires a bill to pass through certain pivot points and allows minorities to block legislation in circumstances such as a Senatorial filibuster. Hence, it is not truly the median legislator that determines passage.

Some have argued that judges should base their statutory interpretation on the positions of this ideologically pivotal legislator, who ultimately controlled the content of the bill that was passed. Given the variety of legislative pivot points, the determination of the pivotal legislator can be quite elusive. Moreover, in the typical law, there are multiple pivotal voters. In the Senate, for example, the committee chairman may control the very consideration of a bill, the pivotal member of the committee will have significant control over the bill as reported out of committee, and the pivotal member of the full legislature will have similar control, not to mention the role of the party leadership. The House has its own distinct pivotal legislators. Professor Eskridge analyzed the original Civil Rights Act and identified Senator Dirksen as pivotal for breaking the Southern filibuster of the bill; Representative McCulloch as pivotal in gaining the bill's report from committee; Representative Brown, for preventing the Rules Committee from blocking the bill; Senator Mansfield, for managing the bill on the floor; and President Johnson, for signing the final bill and for influencing the entire process.[68]

The analysis involves not merely identifying the pivot but also calculating how the various pivots compromised their preferences. The task of reconciling the preferences of the pivotal legislatores in passage of the Civil Rights Act is a daunting one. Moreover, this calculation is complicated by the existence of logrolling. A given act may not reflect the pivotal voter's preference on a given issue but instead represent the preferences of some different legislator who was willing to trade his or her vote on a matter of great consequence to that of the pivotal legislator for the act being analyzed. Interpretive strategies grounded in the pivotal voter hypothesis are surely beyond the ken of the courts.

The best case for use of legislative history is in the internal delegation theory, providing that certain types of legislative history are important merely because of their existence. Thus, the content of a committee report matters, not because of its author or surrounding circumstances but simply because the full legislative body acts as if it matters. Just as pivotal legislators influence the text, they have an ability to negate legislative history that is unacceptable to them. Because the committees themselves are key pivots in the legislative process, legislative history from the committees may be a tool to at least remotely capture the interest of the pivotal legislators.

Legislative history is unlikely to be helpful in the common case of background delegation, where Congress did not anticipate the facts of the particular controversy facing a court. Just as the text will not reveal the congressional principal's legislative command in these cases, neither will the legislative history. Indeed, reliance on legislative history in the case of background delegation may be affirmatively misleading, as courts would use congressional intent regarding foreseen circumstances for those that are unforeseen. This reliability critique does not call for the outright rejection of legislative history as an interpretive factor, because cases may arise where it yields a clear answer. The critique does counsel some modesty in reliance on legislative history, though, and suggests that such materials are not an interpretive panacea. There remains the issue of whether judges can be relied upon to make only modest use of legislative history when they engage in statutory interpretation.

The reliability of use of legislative history is a tricky issue. It seems safe to say from the limitations of the legislative record that judges will sometimes reach the wrong conclusion using legislative history. The frequency of such errors is critical, and there is little information on this fact. In addition, the errors that result from the use of legislative history must be contrasted with the error rate of other methodologies, as no system is perfect. Many critics claim that legislative history is highly unreliable, because it is an insincere interpretive method and serves as a beard for ideological judicial decision making, a position addressed in the following discussion.

Legislative History and Ideological Decision Making

The fundamental case against legislative history, and for textualism, is the desire to control the judiciary and prevent "judicial legislation" that twists statutes to fit the judges' ideological predispositions. Given the plenitude of legislative history, some argue that it simply provides convenient materials for willful ideological judging. More materials will generally facilitate greater judicial choice in interpretation, and with both conservatives and liberals in Congress, one might expect legislative history to be manufactured to suit various ideological positions.

The ideological concern potentially overrides all theoretical arguments for and against a theory of statutory interpretation. In the presence of judicial ideology, the optimal theoretical method of statutory interpretation might in practice be the "second best" method. Suppose that the theory of search for legislative intent was deemed the theoretical optimum. However, suppose that in judicial practice the use of this method did not sincerely seek out the true legislative intent, but its use merely masked the judges' own ideological preferences. If so, use of the "legislative intent" method would fail to advance and might easily undermine its goals. In this scenario, a theoretically suboptimal interpretive method that better constrained the use of judicial ideology could better approach the ultimate theoretical objective. Some make this very argument against reliance on legislative history.

Perhaps the best known cynical comment on legislative history refers to its use as like "looking over a crowd and picking out your friends." Consideration of the legislative materials allegedly allows "judges to pick and choose from the diverse opinions found in much legislative history, and thereby reach result-oriented decisions."[69] A review of securities law opinions concluded that legislative history was used by the justices "for post hoc rationalization of a conclusion reached on other grounds."[70] Yet the degree to which use of legislative history allows such manipulation, as opposed to other interpretive theories, is an unproven empirical question.

As noted above, there is a theoretical hierarchy of sources of legislative history as reliable clues to legislative intent. Committee reports are generally at or near the top of this hierarchy. If the use of legislative history were insincere, though, and judges seized upon any friends available in the legislative record, they might be cited no more frequently than other sources. If this were the case, it would indeed be an indictment of legislative history, but empirical study shows that committee reports are in fact cited far more frequently than floor debates or hearing testimony.[71] This does not prove that the use of legislative history is sincere and not ideological, but it is evidence consistent with that conclusion. This issue will be explored much further in Chapter 7 of this book.

Some claim that "such [judicial] willfulness is equally possible with a textualist approach."[72] Judge Posner has observed that "the irresponsible judge will twist any approach to yield the outcomes that he desires."[73] Insofar as this is the case, no theory can effectively bind the "irresponsible judge." Professor Manning has noted that textualist interpretation, to be effective, must be "faithfully applied."[74] Yet it is the same judges who apply textualism who apply legislative history, and there is no basis for assuming that they would be faithful in one context but not the other. All theories depend in at least some measure upon a responsible judiciary that makes a good-faith effort to find the correct legal resolution of a dispute. The defenders of the use of legislative history characterize it as a "a good-faith effort designed to determine if the balance can be tipped in favor of any one interpretation within the universe of possible interpretations."[75] General intentionalism might seem especially amenable to ideological manipulation, but the classic and practically very important example of general intentionalism, in the *Brown Shoe* decision discussed above, involved a liberal justice (Chief Justice Warren) narrowing the interpretation of the antitrust laws (a conservative outcome). This is but one case, but it documents the plausibility of the suggestion that judges act in good faith, rather than dishonestly, in an attempt to reach a truly legal conclusion.

The fundamental issue is not whether a given theory allows judicial discretion, because such discretion is unavoidable. The issue is which theory can best cabin that discretion for judges acting in at least relative good faith. Judge Easterbrook argues that the consideration of additional materials, as in pluralism that allows consideration of many different theories, allows a series of moves, each of which "greatly increases the discretion, and therefore the power, of the court."[76] He maintains that even a judge acting in good faith "will find that the imagined dialogues of deceased legislators have much in common with today's judges' conceptions of the good."[77]

Judge Easterbrook's position seems a sensible one, but the contrary position is equally plausible, if one believes that judges exercise good faith. In the presence of a textual ambiguity, consulting additional sources provides more information. The additional information certainly could be constraining. If the legislative history provides a clear answer to the dispute before the judge, that history would have a constraining effect. Absent the availability of such a clear answer, the judge might otherwise default to his or her personal conceptions of the good. The legislative history could take a certain textual ambiguity enabling ideological judging and funnel it into a more precise application. Judge Easterbrook's approach contains the implicit presumption that legislative history is unconstraining, because it contains materials to support any interpretation the judge might prefer. This is but an assumption though, lacking in any sort of scientific evidentiary basis.

A central argument for textualism is that it "can cabin that [judicial] leeway and go a long way toward minimizing judicial flexibility."[78] In fact, there is contrary logical reason to think that consideration of legislative history could be more constraining on the ideological impulses of the judiciary.

As textualists recognize, statutory text inevitably contains ambiguities and interstitial gaps without textual direction. A textualist who confronts these ambiguities, without the ability to consider any materials beyond the text, is without any external direction, enabling greater internal judicial discretion, such as the judge's ideology. Imagine a case where the text is ambiguous, but the legislative history appears to provide clear direction as to the case's proper resolution. In this case, legislative history would confine judicial ideological discretion. Thus, "textualism effectively opens the door to seemingly unlimited judicial interpretive discretion every time an ambiguity is found to exist."[79] Textualism could be more confining if judges use legislative history willfully to override unambiguous textual commands. The evidence of such practice is generally lacking and requires empirical examination, not *a priori* assumptions.

Some information is provided from studies of congressional overrides, the adoption of new statutes reversing a judicial statutory interpretation. If an ideological judiciary were placing its preferences above those of Congress, one would expect to see more congressional overrides of those judicial actions. Hence, if use of legislative history conduced to such ideological decision making, Congress would override more decisions that were grounded heavily in legislative history. However, this does not appear to be the case. An early study found that Supreme Court decisions based in "plain meaning" analysis were much more likely to be overridden by the legislature.[80] Professor Eskridge likewise found that Congress is much more likely to override with new legislation a judicial decision that was based on textualist plain meaning than one grounded in legislative history or reference to statutory purpose and policy.[81] Professor Vermeule has criticized Eskridge's study, though, for unclear characterization of variables. A separate study of overrides of bankruptcy decisions reached the same conclusion, though, that textualism was associated with more legislative overrides.[82] This effect is highlighted by a Supreme Court opinion that dissented from a majority's "plain meaning" statutory interpretation on the grounds that recent uses of the principle had been consistently overridden, and Congress promptly overrode that very majority opinion.[83] Given the consistency of the findings of the three studies on textualism and overrides, it is hard to dispute their facial validity.

Vermeule also claimed that the research on legislative overrides suffers from the "fallacy of composition," extrapolating from a subset of cases using formalism to presumptions about all cases using formalism, sometimes called a selection effect. The criticism suggests that the association is an artifact, because some third factor makes it more likely both that textualism will be used in a decision and that the decision will be overridden. In this case, the overrides would be attributable to the third factor, not the use of textualism. This criticism is not persuasive, however, in the absence of some plausible identifiable third factor. I can imagine no rationale why judges, with a choice of interpretive methods, would select textualism for outcomes likely to be overridden by the legislature and other methods for outcomes not likely to be so overridden. The problem is of course a possible one but without further evidence does not seem a likely explanation.

One might question the use of such overrides as a true test of interpretive accuracy. Perhaps the judge got the correct interpretation of the original statute, and the override was attributable to an ideological change in the Congress. For example, suppose that an original statute was passed by a conservative legislature and given a conservative interpretation in court but overridden by a liberal legislature with different policy preferences. Indeed, this hypothesis is addressed by the Eskridgean dynamic statutory interpretation that suggests that interpretation be adapted to contemporaneous legislative preferences. If this were true, the original textualist ruling may have "got it right" on the law. However, the data does not suggest that this is a general explanation of the findings. Only about a quarter of the overrides are plainly ideological in orientation and many of the overriding statutes were "not highly controversial."[84] Indeed, an ideological difference between the Supreme Court and the House of Representatives is actually associated with fewer overrides.[85]

These findings might be viewed as evidence that use of legislative history or intent is more likely to get the "right" interpretation. It does not conclusively prove this fact, though, as it can show only that the use of these tools better conforms to the preferences of the contemporaneous legislature, and not those of the enacting legislature (for which we inevitably have no proof). The lack of ideological association is only a partial answer to this criticism. The findings are plainly contrary to the view that legislative history is judicially aggrandizing, promoting their values at the expense of other branches—decisions based on textualism are the ones most objectionable to the contemporary Congress.

Conclusion

Few interpretive issues have been more debated than the use of legislative history in statutory interpretation, and my above discussion has necessarily abbreviated this analysis. A good deal of this research has focused upon whether the consideration of the legislative history, or particular types of legislative history, is *a priori* legitimate or illegitimate. The claim of theoretical illegitimacy, though, is not a strong one as even some committed textualists, such as Professor Vermeule, emphasize.

The potential theoretical legitimacy of consideration of legislative history, though, does not justify its widespread use in statutory interpretation. While there is sound reason to think that the legislature intends that its legislative history be a relevant material for judicial interpretation, it does not follow that it is regularly useful for this purpose or that it consistently yields better interpretations. There are two potentially strong critiques of at least heavy reliance on legislative history. The first goes to its reliability. While I believe worries about manipulation of the record are overstated, there is still a fair question whether the judiciary's honest efforts to discern the honestly expressed intent of the legislature will be accurate. The evidence on overrides provides some limited evidence, though, that the judiciary may accurately ascertain legislative intent. Second is the concern that legislative history serves in practice to enable ideological manipulation of statutes by the judiciary. This is amenable to empirical testing that will be provided later in the book.

CHAPTER 4

The Canons of Statutory Interpretation

"Canons" of construction have long been used as guides to the interpretation of statutes, as well as other legal documents such as contracts. The use of canons cannot be juxtaposed against textualism, legislative history, and pragmatism because this use is orthogonal to the other theories. Any or all of those theories could theoretically rely on canons of construction or reject them. The canons are judge-created tools for defining the meaning of statutory text. Historically, these rules have not been viewed as mandatory but as guidance, though they have been significant determinants in some cases.

Two very different types of canons should be distinguished. The first, which I call linguistic canons, are rules for interpreting statutory text that are akin to rules of grammar. In general, textualists strongly affirm the use of these canons, though other approaches need not reject them. The second, which I call substantive canons, are rules that create presumptions about the substantive meaning of statutes. For example, the "rule of lenity" creates an interpretive presumption favoring defendants in criminal cases.

These substantive canons commonly have a constitutional footing. The substantive canons sit somewhat uneasily with the other interpretive theories but can be reconciled to their positions. The general rule does not apply to all canons; Justice Scalia embraces linguistic canons but has expressed skepticism about the substantive ones.

This chapter begins by examining the canons themselves and reviewing their content. While canons are so numerous that the review cannot be comprehensive, I address some of the most common linguistic and substantive canons. Then, I examine the now extensive critique of judicial reliance on canons of statutory interpretation, and the response of the canons' defenders.

Linguistic Canons

The most basic linguistic canons are so unexceptional that they are typically unstated. For example, courts assume that legislative language conforms, at least roughly, to the rules of English grammar. In this way, we can discern the subject, verb, and object of a statutory proscription, which is vital to appreciating the meaning of language. Similarly, courts rely on rules of punctuation, so that a period ends a sentence and a stand-alone provision. The Supreme Court has declared that such canons are "simply rules of thumb which will sometimes help courts determine the meaning of legislation."[1] Absent some such canons, there is no basis for concluding that "black" does not encompass "white" or that the affirmative excludes the negative. Such use of canons may be justified as furthering congressional intent or as fairness to the public, which must comply with statutes. Many canons are so historical that they are commonly expressed in the Latin language used by Old English common law courts, and some date to the sixteenth century. Nonetheless, they rely on presumptions that are not incontestable, and the need for some linguistic canons of interpretation does not necessarily support the set of such canons in current use. Given the nature of the legislative process, it may be unrealistic to ascribe a high degree of grammatical precision to a law's text. Indeed, the historic rule was that "punctuation was no part of the statute" and to be disregarded in order "to render the true meaning of the statute."[2]

The basic linguistic canon is now used, though, and provides that statutes should be interpreted in accord with the rules of grammar, on the presumption that Congress drafts its laws with grammar in mind.[3] An example would be the rule of the last antecedent. If a statute contains some qualifying language, a question is to what other words the qualifiers apply. The general grammatical rule dictates that they refer only to the immediately prior reference. Similarly, judges differentiate between words like "and" and "or," presuming that the latter requires only one condition for operation. Judges similarly presume that the use of "may" or "should" in a statute are discretionary and do not invoke a requirement, as would the use of the words "shall" or "must."

Beyond simple grammar, the courts have created a series of other canons of interpretive inference. One of the most common and best known linguistic canons is *expressio unius est exclusio alterius* ("the express mention of one thing excludes all others"). This canon is a presumption that the express inclusion of one thing implies the exclusion of other unmentioned things. While often invoked, the canon is far from absolute. It is considered a tool of construction that is not conclusive and one that must be applied cautiously.

Other common canons provide rules for interpreting words according to associated statutory language. Other traditional canons, *ejusdem generis* ("of the same kind") and *noscitur a sociis* ("known by its associates"), are related and may be viewed in tandem. These hold that if a statute contains a list of words, the meaning of individual words should be determined in part by the content of the other listed language. Suppose a bill were to prohibit transporting a woman across state lines for "prostitution or debauchery, or for any other immoral purpose." *Immoral* is a very broad word that potentially encompasses many arguably immoral purposes on its face, such as a business fraud. The canons would suggest that the bill was limited to issues of sexual immorality, because that was the context of the listed language.

These canons arguably invoke a conservative or libertarian limitation on legislation. It prevents judges from adding unmentioned things to a statute's coverage, even if they seemed to be within the statute's purpose or their inclusion was suggested by legislative history. In this respect, it is consistent with Easterbrook's theory of limiting the domain of statutes. Of course, the canons are hence subject to all the criticisms of that theory, which has seen little explicit usage by courts.

One of the most commonly employed linguistic interpretive devices is known as the rule against surplusage. This rule implies that all terms of a statute are meant to have some independent meaning. Thus, if an interpretation of given statutory words would produce a meaning that was duplicative of other statutory language, it is presumed that this is not the correct interpretation. The given words should carry some meaning beyond that of the rest of the statute. Yet this canon employs an unrealistic view of legislative precision in drafting. Judge Posner notes that "a statute that is the product of compromise may contain redundant language as a byproduct of the strains of the negotiating process."[4]

Other traditional canons, *ejusdem generis* and *noscitur a sociis*, are related and may be viewed in tandem. Both establish a presumption that particular words of a statute should be interpreted according to the company they keep and not viewed in isolation. Like *expressio unius*, these canons tend to have an effect of limiting statutory scope, preventing laws from covering matters unrelated to those expressed in the text. Various other linguistic canons are employed by courts, including all the rules of grammar, when deemed applicable to the interpretive dispute in question. Not all have Latin names but they generally correspond to common sense or grammatical understanding.

Substantive Canons

The substantive canons are based on substantive policy and establish a presumption, a "thumb on the scale," for resolving ambiguous language. An early substantive canon was a principle that statutes should not be interpreted in derogation of the common law. Under this canon, if a statutory text admitted of two different interpretations, judges should choose the interpretation that was most consistent with the preexisting common law. This presumed that the legislature did not intend to change the prevailing legal system, except so far as it explicitly did so, and the rule might be considered a pragmatic canon.

Another of the early substantive canons was the "rule of lenity" favoring criminal defendants over the government. It holds that if the criminal statute "does not clearly outlaw private conduct, the private actor cannot be punished."[5] The effect of this canon is to allow certain defendants, whose actions may be borderline criminal, to escape punishment, in order to force the legislature to clearly prescribe the perimeters of the actions that it wishes to criminalize. The theory of the canon seems grounded in a libertarian position limiting the government and the concern that government provide fair notice or warning of what action is illegal. This canon is sometimes invoked under "rule of law" principles dictating that the government should make explicit what it criminalizes before punishing defendants.

Another substantive canon is the presumption that U.S. statutes have no extraterritorial effect, unless this intended effect is clearly found in the statute. The Supreme Court has found a "longstanding principle of American law that legislation of Congress, unless a contrary intent appears, is meant to apply only" domestically.[6] Although there was some legislative history suggesting that the civil rights law in question was meant to have extraterritorial application, the text did not resolve the issue, so the Court applied the substantive canon to hold that the law lacked extraterritorial effect.

There is a strong canon against giving new statutes retroactive effect. Parties including the government may attempt to apply statutes to actions taken before the statute was adopted, or even to cases pending when the statute was enacted. The presumption is that statutes are not given this retroactive effect. When the Civil Rights Act of 1991 created a new right to compensatory and punitive damages for violations of preexisting employment discrimination prohibitions, the court held that the modification should not apply to pending cases.[7] This was grounded in the theory that elementary considerations of fairness dictate that individuals should have the opportunity to know what law is and to conform their conduct accordingly; settled expectations should not be lightly disrupted. The rule is merely a presumption, though, and Congress may choose to apply its statutes retroactively to past conduct.

An entirely different sort of substantive canon is the principle that statutes be construed so as to avoid creating serious constitutional questions. If a statute admits of two reasonable interpretations, and one of those interpretations would create serious constitutional questions, the canon directs that judges adopt the other interpretation. Significantly, the canon as applied today does not require a finding that an interpretation be unconstitutional, only that it raise serious constitutional questions, sometimes called "grave doubt," about constitutionality. Thus, the canon to some degree may save legislative action from being struck down as unconstitutional but also enables judges to evade difficult, and potentially unnecessary, invalidations of statutes.

The canon of constitutional avoidance is controversial and has been called "a judicial power grab."[8] Courts have used the canon to produce results that were unhinged from the statutory language. The canon gives the judiciary great discretion, as the size of the "avoidance zone" is inevitably indeterminate. In addition, there is no logical basis for believing that it reflects congressional wishes. While Congress presumably wants to adopt constitutional statutes, it might logically want to tread as close to the constitutional line as legal in order to effect its policies.

The Court has recently created federalism-related canons for statutory interpretation. Thus, the justices have demanded a "plain statement" in legislation before finding that a federal law would override state sovereign immunity or create a cause of action against a state government or otherwise interfere with areas traditionally regulated by states. Thus, the Court found that a federal prohibition on mandatory retirement ages did not apply to appointed state judges, because the state's power to determine judicial qualifications was a fundamental state function.[9] The plain statement requirement goes beyond plain meaning. The plain meaning of a federal statute may suggest that it applies to states, but the Court has held to the contrary, unless this meaning was crystal clear. The precise language necessary to provide the demanded plain statement is not entirely clear, but a relatively express application is apparently required.

While use of the linguistic canons is viewed as compatible with textualism, this association does not fit so well for the substantive canons. The substantive canons are judge-made and policy oriented. By their nature, these canons are judicial determinations that the words of a statute mean something different than the conventional understanding of the text would dictate. They have been defended as guides to likely intent of the legislature, though this is unproved as a general matter and inconsistent with textualists' *ex ante* rejection of other guides to the likely intent of the enacting legislature.

The Indeterminacy Critique of the Canons

The linguistic canons facially appear to be logical, uncontroversial, and ideological neutral, but this vision was challenged long ago by the famous legal realist, Karl Llewellyn.[10] He argued that the application of the canons was highly indeterminate and could be deployed by judges to reach whatever result they desired. To demonstrate this, he produced a chart of the canons in "thrusts" and "parries," claiming that, like so many aphorisms, each canon had a counterpoint. A judge could simply choose the thrust or the parry in order to reach his preferred end. Llewellyn concluded that we should give up the "foolish pretense" that judges rely on "mutually contradictory correct rules" of statutory interpretation.[11] He claimed that the canons were convenient beards for ideological decision making, like Scalia's critique of legislative history.

While Llewellyn's critique of the canons is legendary, it has been criticized as "greatly overstated"[12] or "grossly overdone."[13] Some have argued that the canons are useful precisely because they are nonideological and provide a neutral tool in cases where the judiciary is relatively indifferent to outcome.[14] However, the canons, like any interpretive tool, may be used in a manipulative fashion. Others argue that "[f]ederal judges regularly exercise broad discretion in deciding when the canons should apply, which ones to invoke in a particular setting, and how to reconcile them with other contextual resources such as specific legislative history, general statutory policy or purpose, and deference to agency determinations."[15]

For some, the canons cannot resolve most interpretive disputes but remain useful on occasion. As noted in preceding chapters, there are many close questions in statutory interpretation. The text may not resolve a particular case, and the legislative history may be unhelpful or conflicted. Unfortunately, one cannot assume that the canons will be helpful and unconflicted. Professor Eskridge argues that "a variety of canons will typically be applicable to any given statutory issue, and they will often cut in different directions."[16] Judge Posner claims that use of the canons makes interpretation seem misleadingly "mechanical," which conceals "the extent to which the judge is making new law in the guise of interpreting a statute."[17]

This criticism may presume too much reliance on the canons, which were not meant to resolve all potential interpretive disputes. Sometimes, the canons may provide a helpful decision rule. This defense, though, may simply reduce the canons to tie-breakers that are "at best of modest utility."[18] Moreover, the canons may not even be helpful interpretive tools in close cases.

The Logical Critique of the Canons

Even if the canons were not insincere or self-contradictory, many of them can be challenged on logical grounds. Consider the well-accepted *expressio unius* canon. Suppose you ask a friend what foods he likes, and he gives you a list of his favorite foods. It would be unlikely that he means to convey a dislike of every single food not contained on that list. He may have forgotten some foods and certainly failed to consider food products that he has not yet sampled. Cass Sunstein notes that a legislature's failure to include an item on a list may similarly "reflect inadvertence, inability to reach consensus, or a decision to delegate the decision to the courts."[19] Judge Posner suggests that a legislature "might create an exception to a general grant without thereby wanting to prevent the courts from recognizing additional exceptions, unforeseen at the time of enactment that would be consistent with the grant's purposes."[20] This is especially trenchant in the context of societal change; Congress can hardly be expected to list a technology or practice that was unknown at the time of enactment. The Court itself has recognized that the canon is only appropriate when it can draw "the inference that items not mentioned were excluded by deliberate choice, not inadvertence."[21] Of course, this exception is broad and vague and potentially swallows the canon.

Many other examples can be used to describe the shortcomings of the *expressio unius* presumption. Max Radin noted that "to say that all men are mortal does not mean that all women are not or that all other animals are not."[22] Suppose a parent tells a son, "don't hit or kick your sister." *Expressio unius* would imply that the son is authorized to bite or choke her, but this would seem to be an erroneous interpretation of the parental command. In this case, an intentionalist or purposive approach might seem to be a more accurate interpretation of the directions. Of course, statutes are not parental commands, and defenders of the canon could argue that regulated parties, unlike children, have a presumption of freedom of action unless expressly limited by government. This response, however persuasive, removes the "linguistic" part of the linguistic canons, though. It transforms them from inquiries into the true meaning of language into substantive presumptions about individual freedom.

Indeed, even the most basic grammar canons are not uncontroversial. Consider the rule of the "last antecedent." In a complex sentence, it may be unclear to what subject a pronoun or verb or phrase applies. The general rule of grammar is that qualifying words or phrases apply to the language immediately preceding the qualifier and not to earlier language. This arose in a famous 1900 case interpreting a statute prohibiting the sale of alcohol between 11:00 P.M. and 6:00 A.M., or on Sunday, *except* that an innkeeper could supply liquor to guests.[23] The court applied the rule of the last antecedent and interpreted the innkeeper exception to be limited to the Sunday prohibition and inapplicable to the nighttime prohibition under the rule of the last antecedent. Some have suggested that this was an erroneous interpretation of the statute. The limitations of the linguistic canons have been well catalogued, with explanations of their questionable application to particular statutes.[24]

Even the obeisance to rules of grammar may thus be questionable. Anyone listening to a congressperson speak is aware that grammatical errors are not uncommon. A statute hastily cobbled together as a compromise among multiple congresspersons may be more subject to mistake. Gadamerian theory shows that language is a set of signals within a community about meaning. Rejection of evidence about intentionalism to determine meaning can thus be counterproductive. Posner's concluding word is that "most of the canons are just wrong" and do not even reflect common sense.[25]

The defense of the canons is simply that the legislature must have intended their use. They "rest ultimately on assumptions about, and theories of, the legislative process."[26] Thus, a canon that did not reflect common sense would not be appropriately employed by judges. This limitation calls into some question the validity of the canons, however. One might question the aptitude of the judiciary in accurately comprehending the legislative process or intent. For at least some of the grammatical canons, though, the assumption of their use is at least plausible and presumably better than believing that the legislature is typically ungrammatical in its phrasing.

Critiquing the Substantive Canons

The substantive canons are subject to an entirely different theoretical critique. They "are generally meant to reflect a judicially preferred policy position"[27] and surely represent judicial "legislation" by their very nature. Their presumptions place a thumb on the scale for certain outcomes, often ideological ones. One might reasonably question what authorizes such judicial presumption-creating. This general attack is potentially answerable, though, insofar as the substantive canons are constitutionally grounded, as they often are. The judiciary of the United States is clearly empowered to use the Constitution to override statutes, and using the Constitution to interpret them is a lesser power that might be encompassed by the greater power to invalidate. And given a congressional power to override the use of substantive canons, which are only presumptions, the judges are not entirely taking legislative power out of the hands of the legislature.

Justice Scalia's position on the substantive canons has produced some controversy. They are judicially empowering and he has written that for "an honest textualist, all of these preferential rules and presumptions are a lot of trouble."[28] In practice, however, he has used the substantive canons, even in dissenting opinions that he has authored.[29] Nevertheless, reliance on such policy-based canons involves placing a judicial thumb on the scale and is difficult to square with textualism or any theory of legislative supremacy. These canons might seem vulnerable to criticism under my delegation theory, though they are consistent with a theory that the legislature intended to delegate some policy-making authority to the judiciary.

Individual substantive canons are still subject to reasonable criticism. The traditional canon against interpreting statutes in derogation of common law is especially questionable. It may have been a logical rule in the early days of statutes, when common law governance prevailed, but now "seems woefully anachronistic."[30] Indeed, the intrinsic logic of the canon is questionable as the very reason for statutes is to derogate the common law—if the existing common law were deemed satisfactory, no statute would have been necessary. Some suggest that this canon is grounded in conservative ideology, by limiting the impact of federal legislation, though this effect would not be universal. Such ideological direction is an implication of most of the substantive canons.

The liberal parry to the "derogation of common law" thrust is the canon calling for broad or liberal interpretation of "remedial" statutes. The theory of such a canon is that when the legislature acts to address a particular societal problem, such as air pollution, it wants such legislative authority to be interpreted broadly in order to effect its desired consequence. This canon, once more broadly invoked, has seen relatively little use in recent years.

The canon of liberal interpretation of remedial statutes is problematic, given the compromise nature of legislation, discussed in Chapter 2. The fact that Congress wants to reduce air pollution does not imply that it wants to take any measures plausible to achieve that end. The legislation may have wanted to "go so far and no further," perhaps to avoid excessive economic costs of compliance. In this case, the liberal interpretation of remedial statutes may go well beyond the legislature's compromise solution. Justice Scalia has referred to the canon as an example of "lego-babble."[31] Standing alone, the canon offers relatively little, though it might add to other evidence that a broad interpretation was intended.

The rule of lenity for criminal defendants is another substantive canon with a more liberal direction. This longstanding canon declares that "before a man can be punished as a criminal . . . his case must be plainly and unmistakably within the provisions of some statute."[32] Where statutory language is unambiguous, the rule of lenity is inapplicable. In the presence of ambiguity, though, the Court has held that principles of fair notice preclude criminal prosecution. It has also expressed some worry about the judiciary creating new crimes through its interpretive efforts. A related canon presumes that a criminal statute has a *mens rea* component, even if not expressed on its face.

As discussed above, a number of the recently developed substantive canons involve federalism. A more historic federalism canon involves preemption of state statutes. The Supremacy Clause empowers the federal government to preempt state laws that conflict or even address matters involving federal legislation. However, there is a judicially created presumption against preemption, unless clearly expressed in the statute.[33] This presumption reflects federalism values and respect for state decision making. Ernie Young has urged that the presumption against preemption is especially important in protecting federalism.[34]

The preemption canon, though, has not carried the weight of other federalism canons, such as the presumption against abrogation of state sovereign immunity. The justices most devoted to protection of federalism through the other substantive canons have "exhibited blindness to those values when presented with a preemption case."[35] Some have suggested that this consequence simply reflects a conservative antiregulatory animus. The other federalism canons are strong because they limit federal regulation but the preemption canon is weak because it strengthens state regulation. The claim is that "the Court's pro-business, anti-regulatory leanings . . . trump its more abstract states' rights leanings."[36]

The relative weakness of the preemption canon illustrates the indeterminacy problem with the substantive canons' clear statement rules. The precise degree of clarity required is vague, and the standard is therefore a malleable one. The judge's thumb may weigh more heavily or lightly on the scale in different instances, perhaps depending on the ideological orientation of the case circumstances.

The substantive canons contain both conservative and liberal directional guidance. This does not mean that the canons are nonideological, though, but may have the reverse effect. The availability of additional interpretive tools can simply ease ideological decision making. When the common law canon conflicts with the remedial statute canon, the judge can choose the one that produces his or her preferred result. The canons may thereby further judicial ideological decision making. Justice Scalia has criticized the substantive canons as a "lot of trouble" for adding a "thumb of indeterminate weight" to the decision-making scale, which will not yield "uniformity or objectivity."[37] Judge Posner argues that the canons promote judicial activism because they do not constrain decision making as much as they create an illusion of constraint.

Answering the Critiques

While the criticism of the canons clearly has logical merit, it can be answered with a defense much like the defense of legislative history. Congress drafts legislation against a background of judicial interpretation and is surely aware of at least the most common statutory canons. Eskridge and Frickey suggest that the canons' "off the rack" principles provide guidance in advance for legislators drafting statutes.[38] Thus, if legislators intend to abrogate state sovereign immunity, they should do so with clear and conclusive language. If they do not wish a list to be exclusive of unmentioned items, they can say so in the language of the statute itself. A survey of the canons has found that cases relying upon them "often invoke purposive justifications—gleaned from the legislative record evidence or imputed to Congress—thereby attributing its result in part to the policy preferences of the legislative branch."[39] Given the acknowledged difficulties associated with judicial discernment of true legislative intent, Professor Manning argues that "it may be important, if not essential, to emphasize and develop effective rules of thumb to resolve the doubts that inevitably arise out of statutory language."[40]

The delegation answer to the critique of the canons is somewhat less effective than for legislative history, though. While Llewellyn's thrusts and parries may be somewhat overstated, they contain some material truth. When Congress drafts against a canonical background, it is unaware of which of the conflicting canons a judge may choose to employ. As long as judges employ a multiplicity of canons that have a self-contradictory component, it is more difficult for Congress to design statutory language to achieve a given result. Moreover, some research suggests that legislative drafters are unaware of the canons themselves when writing language.[41] Judge Mikva has declared that when he was in Congress "the only 'canons' we talked about were the ones the Pentagon bought."[42]

The delegation answer may be particularly problematic with respect to the substantive canons. The rule of lenity suggests that ambiguous language be interpreted to favor the criminal defendant, but the determination of the presence of ambiguity is itself ambiguous. A willful and intelligent judge can surely find ambiguity in nearly any statutory language, given the indeterminacy of language itself, as discussed in Chapter 2. When the judiciary commands a "clear statement" to overcome presumptions such as sovereign immunity, it leaves unsettled exactly what sort of statement is clear enough. Judge Wald has described the presumption as requiring that Congress signal its intent in "neon lights,"[43] but there is no linguistic tool that is clearly neon. Eventually, the necessarily clear "magic words" may be established through subsequent precedent, but this is not inevitable and at minimum leaves a potentially considerable period of uncertainty until the nature of such words is judicially determined. The clear statement canons are criticized as too vague on this basis, providing only "a thumb of indeterminate weight."[44]

This problem is evident in the federalism canon presuming that Congress does not intend to revoke state statutory immunity. The issue is illustrated by the decision in *Dellmuth v. Muth*, where the majority found the Employment of the Handicapped Act lacked the necessary unequivocal clear statement of abrogation of state sovereign immunity.[45] In dissent, however, Justices Brennan, Marshall, Blackmun, and Stevens maintained that the statute contained such a clear statement, a position that the Eleventh Circuit had previously taken. Professor Eskridge has suggested that the Court ruling was an example of a "bait and switch" played by the Court on Congress, which was illustrated by the fact that Congress overrode the outcome with a clearer statement just one year later.[46] The rule has evolved from a "clear statement" rule into a "superstrong clear statement rule," as the Court determined that congressional statements revoking sovereign immunity were insufficiently clear. Justice Scalia would not read a statute to have abrogated the sovereign immunity of states unless it speaks "with unmistakable clarity."[47] The lineup of justices in *Dellmuth* suggests that the necessary clarity of statutory language may just be a function of the justices' individual ideological preferences.

In addition, it may be more difficult for Congress to control judicial agents' use of canons as the interpretive principle. Declaring the inapplicability of a canon typically requires such a declaration in the statutory language itself. If a member or even a majority of Congress disagrees with legislative history, it is relatively easy to create contrary legislative history, but it is more difficult to anticipate all the potential canonical applications and include them in the legislative history or the text itself, especially when the Court creates new canons.

This presents another legislative problem with delegation and canons, which is temporal instability. While the linguistic canons have lived for centuries, the Court seems to intermittently alter the substantive canons or create new ones. In general, the "canons are not stable over time, and legislators and their staff members, even if they are aware of relevant canons, can never be sure when a canon will be disregarded or outweighed by other considerations."[48] In the 1960s and 1970s, the courts interpreted statutes liberally to expand their scope, but more recently, the courts' substantive canons have produced more conservative decision rules.[49] A Congress adopting a statute in the earlier period could not be expected to foresee this alteration in judicial canons, demanding express abrogation of sovereign immunity, for example.

As with textualism, reliance on canons may reflect an unrealistic view of the legislative process. Given legislative time constraints and difficulties in reaching linguistic compromise, it may be unreasonable to expect the Congress to appreciate the influence of canons when drafting and enacting statutes. Even if the initial drafter were quite knowledgeable about the use of the canons in interpretation, which seems uncertain, subsequent amendments in the often harried legislative process are likely to reflect consideration of such canonical principles.

Finally, there is the omnipresent question of the canons' effect on ideological decision making by courts. This effect may show up due to the indeterminacy and inconsistency of canons, as claimed by Llewellyn, which enables judges to reach whatever result they desire. Or it may appear in the impact of substantive canons to direct future decisions in a particular ideological direction. Some have argued that the canons by their very nature are conservative in promoting continuity over change. The theoretical arguments on ideological impact of canons are plausible, but once again the ultimate test must be an empirical analysis.

Study of the Canons

Like most legal issues, use of the canons has seen relatively little empirical analysis of their functioning in practice. Yet such analysis is vital to resolving the disputes over the legitimacy of the canons. Some embrace Llewellyn's legal realist approach to the canons; others dismiss it or claim it to be vastly overstated. Yet these are little more than assertions backed at best by anecdotes, absent more rigorous analysis of how the canons function in practice.

In the case of the canons, though, a recent article has provided a very thorough analysis of the canons' usage at the Supreme Court, albeit one that is limited to the law involving workplace disputes.[50] The study found that the use of canons at the Court, both linguistic and substantive, had increased in recent years. Neither type of canon appeared to have much constraining effect, though, as conservative justices deployed canons to achieve conservative results and liberal justices did so to reach liberal ends. The research concluded that "canons are regularly used in an instrumental if not ideologically conscious manner."[51] This is consistent with Judge Posner's claim that the use of canons is conducive to ideological decision making, because the canons provide a convenient neutral beard behind which to hide.[52]

The study supported Llewellyn's basic claim in noting "a number of decisions in which majority and dissent rely on canons" and "majority reliance on language canons is likely to be accompanied by dissent invocation of language canons."[53] Indeed, the research goes beyond Llewellyn's claim and finds cases in which the majority and the dissent relied on the same "thrusting" canon without even requiring a parry.[54] The individual canon may itself be so ambiguous that no countering parry is necessary to manipulate its use. These findings are discussed further in the empirical analyses of Chapters 6 and 7.

Conclusion

The linguistic canons of interpretation are historically grounded and almost universally accepted as helpful statutory interpretive devices. Their use has been subject to much criticism on grounds that they unduly presume legislators are capable English teachers and may yield erroneous results. While this criticism is difficult to dispute, it does not invalidate the use of canons as an interpretive aid. They may provide a useful aid to interpretation, so long as they may be rebutted.

The canons sit uncertainly in the context of legislative delegation of interpretive theory. Alexander Hamilton noted that the canons were "not enjoined upon the courts by the legislative provision, but adopted by themselves, as consonant to truth and propriety."[55] Unlike the text or the legislative history of statutes, the canons are not provided by Congress but are created by the judiciary. However, the historic nature of the linguistic canons provides interpretive rules to which the legislature may adapt. Such canons may facilitate effective delegation, by informing the legislature of how its words will be read. The substantive canons, by contrast, fit poorly with legislative delegation; indeed, they appear to make the judiciary the principal who tells the agent legislature what it cannot do or how it must legislate.

The overall evaluation of any of the canons, as with any other interpretive device, requires an empirical examination of their application in practice. The evidence of the effect of even the linguistic canons is not entirely sanguine. The canons are too often indeterminate in direction, making them vulnerable to easy manipulation, much like the criticism of other interpretive tools. This problem is exacerbated by the facts that these canons are often conflicting, and they lack a clear hierarchy of relative importance, as exists for the legislative history tools. This problem is explored further in the subsequent empirical analyses of the book.

CHAPTER 5

Pragmatism and Dynamic Statutory Interpretation

Perhaps the most controversial contemporary theory of statutory interpretation is pragmatism. Unlike the theories discussed in the above chapters, pragmatism does not rely on particular legislative materials or particular interpretive rules that constrain judicial discretion. By contrast, pragmatism embraces judicial discretion and seeks to direct it toward the best outcome for society. Pragmatic interpretation may reject as fiction the claim that judges merely "interpret" the preexisting defined law, contending that judges are partners in creating the law that governs America. As such, judges should dedicate their efforts to creating the wisest rules of law.

Pragmatism is distinguished from other theories by its broader philosophical pedigree. It developed in the latter part of the nineteenth century in the United States. Pragmatism evolved out of a small group of Massachusetts intellectuals, including lawyers, who called themselves the Metaphysical Club. They included William James, John Dewey, and Oliver Wendell Holmes. Rather than pursuing a notion of absolute truth, the pragmatists simply sought to find "what worked" in the world. The philosophy was a consequentialist one. The morality of action was grounded in its consequences, and action was evaluated based upon its results. The theory is plainly instrumentalist and abandons all pretenses that the law is a self-contained system ruled by logic. For Holmes, law was not based on a "syllogism" but on the "felt necessities of the time," and "intuitions of public policy, avowed or unconscious." This may be what Alexander Hamilton meant when he spoke of the important role of the judiciary in "civilizing" statutes.[1]

Only recently have these historic theories of pragmatic law assumed prominence in statutory interpretation. Judge Richard Posner of the Seventh Circuit Court of Appeals and the University of Chicago Law School has vigorously argued for a pragmatic approach to decision making generally, and the law in particular. On a separate track, William Eskridge of Yale Law School propounded a theory he called "dynamic statutory interpretation," in which judges adapted the law to present-day circumstances, including the prevailing political preferences. This chapter reviews the arguments for and against pragmatism in statutory interpretation.

Legal Pragmatism

Legal pragmatism is most famously expounded today by Judge Richard Posner of the Seventh Circuit Court of Appeals. In an early exposition of his theory, he characterized legal reasoning as practical reasoning. While such reasoning is "a grab bag that includes anecdote, introspection, imagination, common sense, empathy" and other factors, Posner argues that it still could provide "as high a degree of certainty as do logical demonstrations."[2] Central to pragmatic interpretation is "the primacy of consequences" and "reasonableness" in decision making.[3] In the context of statutory interpretation, Judge Posner has suggested that the competing theories of the legislative process expressed by textualism and legislative history depend on "controversial political theories" that "do not provide sure footing for judicial decisions."[4]

Judge Posner has amplified his theory over succeeding years and defines its core as "merely a disposition to base action on facts and consequences rather than on conceptualisms, generalities, pieties, and slogans."[5] He emphasizes that pragmatism recognizes the "standard rule-of-law virtues of generality, predictability, and impartiality," such that the doctrine's results might be expected to overlap considerably with more conventionally formalistic forms of legal analysis.[6] However, these formalistic considerations are not dispositive in Posnerian formalism, because the pragmatic judge will depart from them when they appear consequentially perverse. Perhaps more important, pragmatism provides some guidance for judges when the traditional formalistic materials for decision making fail to determine an outcome. Thus, in the presence of ambiguity, pragmatism provides a path for resolution that need not pretend that the law is universally determinate. Pragmatism has been called simply "practical reason," but even its advocates recognize that the notion "is easier to invoke than to define."[7]

The contemporary pragmatism has substantial traditional underpinnings. Tom Merrill suggests that U.S. judges have "been pragmatists when it comes to interpreting statutes" for "most of our history."[8] The legal process school of postwar ascendancy suggested that "courts should attempt to 'make sense' of regulatory statutes or treat them as would 'reasonable people acting reasonably,'" which rings of pragmatism.[9] By 1990, Richard Rorty proclaimed that pragmatism generally was so widely accepted as to have become banal.[10] This claim was too broad in statutory interpretation, though, as traditional formalism retained its hold. Within statutory interpretation, pragmatism has always taken a back set to the alternative approaches of plain meaning and legislative history. Moreover, pragmatism's theoretical popularity may speak to little more than its broad vagueness.

Pragmatism may become "a grab bag that includes anecdote, introspection, imagination, common sense, empathy, imputation of motives, speaker's authority, metaphor, analogy, precedent, custom, memory, 'experience,' intuition, and induction. . . ."[11] It bears some resemblance to the pluralism of approaches to statutory interpretation or to the "ordinary judging" paradigm. The "essence of ordinary judging" is said to be the fitting of statutes to their temporal circumstances.[12] Llewellyn's defense of pragmatic statutory interpretation suggested that courts should consider the statutory language, the legislative history, the purpose of the statute, the coherence of the legal system, and the court's overall sense of the situation.[13] This is pluralism, with all its discretionary indeterminacy.

Unfortunately, this indeterminacy calls into question the virtues of pragmatism. For some, such as the legal process traditionalists, pragmatism means fitting the statute to the circumstances of the underlying statute and the individual case. For others, the judge should look to the broader legal environment and interpret statutes in order to promote coherency among statutory programs and consider the systemic effects of a given interpretation.[14] Cass Sunstein, sometimes regarded as a pragmatist, has suggested that it might be more pragmatic generally to use a formalistic standard, given the limitations of the judiciary in developing coherent policy on a case-by-case basis.[15] The latter process might introduce an "unacceptable amount of uncertainty . . . into the interpretive system."[16] Long ago, pragmatism was criticized as being "in a sense anarchistic and devoid of standards or principles," when "law requires an appreciable degree of uniformity, stability and certainty."[17] The case-by-case discretionary judgment often associated with pragmatism may not be the wisest approach.

Pragmatism surely must be judged by its own standard. If case-by-case pragmatic judging is systemically unpragmatic, it is not to be recommended. But the argument that pragmatism is unduly indeterminate or discretionary or otherwise imprudent is only asserted and not proved. The theoretical case requires some actual testing of its assumptions. Before proceeding to the testing of pragmatism, though, I examine a variant of the theory known as dynamic statutory interpretation.

Dynamic Statutory Interpretation

William Eskridge has propounded a theory of "dynamic statutory interpretation" that is often associated with pragmatism but not necessarily the same theory. Dynamic statutory interpretation can confuse, because it contains both a descriptive and a normative component that need to be distinguished. Descriptively, the theory suggests that judges *will* adapt their decisions to the contemporary preferences of other institutions, such as the legislature. As a descriptive, this theory can be evaluated empirically. Although the testing is inconclusive, one major article called the claims of the descriptive theory into question. Jeff Segal examined whether the Supreme Court's statutory decisions became more liberal as the legislature became more liberal.[18] He noted the difficulties of affirmative congressional action as reason to question the degree to which justices would respond to threatened action. Moreover, under different theoretical models of congressional action, he found no evidence that justices modified their decisions in response to the ideological preferences of Congress.

Normatively, the theory suggests that judges *should* adapt their decisions to the circumstances of the present day, including but not limited to the contemporary preferences of other institutions. The distinction between the two approaches must be maintained, and the normative one is central to the theoretical case for pragmatism. Even if the descriptive claim about response to Congress is incorrect, that doesn't invalidate the normative pragmatic argument. Congressional preferences are just one form of evidence for the pragmatist. Moreover, the congressional ideology by itself is not particularly illuminating to the pragmatist, who should be aspiring to a non-ideological welfare-maximizing optimum answer.

A study of bankruptcy decisions and statutory amendments informs this discussion.[19] It considered fifty-eight bankruptcy law rulings that were overruled, compared with a control group of decisions that were not altered by the Congress. The overruled decisions were disproportionately based on textualist reasoning in the courts. While most of the decisions in the control group were pragmatic (37%), few of these decisions were found in the overruled group (7%). By contrast, only 10% of the decisions in the control group were exclusively textualist, but such reasoning made up 33% of the overruled group sample. This finding does not necessarily mean that the courts are deciding with an eye to congressional response, though, and the author did not so interpret the findings. Rather, he suggested that the pragmatic decisions produced the most sensible result, independent of ideological preferences, which Congress saw no need to disturb, while the textualist decisions yielded an unwise law, which Congress had to correct.

The Case for Pragmatism

The basic case for pragmatism, in statutory interpretation or elsewhere, is simple: it should produce the most beneficial societal outcome. Rather than apply the law rigidly, where it would produce unfair or counterproductive results, the pragmatist will apply the law more flexibly to produce fair and socially beneficial consequences. Pragmatism thus reflects a certain theory of delegation, that the Congress adopting the statute did not have all the answers and sought to delegate the case-by-case fleshing out of the statute to judicial discretion. As previous chapters have shown, this is at least sometimes the case.

Pragmatists also point to the structural biases of the legislative process. Political scientists have amply demonstrated that it is very difficult to pass new legislation. As discussed in Chapter 3, more than a majority is required to pass a law. Ideally, each legislature would modify past legislation as appropriate for modern circumstances. In practice, the ideal is unapproachable, as a minority can block the passage of a new law. Moreover, the Congress is "busy," with many policy issues to address. Even if a supermajority of the Congress preferred to amend an existing law, the body might simply lack the necessary time to take this action. Consequently, a given statute may not reflect contemporary realities. Pragmatism suggests that judges may compensate for this effect.

Given this structure, one might expect that statutes would become obsolete or inapt for modern circumstances. Pragmatism is embraced as a tool for fitting old statutes into contemporary realities. For textualists, this is unpersuasive. Legislation is to be written by Congress, and if it is obsolete it should be applied nonetheless, until the legislature changes it. While pragmatists are oriented toward the best consequential outcome, textualists are oriented to a certain principle, regardless of consequences.

One famous case of pragmatism involved the Sherman Antitrust Act. The language of the law was very abbreviated and prohibited "any contract . . . in restraint of trade." Yet every contract restrains trade, by its very nature, committing one contracting party to the other, exclusively, regarding the substance of the contract. To avoid the literal result of the statutory language, the Court essentially just inserted the term "unreasonable" before the statutorily prohibited "restraint of trade."[20] Courts have developed antitrust law under the Sherman Act through a common law process. More recently, courts have commonly employed economic principles in the interpretation of the act and the definition of what restraints are unreasonable, though nothing in the text calls for such an approach. This is classical pragmatism, interpreting a law so as to further the optimal societal consequences.

Bear in mind that pragmatists need not demonstrate nor even argue that the judiciary will reach perfect results in its application of the theory. Judges may get the pragmatic balance wrong. Rather, pragmatists need only claim that the use of the theory will produce relatively better results than the use of any competing theory. Once again, this is ultimately an empirical question and a difficult one to test, given the uncertainty of what results are "better." Pure theory cannot provide an answer to this dispute, however.

While "common sense" pragmatism is intuitively appealing, its implications can be theoretically troubling. Pragmatism suggests that judges may "update" or even ignore statutory commands that seem unwise, which seems institutionally discomfiting if not unconstitutional, to have judges rewriting legislation. While few would seriously challenge the judicial approach to the Sherman Act, the overarching theory seems to grant inappropriate power to the judiciary. Before analyzing those concerns, though, I address a pragmatism doctrine that is nearly universally accepted.

The Absurdity Doctrine

By its nature, pragmatism seldom fits within the dogma of legal doctrines. Pragmatism is fundamentally a circumstantial, rather than rigidly doctrinal, approach to adjudicative decision making. Pragmatic considerations are occasionally captured in doctrinal authority, though, and the most obvious of these in the context of statutory interpretation is known as the "absurdity" doctrine of statutory interpretation. This principle simply states that laws will not be interpreted in a fashion so as to yield absurd results, even when the text superficially seems to command such an interpretation. Lon Fuller observed that it is plainly apparent that when the master tells the housemaid "to 'drop everything and come running' he has overlooked the possibility that she is at the moment in the act of rescuing the baby from the rain barrel."[21] In the statutory context, this would mean that a statute making it a crime to "spill blood on the street" should not be applied to a "physician doing emergency surgery at the scene of an accident."[22] Most findings of absurdity are not so dramatic, and its application is usually an assessment of the "reasonableness, rationality, and common sense" of an interpretation.[23]

Significantly, advocates of virtually all theories of statutory interpretation accept the validity of the absurdity doctrine. The doctrine is consistent with the theory of delegation of judgment to the courts. Absurd results may well only reflect the unforeseen circumstances that result in the background delegation. The absurdity doctrine is most comfortably consistent with pragmatism. Intentionalists have embraced the doctrine on the grounds that the legislature would surely not intend to create absurd results. The very core of formalistic textualist theories, by contrast, seemingly rejects the judicial discretion implicit in the absurdity doctrine, though textualists such as Justice Scalia are untroubled by the doctrine.

The absurdity doctrine turns some of the arguments for textualism on their heads. For example, textualists have suggested that the legislative process might be improved if judges limited their consideration to text. Conversely, the judicial process might be improved if judges could less easily evade responsibility by deference to text or other legislative materials. W. David Slawson suggests that judges "are increasingly reluctant to accept responsibility for making difficult policy decisions or to offer reasoned justifications" and therefore may rely on legislative history to "deflect responsibility onto past Congresses."[24] By using tools like legislative history or text, judges can generally save time and effort, as well as evading responsibility. The absurdity doctrine, though, is contrary to this concern; it shows a judiciary assuming responsibility for righting a bad statute. It is the essence of pragmatic judging and the real question is how constrained the theory should be.

While textualists have universally not rejected the absurdity doctrine, they necessarily have some unease with its principles, and John Manning has directly criticized the approach. The legal process school's view of interpretation sought to apply statutes from the perspective of a "reasonable policymaker." It questioned how a reasonable policymaker would apply given language. A prominent textualist like John Manning rejects this position, though, arguing that statutory coherence should not be presumed in light of the complexity of the legislative process and its necessary compromises.[25] Thus, the textualists can take a bold standard in favor of *unreasonable* policy outcomes. This is consistent with their vision of a limited judicial role as agent of an even unreasonable legislature. But the position once again evades the delegation question; a legislature might intend that an interpreting court try to make reasonable its legislation on a case-by-case basis. Moreover, the textualist critique ascribes undue intentionalism to the legislature. In many disputes involving background delegation, the legislature gave no consideration whatsoever to the facts before the court. Surely it seems likely that in these circumstances the legislature would prefer the court to adopt the reasonable, rather than the unreasonable, interpretation.

An alternative critique of the absurdity doctrine questions its reliable accuracy. What appears absurd to some may in truth be sensible. Even an authentically absurd result in a particular case might be appropriate if necessary for application of a stable and uniform rule. Professor Vermeule suggests that a "judicial power to avoid absurd results is also a judicial power to avoid results that the judges mistakenly think are absurd merely because, as ill-informed generalists, they have misunderstood the statutory scheme."[26] As is always the case, the functioning of the absurdity doctrine must be assessed in practice, not purely in hypothetical theory.

The Chevron *Doctrine*

The *Chevron* doctrine of judicial deference to agency decisions was discussed above in the context of textualism because it indicated an apparent inconsistency in that theory. The doctrine fits far more comfortably in a context of pragmatic statutory interpretation. Agencies are directly involved in the administration of statutes and see their day-to-day application. Agencies also have great resources for fact finding about the broad effects of particular statutory interpretations. Cass Sunstein, for reasons such as these, defends such deference to agencies as a recognition that agency interpretations are best suited to making extratextual "judgments about how a statute is best or most sensibly interpreted."[27] Professor Vermeule urges that agencies "will often possess far better information about the legislative process that produced the statute, about the specialized policy context surrounding the statute's enactment, and about the resulting legislative deal."[28] Professor Eskridge suggested that agencies are best suited to update the meaning of statutes for new societal developments.[29] Many of the "substantive statutes that administrative agencies implement are designed to be flexible enough to last for generations, with agencies updating their meaning to accommodate changed circumstances."[30] This reflects dynamic, pragmatic statutory interpretation.

There is a consensus among a diverse group of experts that administrative interpretations of a statute warrant deference. This may be because those interpretations are the most accurate evidence of the original legislative intent or the most reliable evidence of the pragmatic effects of a given interpretive approach. Agencies "may adjust their interpretations to new facts, policies, and even political values."[31] A deference doctrine thus represents a pragmatic recognition of the ability of agencies to discern the statutory interpretation most in the public interest.

Although support for *Chevron* deference to agency interpretation is often associated with textualists, it is best considered a pragmatic doctrine. As discussed in Chapter 2, nothing in textualism intrinsically counsels for deference to agencies, while pragmatism would recommend this course. Features of the deference doctrines illustrate this effect. The Court has adjusted its doctrine and called for relatively less deference when agency decisions are less procedurally formal.[32] Matthew Stephenson has explained how this is a rational and pragmatic apportionment that grants greater deference when the agency has devoted more resources to finding the correct answer to a particular problem.[33]

Some might maintain that *only* agencies and not the judiciary should engage in such pragmatic decision making. Professor Sunstein has a strong version of this argument for pragmatic administrative deference, counseling that dynamic interpretation of statutes is "an administrative task not a judicial one,"[34] a position to which Professor Vermeule also subscribes. Sunstein's argument was made in the context of a statute for which there *was* an administrative statutory interpretation, though, and does not help in its absence. However, "flexibility arguably is more important in the interpretation of non-administrative statutes than it is in the interpretation of administrative statutes."[35] Some statutes are not subject to administrative interpretation and, for others, the agency may not have addressed the issue in the case. In these circumstances, agency expertise is not helpful.

The preference for dynamic agency interpretation over dynamic judicial interpretation is not a plain one. Agency decisions will generally reflect the ideological preferences of the current administration, which has some contemporaneous democratic imprimatur but only for the executive branch and not the legislative. Nor is it clear that Congress intends for total deference to administrative interpretations. Indeed, its provision for judicial checks on administrative interpretations in the Administrative Procedure Act and elsewhere strongly suggests the opposite. Moreover, the "bottom up" dynamism of case-by-case judicial processes may be superior to the "top down" dynamism characteristic of administrative rule-making processes, a theory discussed below. Nevertheless, the agencies have some advantages over the courts, and a prudent judicial dynamism would give substantial weight to their conclusions as reflected in the *Chevron* doctrine. Indeed, this deference answers one of the most common criticisms of pragmatism—that it leaves the judiciary unconstrained, because deference to agency interpretations is a self-denying practice.

Other interpretive standards are also compatible with pragmatism. Indeed, some use of legislative history would generally be embraced by pragmatists. Just as an executive interpretation warrants deference due to the pragmatic judgment of an agency, the legislature's intent or the advice of a relatively expert congressional committee could warrant consideration for the same reason. Thus, in one decision, the majority explained that a "jurisprudence that confines a court's inquiry to the "law as it is passed," and is wholly unconcerned about "the intentions of legislators," would enforce an unambiguous statutory text even when it produces manifestly unintended and profoundly unwise consequences.[36]

Judicial Power

The most fundamental objection to pragmatism is its presumed empowerment of the judiciary to engage in "lawmaking" rather than mere interpretation. Indeed, this may explain the textualists' acceptance of executive discretionary interpretation under *Chevron* and rejection of such pragmatic discretionary interpretation by judges. Such judicial lawmaking is regarded by the critics as illegitimate, either on technical legal constitutional grounds or on broader philosophical democratic grounds, themselves grounded in constitutional principle. Judge Posner notes the criticism that pragmatism counsels judicial "lawlessness" and threatens that pragmatic judges may "override precedent, 'plain meaning,' settled doctrine, and other formalist obstacles to legal change, just as German judges did in the Hitler era."[37]

Put simply if strongly, the critics argue that pragmatism or dynamic statutory interpretation "effectively represents a dramatic and pernicious reordering of our democratic form of government" that "would establish the judiciary as a largely unaccountable ruling elite, the virtual equivalent of philosopher kings."[38] This rather florid critique of pragmatism proves far too much, however. If we are to have judges decide cases, they will to some degree act as such a ruling elite. The ability of judges to strike down statutes as unconstitutional is far more akin to philosopher-kingship than is the use of pragmatism in statutory interpretation. Some might answer that it is the "law" and not judges striking down statutes, but the alleged constraint of the "law" in these decisions is merely presumed rather than proven. A typical pragmatic statutory interpretation will be far less consequential than constitutional rulings and can be readily reversed by the legislature, should the judiciary become too kingly.

As is so often the case in the battles over statutory interpretation, the constitutional criticism of the illegitimate transfer of legislative power to the judiciary of pragmatism begs the vital question. The Constitution assigns legislative power to the Congress and adjudicative power to the judiciary. Neither pragmatism nor any other statutory interpretation theory is likely to change that. Any time that a court elaborates on statutory meaning or fills a statutory gap, it is "legislating" in some metaphysical sense, regardless of the interpretive method that the court employs. Judges cannot certify questions to the enacting legislature, so when a statute does not settle a question, the judge must fill in the gap. So long as the court is merely exercising its adjudicatory authority, though, and not literally rewriting the formal statute books, the court is not legislating in a technical sense. Our Constitution and Congress delegate to the courts the authority to interpret statutes in adjudication. Whenever a court resolves a statutory uncertainty, under any method, it "makes law." Nothing in the text of that delegation dictates that the courts employ a particular interpretive method. The delegation of regulatory (or statutory interpretive) authority to administrative agencies of the executive branch raises far more serious constitutional issues about "legislating" than does a judge's choice of interpretive method for statutes.

In this context, the judges are delegatees of Congress. The legislature adopts statutes and delegates to the judiciary the authority to apply those statutes in adjudication, as the Constitution requires. The delegation does not explicitly preclude the use of pragmatism in interpretation. Although Congress theoretically might attempt to legislate interpretive standards and reject pragmatism, it has not done so. Critics of pragmatism sometimes argue that such a legislative delegation of authority to courts is not constitutionally permitted, but once again this argument proves too much to be logically sustained.

The limits of language mean that no statutory text can be perfectly determinate for all cases that may arise. While contemporary statutes are quite detailed, they still cannot set forth every conceivable factual scenario that might arise and how it should be resolved. Even if language could be perfectly determinate, it is unrealistic to presume that our busy legislature could foresee all cases that may arise under the statute and write the corresponding perfectly determinate language. Even while criticizing pragmatism, Judge Barak notes that "[e]very system of interpretation—including both old and new textualism—must be based on at least a modicum of discretion."[39] There is some logic to exercising that discretion sagaciously, to employ the pragmatic policy that is in the best interests of society.

Adamant critics of pragmatism, Redish and Chung, acknowledge that Congress may sometimes in statutes "delegate discretionary authority to the judiciary to fashion its own substantive common-law principles."[40] Yet this sort of concession potentially obliterates the judicial empowerment criticism of pragmatism. If Congress *may* delegate such discretionary authority to the judiciary, why presume that it has not in fact made such a delegation. Pragmatism essentially rests on an assumption that the Congress has delegated to the judiciary the authority to make pragmatic judgments about the proper way to adapt statutory text to individual cases. While this assumption has not been conclusively demonstrated, neither do the alternative hypotheses (e.g., textualism, legislative history, canons) have such a conclusive demonstration. If it is fair to assume that the judicial canons may be used to interpret statutes, it is equally fair to assume that pragmatic considerations may be used.

Presumably, if judges were employing a pragmatic approach to statutory interpretation, as some are, and the legislature affirmatively disapproved of this approach, the legislature could say so. There is no sign of such disapproval. While individual legislators occasionally rebuke the judiciary for its "activism" or the outcomes of particular cases, there is no sign that interpretive pragmatism is the source of the decisions. On occasion, the legislature functionally reverses a judicial decision by rewriting a statute, but pragmatism is the one theory that takes this practice into account. As discussed in the section on dynamic statutory interpretation, the pragmatic judge seems to have been the more faithful delagatee in these circumstances than was the textualist judge.

The critics of pragmatism appear to fear that it would authorize judges to run wild and impose their personal preferences in statutory interpretation cases, without regard to statutory text or congressional intent. Advocates of pragmatism typically downplay its significance, suggesting that clear text or legislative history will generally dictate a statute's interpretation. For Judge Posner, even if a statute seems intrinsically "foolish," judges must obey its commands.[41] He recognizes the pragmatic value of having some clear legal rules. One can limit the determinative role of judicial pragmatism to certain "hard cases," not readily resolved by more traditional methods of interpretation. This pragmatism is far less aggressive than, say, the purposive theories of a Ronald Dworkin. The critics do not buy this claim of the modesty of pragmatism, though. They contend that the authorization of judicial discretion in the hard cases is letting the camel's nose into the tent, which will be inexorably followed by the whole camel, or unbridled judicial discretion.

This criticism ignores the plain fact that far more of the camel than just its nose is already present in the judicial tent. "Legal doctrine is something a court of last resort can always (well, almost always) get around and it will do so if the judges' feelings are sufficiently engaged."[42] Claims about the prevalence of judicial subjectivity in decision making are not merely asserted; they have been convincingly demonstrated through empirical methods. I have already addressed the considerable quantitative evidence that the justices are strongly influenced by their personal ideological preferences in many contexts. Chapter 7 will consider the interaction of this ideology with statutory interpretive methods.

One adaptation of the judicial empowerment theory argues that pragmatism will have adverse structural incentives. It maintains that judicial empowerment will lead to poorer legislation, because legislators cannot trust the judiciary to implement its clear textual commands. Or perhaps pragmatism is intrinsically conservative, like the argument regarding textualism, and will discourage legislation more generally. Thus, some stress that "[i]f the legislature cannot trust the implementing authorities to respect its collective understanding, it may be reluctant to legislate at all; and if it does legislate, it will be forced to make substantial efforts to ensure that its intended meaning cannot be willfully ignored."[43] This once again assumes the conclusion and rejects without explanation the possibility that the legislature wishes for the judiciary to decide cases pragmatically. Pragmatism might encourage legislation, by dispelling the fear that unforeseen circumstances will cause a statute to produce some negative societal consequences.

The judicial empowerment critique of pragmatism relies upon the presumption that this exercise of judicial interpretive power is inappropriate or unwise or unconstitutional. This claim is typically too facile in its presentation. The strong version of the claim is patently overbroad. If delegation of metaphysical legislative authority is to be disallowed, pragmatic statutory interpretation is far down the list of delegation problems. The weaker version of the claim, that this delegation is a "bridge too far," is theoretically plausible but lacks necessary supporting evidence. Given the inevitability of interpretive delegation to courts, claims of excess delegation involve merely an exercise in line drawing.

The typical case for drawing the line short of pragmatic interpretation returns to intentionalism. Alternative approaches, such as textualism or use of legislative history, direct the judge to consider at some level the intent of the legislature. The ultimate question, in this view, should be what the legislature thinks best, not what the judges believe to be best. The critics claim that pragmatism lacks this basic regard for the intent of the legislature, but again we have a question-begging problem. Perhaps the legislature *intends* that judges apply its statutes in a pragmatic fashion. If so, pragmatism conforms to legislative intention, and no one has presented evidence that this is not so. And if this is the legislative intention, the pragmatic practice gains its necessary democratic imprimatur.

The judicial empowerment criticism of pragmatism rests centrally upon another undemonstrated assumption: that the alternative methods of interpretation are more binding on the judiciary. Superficially, this assumption might seem plausible. "Do what seems most pragmatic" appears to admit of more flexibility than "Do what the statutory text commands." Pragmatic interpretation might therefore unleash unchecked judicial choice in statutory cases. However, as previous chapters have shown, this superficial appearance of relative discretion is not necessarily accurate, and text alone may enable great scope for judicial manipulation. Ultimately, this question is an empirical one, not to be resolved by casual assumptions. It may be that pragmatism can be as constraining as textualism, as later chapters will explore.

Some of the defenders of pragmatism have essentially bought into the premises of the critics of the theory. Eskridge, for example, openly characterizes his dynamic statutory interpretation as "judicial lawmaking" and maintains that such activist judging is "constructive" and preferable to a strict separation of powers that reserves legislation for the legislature, which has difficulty remaining up-to-date and producing logically integrated policies. This defense seems to accept the critique of judicial empowerment and justifies such empowerment. However, this defense of pragmatism may be as misguided as the critique, and Eskridge does not counsel for unbridled judicial discretion. As shown above, pragmatism is not intrinsically "lawmaking," any more than are other interpretive theories.

Judge Barak presents a slightly different critique of the practical wisdom of pragmatism. His objection is that pragmatism provides no polestar measure for the good, leaving that determination to the judiciary.[44] In this sense, he argues pragmatism uniquely empowers the judiciary to discretionarily set goals, rather than just discretionarily implementing them. He argues that the goal should be the legislative purpose, and judges should interpret so as to maximize that purpose. Posner and other pragmatists largely accept this critique and place their faith in judges to discern "the good" outcome. Barak's argument runs afoul of many of the weaknesses addressed above. To the extent that statutory text is indeterminate, legislative purpose may be more so. The ability of a theoretical fealty to legislative purpose to constrain decision making in any meaningful way is utterly undemonstrated. Moreover, this argument again runs into the circularity problem; perhaps the legislative purpose *was* for judges to apply the statute pragmatically. Federal judges are chosen by the legislature, perhaps with an eye to their goals for society.

There is also the question of why we would prefer maximizing the goals of a past, possibly a distant past, legislature to the goals set by contemporary judges. Professor Eskridge observes that "[t]emporal distance may produce a better understanding of what is good or useful about the statutory text and what is not."[45] The response to this position might be that it is not for judges to make this call and that the legislature is perfectly capable of updating statutes in response to developing understanding of their operation in practice. The rebuttal is that legislative action is difficult and easily blocked by minority interests. The pragmatic judge is "more responsive to the current preferences of Congress and the president than to the historical preferences of the original enacting coalition."[46] In this approach, the pragmatic judge is quite deferential to the legislature, just the current one rather than the enacting one.

Judge Barak implicitly acknowledges this question and emphasizes that his purposivism may be as dynamic as pragmatism, adapting the original purpose to contemporary circumstances.[47] This concession may largely give away the game, though. Such an adaptation of purpose to circumstances sounds like pragmatic decision making, and such decision making may be the legislature's end. Indeed, it would seem that a judiciary may be better and more determinately able to identify the pragmatic outcome than to imaginatively reconstruct how the legislature would wish its general purpose to be applied to changing circumstances. More centrally, pragmatic application may well itself be the legislative purpose from the beginning. Indeed, this is a reasonable inference for explaining the interstices commonly left in statutes, such as those described in Chapter 1.

This legislative purpose, though, is not established, and pragmatism might seem especially vulnerable to the concern of ideological bias and willful judging. The philosophical notion of pragmatism can be ideologically neutral, and "advocates of practical reason are a diverse group, both politically and intellectually."[48] Nevertheless, there remains the concern that each of those groups may inject their own diverse preferences into interpretation, rather than finding a more pragmatic middle ground. This must be an empirical question.

There is a contrary view that judges' willful interpolation of personal policy preferences into law would actually be "constrained if judges acknowledged" that they were considering pragmatic issues.[49] Judge Posner suggests that the transparent discretion provided by interpretive pragmatism may actually constrain judicial activism, arguing that "[j]udges are less rather than more likely to be power-mad if they know they are exercising discretion than if they think they're just a transmission belt for decisions made elsewhere."[50] Similarly, it's been said that "there are only two kinds of judges at all levels of courts: those who are admittedly . . . result-oriented, and those who are also result-oriented, but either do not know it or decline for various purposes to admit it."[51] The former more introspective judges are more "inhibited by the knowledge that they may put into judicial decisions value judgments that may not have enduring validity and may even turn out to be wrong."[52]

Anecdotally, one might find some support for this claim by observing today's Supreme Court. Justices Thomas and Scalia appear to be the justices most dedicated to the original text and understanding. They also seem to be among the more activist judges on the Court, in the sense of upsetting precedent and settled understanding of the law, and they are also among the most ideologically consistent justices. Ultimately, of course, the association of pragmatism and activism, whether positive or negative, can be empirically measured. Reliance on assumptions in either direction doesn't resolve the question.

Pragmatism does not obviously or necessarily grant the judiciary more discretion than the alternative theories. Indeed, as subsequent chapters will demonstrate, the evidence does not strongly support the excessive judicial empowerment hypothesis. The real question may not be the absolute amount of judicial discretion enabled by an interpretive theory but the manner in which the discretion is channeled by that theory, when exercised in good faith. This leads to a more substantial critique of pragmatism, that the theory itself is unpragmatic in its practice.

The Pragmatism of Pragmatism

One of the more trenchant criticisms of pragmatism challenges whether the practice is even pragmatic in its application. This criticism reflects an institutional criticism of the judiciary. Even if pragmatic statutory interpretation was deemed to be theoretically optimal for the ideal body, it is not necessarily true that judges could effectively provide this optimal interpretation. Perhaps the characteristics of the judicial process (or the characteristics of judges themselves) conspire against the ability of the judiciary to identify the pragmatically best policy.

Some defenders of pragmatism argue that the courts' "independence and their deliberative capacities" give them "significant advantages over a legislature that may be influenced by parochial interests and is frequently responsive to monetary demands."[53] The judiciary may be considered something like a traditional council of "wise elders" with good policy judgment who may be entrusted "with responsibility for deciding cases in a way that will produce the best results in the circumstances."[54] This strong argument appears to prove too much—why even have a legislature if judges are so superior? Moreover, the superiority of judges is not so evident.

Being unelected and circumstantially removed from the situation of most people (e.g., in terms of income), judges might not be the best group to ascertain the best policy. If the general welfare were an objectively obvious finding, amenable to judicial interpretation, pragmatism would be more defensible. But the critics contend that this is not the case. What is "best" necessarily involves some moral judgment, and the critics of pragmatism argue that unelected judges are ill-positioned to make these moral determinations. Federal judges are not elected, nor is their membership highly representative of the United States population. Consequently, their values may differ from those held by the democratic majority.

The difficulties of such a judicial determination of best policy are compounded by the legal process. Judges are largely confined to the arguments and evidence presented by the advocates for the particular parties to the dispute. Judges cannot conduct policy hearings and call their own expert witnesses. Instead, judges get a cramped and strategically selected set of evidence on which to decide. While *amicus* briefs may provide the judiciary with a broader perspective, they may still fail to obtain necessary information. Unlike legislatures or administrative agencies, the judiciary cannot hold hearings and take all available evidence.

Moreover, the judicial process yields only individual case outcomes, and the adjudicatory process may be ill-suited to pragmatic policymaking. Thus, judges "might, by treating statutes flexibly, be purchasing case-specific benefits at the price of increased uncertainty."[55] This risk is compounded by the nonrandom nature of the cases that arise to be adjudicated. The U.S. judiciary lacks the ability to give advisory opinions and is limited to the cases and controversies that come before it. Those cases are selected by the litigants that choose to pursue a dispute to adjudicatory finality. Unlike the other branches of government, judges cannot set their own agenda and are limited to the cases that arise.

A body of research has developed questioning the ability of the judiciary to make wise programmatic choices. A classic early work by Donald Horowitz, which focused on constitutional controversies, used case studies to show that the judicial process undermined the institution's ability to make sound policy choices.[56] Justice Breyer, typically regarded as a leading pragmatist, has noted that "courts work within institutional rules that deliberately disable them from seeking out information relevant to the inquiry at hand."[57] A study of judicial interpretations of environmental laws concluded that this led to perverse consequences, even when judges were properly motivated and exercising good faith.[58] Professor Vermeule notes that "vivid costs in particular cases may trigger cognitive failings in both theorists and judges, causing them to overreact to the specifics of particular cases while ignoring the overall systemic effects of the interpretive rules they defend or adopt."[59]

Despite these shortcomings, Posner and others believe that judges are up to the task of pragmatism. Judge Posner views the courts as "councils of wise elders" who may be trusted to resolve disputes "in a way that will produce the best results in the circumstances rather than resolving them purely on the basis of rules created by other organs of government or by their own previous decisions."[60] The response to the democratic critique is that most decisions do not involve marginal questions about moral good or bad. While there is great disagreement on the margin about moral goodness, Americans also have a vast dimension of shared morality. Pragmatism essentially makes the case that, within this area of shared morality, judges should find the interpretation that best suits it through the exercise of "practical reason."

Pragmatists, especially Judge Posner, downplay the significance of grand moral theory as a decision-making tool. This frustrates his critics who lament that he claims that pragmatism produces "better" consequences but then fails to define what good consequences are. The position is called a "stunted form of consequentialism" with "no value theory."[61] Dworkin complains that it is pointless to tell judges to do what "works" without establishing a criterion for what "works." In fact, Posner's position is sensibly humble. He does not claim that he (or any other individual philosopher) has all the answers about what is "better" or what "works." Rather, his claim is an institutional one, that allowing judges to make pragmatic decisions in the interests of what *they* believe to be better will generally conform more to what society considers better than would any alternative method. Of course, such an institutional position can fall prey to responses about the institution's deficiencies.

With respect to the shortcomings of the judicial process, pragmatists can concede them but maintain that the process has countervailing advantages. When Congress legislates, it inevitably does so for the typical case circumstances. Congress may not mean for its rules designed for the typical circumstances to extend to atypical ones. Yet Congress has difficulty designing exceptions to its rules for the atypical circumstances. Plainly, Congress cannot foresee all the possible future scenarios in which its rules may be applied, even in the short term. Given the indefinite duration of statutes, the foreseeability problem is much greater. When Congress wrote the Sherman Antitrust Act, it did not know of computers, much less the details of the business practices of Microsoft. One could hardly expect Congress to adapt the legislative commands of the Sherman Act to these circumstances. It is unrealistic to expect Congress to revise the entire body of statutes every year, and requiring such revisions may only draw legislative attention away from more pressing contemporaneous social problems. If Congress addresses the more pressing problems, but not the revisions, then the old statutory language survives only due to inertia and limited resources, not any constitutionally appropriate basis.

The judiciary, by contrast, is intimately familiar with the circumstances of the cases it adjudicates. Even assuming that judicial decisions produce the optimal resolution of particular cases, the associated opinions set precedents that govern future cases with different facts. The optimal decision for a given case may yield suboptimal outcomes for those future cases. The unrepresentative nature of cases obviously creates a potential problem. If a judge defines a statutory interpretation based on atypical circumstances, that definition could be erroneous for other circumstances, which may be much more common.

This problem of institutional capacity is not quite so severe as it might seem, however. First, it is cured by "judicial minimalism." Judges are, by nature, adjudicators, not policymakers and lower courts that decide most cases seem largely minimalist. Moreover, the overriding law is not made by individual decisions but by their systemic production. Governing law is usually the product of a series of decisions, through which pragmatic interpretation may incorporate a variety of factual scenarios.

All decisions set precedents that obviously establish statutory interpretations to be followed in subsequent adjudications, but such precedents admit of considerable flexibility and adaptation in subsequent adjudications. For most courts, though, an erroneous decision does not set any sort of national policy. Circuit splits, in which different circuit courts adopt different statutory interpretations, are relatively common. Even absent such splits, precedents, including Supreme Court precedents, are readily distinguished by future courts. While precedents are said to characterize a path-dependent system, in which early rulings influence later ones, empirical research has shown that the extent of such path dependence is quite weak.[62] Hence, there is relatively little danger that a "wrong" decision would lock in a terrible unwise statutory interpretation, though this risk is clearly greater for Supreme Court rulings than for those of lower courts. In addition, the less frequent legislative determinations also run some of this same risk. Congress adopts statutes to address a contemporaneous social issue, and changing facts may make the congressional determination inapt as societal circumstances change.

The case for pragmatism is not dependent on the results in individual cases so much as in its overall systemic effect. Like the legislature, the judiciary is a "them, not an it" and only determinations that are integrated and survive numerous judicial decisions make policy.[63] This is the Hayekian or common law justification for judicial discretion, discussed below. Despite the shortcomings of judges making polycentric policy decisions, the overall judicial process ameliorates some of these problems. Moreover, the goal is not the unachievable perfect system but simply the best available.

The manner by which the law evolves through a coordinated system of judicial decision making has been assessed in a thorough study of prison reform litigation.[64] Up until 1964, no U.S. court "had ever ordered a prison to change its practices or conditions."[65] They adhered to precedents that such conditions were not subject to constitutional review. After the initial decision declaring that certain conditions were cruel and unusual and issuing injunctions to reform the prisons, the legal culture adapted. Just one decade later, "prisons in a total of forty-one states, as well as the District of Columbia, Puerto Rico, and the Virgin Islands, had at one time or another been under comprehensive court orders, as had the entire correctional systems of at least ten states."[66] This evolutionary policymaking by precedent was the "result of an incremental, intuitive process of muddling through," much like cultural evolution.[67] Although a single initial decision provided the variant for other judges to consider, the change in the law "represented the collective actions of literally hundreds of federal judges" who were "middle-of-the-road, upper-middle-class Americans, largely white and male, appointed by Republican and Democratic presidents."[68] While not a statutory example, the constitutional experience illustrates how judicial ideology does not dominate such pragmatic decision making and supports a Posnerian view of evolution through common societal values. This is but a single case study but it provides an example of the functional operation of pragmatism.

Professor Vermeule is the foremost expounder of the pragmatic value of relatively formalist rule-following, rather than the case-by-case evaluations of pragmatic judicial decision making. He argues that the predictability of this approach provides a better set of governing rules than would the case-by-case assessment of consequences. Formalism may be more pragmatic than case-by-case pragmatism by virtue of providing more certainty of resolution.[69] If the meaning of a statute varies too widely depending on case circumstances, it may be more difficult for actors to predict its meaning and order their affairs accordingly. A system of rule-following, rather than circumstantial analysis, has obvious disadvantages, though. For example, the Three Mile Island accident occurred because "nuclear power plant operators had become rule-following automatons," and the incident caused a shift in nuclear safety decision making, from rules to more flexible, case-by-case standards.[70] As always, the answer requires empirical investigation.

Some defenders of pragmatism have dwelt on the inherent limitations of the legislative process and have presented the "rent-seeking" justification for judicial policy making. In this view, the legislature is in thrall to narrow private interests, sometimes called factions or interest groups, due to campaign contributions or other favors they may bestow upon legislators. Judge Easterbrook declared that "many laws are designed to serve private rather than public interests."[71] Federal judges, with life tenure, are viewed as less susceptible to this influence. The theory has been used as "a rationale for remedying alleged deficiencies of electoral and legislative politics through judicial intervention."[72]

This very defense of an activist judicial pragmatism, though, can also be used as an argument against judicial authority. Critics of the legislature have been far too sanguine about the judiciary's freedom from such rent-seeking behavior. Judicial decision making is, by its nature, a prisoner of litigated cases. Litigants can, to some degree, manipulate the development of law through the cases they select to litigate to a decision and appeal. Some have greater resources that better enable them to litigate.[73] Perhaps more significantly, litigants can manipulate the course of the law through strategic case selection, presenting to judges the more atypical disputes that conduce to favorable results and the consequent precedents.[74] This is counteracted, to a degree at least, by the occasionally inefficient decision making of litigants.[75] Nevertheless, the rent-seeking problem exists, and the comparative vulnerability of legislative and judicial decision making is not theoretically determinate.

Of course, the institutional problems of the judiciary are not unique to pragmatism. Adrian Vermeule notes that "litigant error and strategy behavior may distort the presentation of legislative history to the court."[76] The same might be said of textualism, given the great length and detail of statutes and external sources such as dictionaries and the full body of legislation used by textualists. Although pragmatism seems to leave the judiciary more discretion and room for error, that conclusion has not been proved.

Principled pragmatism would use the text heavily and also place significant weight on legislative purpose. The pragmatic method is more a means than an end, and adopting the best decision to achieve the legislative purpose is the pragmatic approach, even if the judge might disagree with that overarching legislative purpose. In this sense, one might expect pragmatism to be somewhat complementary to intentionalist methodologies, but it would not assume that the legislature itself had determined all the answers. Of course, the ability of judges to fulfill this aim is undetermined. The critique and the defenses of pragmatism are overly theoretical. The pragmatism of pragmatism is essentially a consequentialist question that requires empirical investigation. Pragmatism may indeed be unpragmatic, but this can be discovered only by testing. It is difficult to design a direct test of the system in the context of statutory interpretation, but we have some indirect evidence of the value of a pragmatic approach to judicial decision making.

The Common Law

When evaluating the realistic consequences of judicial pragmatism, the common law is instructive. Common law is explicitly and openly "judge made" on a case-by-case basis with all the institutional limitations on judicial authority and judgment. Hence, it is tantamount to the metaphysical concept of judicial decisions as legislation. *Ab initio*, common law was utterly about judicial discretion. Although a considerable body of common law precedent exists, judges retain the authority to distinguish it, change it, and adapt it to new circumstances, such creating new torts to suit modern circumstances. Justice Scalia describes the common law mindset as one that asks: "What is the most desirable resolution of this case, and how can any impediments to the achievement of that result be evaded?"[77] This is the pragmatic approach (though Scalia criticizes its use in statutory interpretation). The common law approach correlates to the "ordinary judging" paradigm discussed above.

Some have intermittently suggested that the common law's pragmatism is seen in its tendency to produce economically efficient rules and results, superior to those achieved by legislation. Various theories were propounded for why the judicial process, in common law cases at least, tended to produce economically efficient results. These theoretical analyses proved difficult to sustain, though, for reasons including the special interest manipulation discussed above.

There is a growing body of empirical evidence that provides support for the economic value of the common law process. Professor Mahoney recently presented empirical data indicating that common law nations were economically more successful.[78] At around the same time, a group of economists, Rafael LaPorta, Florencio Lopez-de-Silanes, Andrei Shleifer, and Robert Vishny (the LaPorta group), reported that nations of English legal origin (common law nations) had greater financial development than other nations.[79] This research group has also found that English legal origin, using the common law, is associated with greater economic freedom than found in civil law nations.[80] An independent group of World Bank researchers have recently confirmed these general results.[81] One study measured comparative degrees of legal formalism and found that more formalistic systems had lesser economic growth.[82] While the research has been primarily performed by economists and addressed only economic outcomes, other recent research indicates that common law systems may better deter personal injuries.[83]

The evidence on the success of common law systems is supportive of pragmatic judicial interpretation. The precise reasons why common law systems are superior is unproved, but the research on relative formalism suggests that case-by-case adjudication through precedent is at least a part of the explanation. Even though we now live in an age where statutory law is arguably more important than common law, the association survives, probably because common law judicial systems employ a more "common law–like" process for interpreting those statutes.

Judge Posner has drawn this contrast of the American legal system to those of the European continent. Those European systems generally apply a form of interpretation of statutory civil law, where judges lack authority to create common law rules but may only interpret legislation. Their legislative codes, moreover, "generally are clearer and more detailed than ours."[84] In consequence, he suggests that the European judiciary is more formalist and less pragmatic. Hence, the comparison between the European system and the Anglo-American common law system serves as something of a test case for formalism vs. pragmatism.

Statutory interpretation is not strictly a common law process, though the parallels are significant. For a variety of statutes, ranging from antitrust law, to private securities fraud actions, to CERCLA liability, the development of statutory law has closely followed the common law practice. Professor Manning recognizes the aptness of the comparison when he favors textualism precisely because he believes the Constitution meant for statutory interpretation to depart from common law methodologies.[85] There is some contrary evidence, though, for example in Alexander Hamilton's profession that the judiciary should react to "unjust and partial laws" by "mitigating the severity and confining the operation of such law."[86] A review of *The Federalist* concluded that the framers generally endorsed an equity-based approach to statutory interpretation.[87] Justice Scalia, though, has been especially critical of the common law analogy. He notes that we "live in an era of legislation" and fears that the pragmatic judicial approach associated with common law decision making is not "appropriate" for statutory interpretation.[88] This, ironically, is itself something of a dynamic approach to interpretation that suggests that changing times require changing interpretive methods. Yet the empirical evidence suggests that common law systems are preferable in today's world.

Professor Vermeule argues that the "common-law style of interpretation presupposes a fanciful, even romantic account of judicial capacities."[89] Yet he also recognizes that the issue is centrally an empirical one, and the empirical evidence strongly supports this common law style of interpretation. This claim should not be overstated, as the empirical evidence on the value of common law processes has its shortcomings and is far from dispositive. Nevertheless, the studies are informative about the potential virtues of a case-by-case pragmatic judicial resolution of legal controversies.

Hayek and Judicial Decision Making

Friedrich Hayek is not generally considered a pragmatist. His devotion to the rule of law and liberty as a supreme value does not immediately seem pragmatic in nature. Yet Hayek's free market approach had a core of pragmatism. Hayek has traditionally been seen as a formalist, because his theory of judging was dedicated to the application of clear rules, on which private parties might rely. Yet he was also devoted to the common law system of judicial discretion in the law's application to case circumstances.

The Hayekian formalistic legal certainty goal is an unachievable one. As discussed above, no language can yield such certainty. Nor are judges, being human, able to create such determinate certainty out of the available legal materials. Nor can any certain rules realistically predict the future developments, whether technological or sociological, that could alter the circumstances of their future application. Simple formalistic rule-following cannot alone create valuable or even certain law.

Hayek suggested that the optimal law developed out of a "spontaneous order," rather than from any central organizing principle.[90] His great defense of capitalism arose from the inability of a central authority to gather the information necessary to set the best standards, and the ability of unorganized individual choices to create a better overall system.[91] Rules are better formulated from the bottom up than from the top down. This is easily analogized to judicial discretion in individual cases, the spontaneous part of the order. The legislature lacks the information about all possible disputes to set clear and universal rules. Judges hearing specific disputes can better reach sensible decisions, just as individuals making business transactions can better determine sensible economic outcomes than can any top-down rigid legislative process.

The development of the law in this respect can be analogized to studies of cultural evolution. Researchers in anthropology, sociology, and other disciplines have studied this cultural evolution. Humans have developed culture, which has "made the human species a spectacular ecological success."[92] Researchers have increasingly studied how human culture develops and how it changes, sometimes called cultural evolution. A non-mathematical explanation of the process from an interdisciplinary perspective can be found in a recent book by Professors Richerson and Boyd.[93] They address the significance of culture to humanity and its absence from the lives of other species.

Culture exists due to the transmission of its concepts among individuals. In many cases, it is imitative—there is a "tendency to conform to the beliefs of the majority."[94] Many children initially adopt the cultural views of their parents. This imitation has real efficiency benefits, because it allows selective learning and enables cumulative improvement over time.[95] Eventually, however, children grow and are exposed to alternative cultures that transmit their different cultural beliefs. While many adhere to the culture of their parents, some engage in "comparison shopping" and switch to cultural beliefs that they now prefer or perhaps adopt a variant that combines their existing culture with new aspects.[96] Other individuals may shift in the opposite cultural direction. The group culture overall will change when one variant is sufficiently more appealing that it becomes the dominant choice.[97] Change will be more likely when its consequences are more knowable and less risky, otherwise imitation is the preferable strategy. Other factors also influence this choice. Thus, "we are predisposed to imitate successful, prestigious people."[98]

The analogy of this cultural evolution to pragmatic statutory interpretation is straightforward. Reliance on textualism may create an imitative component that tracks that aspect of culture. This imitation may create errors, but it saves on decision making effort and helps avoid the risks of costly mistakes. However, when confronted with new case facts and new legal arguments, some pragmatic judges with varying views of justice will depart from rigid adherence to formalistic tools. A certain number of departures are necessary for adaptation.[99] If those departures are persuasive to other judges, they will grow and become a new precedential paradigm that potentially might displace the earlier rules and become the source of future imitative behavior. Of course, this occurs only incrementally over time. The legal rules deemed more fit are the ones that survive. Judge Easterbrook has observed that the accretion of precedent allows judges to "improve on the treatment of the earlier case," thanks to the learning process.[100] The same might be said of pragmatic statutory interpretation.

Hayek's case for relative legal formalism, like Vermeule's, was a pragmatic one. He believed that relative formalism produced the best results for society. His disagreement thus was not with pragmatism as a guide to law but at most to the legal strategy that would prove most pragmatic. And he recognized the wisdom of "piecemeal tinkering" that could make the law "more consistent both internally as well as with the facts to which the rules are applied."[101] This language clothes an appreciation of pragmatic decision making, the value of which is largely confirmed by the empirical evidence on the effects of the common law as discussed above. Too much formalism obviously would interfere with the spontaneous order of the law by imposing "top down" strictures on case-by-case decision making.

Of course, free-wheeling pragmatism that ignored text and precedent would also be suboptimal. Pragmatic statutory interpretation that amounted to nothing more than an equitable "best results" standard would be costly and excessively unstable. But this is not the appropriate model of pragmatic statutory interpretation. Pragmatism does not imply judges who ignore the text, or legislative intent, or other approaches; it simply suggests that in difficult, unforeseen circumstances, judges should consider the pragmatic implications of their decisions. The ability of judges to do so is at least somewhat confirmed by the experience with common law, as discussed above. It is in this sense that pragmatism parallels the paradigm of cultural evolution.

The textualist/formalist critique of pragmatic interpretation suffers another flaw in its presumption that textualism is indeed predictable and formalist. As noted in Chapter 2 and elsewhere in the book, there is a plausible argument that textualism is as judicially manipulable as other interpretive methods. Insofar as this is true, the approach suffers some of the same problems as does the critique of pragmatism. This will be explored empirically in Chapter 7.

Application to Statutory Interpretation

The association of pragmatism with the practice of the common law is informative. Common law is "ordinary judging" of the conventional sort, and the empirically demonstrated advantages of common law commend the theory. Advocates of "ordinary judging" have criticized dynamic statutory interpretation as placing "too much emphasis on the judge's role in fitting statutes into an evolving legal landscape as *the* justifying principle for the judge's collaborative interpretive role."[102] This criticism is overly theoretical, though, and goes not to actual judicial practice but to law review justifications. Differences at the theoretical level pale if the fundamental practice is the same.

Critics raise the easy objection that the common law is "judge-made," so that the same approach should not be employed for statutes that are intended to be "legislature-made." They could argue that the common law is the appropriate zone for pragmatism, while statutory interpretation should be a more formalistic endeavor. This criticism is only persuasive, though, when combined with a showing that the legislature *does not want* judges to employ such pragmatism, and this showing is entirely absent. The pervasive presence of statutory gaps and ambiguities testifies that the legislature intends common law judicial discretion to be employed. A rational legislature could easily recognize its own inability to foresee all possible future disputes and delegate the resolution of at least the atypical ones to a discretionary judiciary accustomed to common sense adjudicative rationality.

One must be cautious about the common law analogy. Statutes are often passed precisely because the common law was deficient in its resolution of a problem. It would be unwise to return to the late-nineteenth-century practice of derogating statutes that are contrary to the common law. Viewed in its most aggressive formulation, pragmatism might yield this result. But a more modest pragmatism, that was limited to interstices or ambiguities or the very atypical case, is not so intrusive. The attack on pragmatism reduces to a mistrust of the judiciary to apply pragmatism wisely and not impose the judicial ideology willy-nilly, contrary to statutory meaning. Yet this attack suggests that the judiciary cannot faithfully apply a theory, and it would apply equally to every interpretive approach. To be effective, the attack would have to maintain that pragmatism is more "willful" than the alternatives. The validity of this attack needs to be tested empirically in practice, not simply assumed.

Conclusion

There is much to be said for pragmatic statutory interpretation, for reasons explicated in this chapter and the remainder of the book. However, some of the advocates for pragmatism or dynamic statutory interpretation are their own worst enemies, in my conception. These advocates have painted the theory as a dramatic empowerment of judicial activism and claimed that this is institutionally for the better (e.g., in the judiciary's ability to avoid rent-seeking or other pathologies of the legislative process). In reality, that pragmatism is, and is best defended as, a rechanneling of an existing empowerment. On the presumption that judges are flawed vessels but acting in good faith, the true question is whether this rechanneling is wise. When the text is relatively clear, directly applicable, and produces no absurd results, the pragmatist should employ a textualist approach.

Appropriately exercised, pragmatism does not simply tell judges to resolve a case however they think best or fairest. The institutional limitations of the judicial process counsel against such a broad exercise of judicial discretion. Pragmatists should not totally ignore text, except in cases where the literal text produces absurdity. Professor Eskridge thus calls for a "cautious model" of pragmatism that would not readily ignore reasonably determinate text. Pragmatism first identifies a legislative delegation to the judiciary, whether inescapable background delegation or a direct intentionalist delegation due to the limitations of the statutory text. The pragmatist then presumes that the presence of this delegation authorizes the judge to resolve the case pragmatically, with an eye to the consequences of the resolution.

These consequences incorporate the importance of adherence to text and precedent and stable understanding of the law. The common law experience supports the wisdom of pragmatism, though additional empirical analysis is required in the particular context of statutory interpretation, in order to evaluate the effects of pragmatic interpretation in this field.

CHAPTER 6

The Justices and Their Practice of Statutory Interpretation

The conventional wisdom is that "the Supreme Court's approach to statutory interpretation has become increasingly 'textualist' in character; that is,
more oriented to statutory language and the assertedly 'objective' meaning
of statutory text than to the collective subjective intent behind the legislation."[1] Jonathan Molot suggests that "even those who question textualism's
more extreme assertions have gone a long way toward accepting textualism's
core insights."[2] Some proclaimed the death of legislative history as an interpretive tool, but a casual inspection of opinions demonstrates that the procla-
mation was overstated. Legislative history continues to be invoked, at least
occasionally, by the Supreme Court and lower courts. This chapter considers the pattern of use of different methods of statutory interpretation during
the Rehnquist Court.

It is unrealistic for research to attempt to discern the "true" or even primary reason for a Supreme Court decision. However, it is relatively easy to
compile the reasons given by the Court. The use of citations may not fully

capture the Court's reasoning. A justice's awareness of a source may be influential even if it is not used in the opinion. However, it is the best objective tool for empirical analysis and given the extensive opinions now common, it seems fair to assume that the vast majority of resources used by the Court are cited therein.

Research on Judicial Practice

Although political scientists have extensively studied judicial decision making, they have overwhelmingly focused on constitutional issues and done little to examine statutory interpretation. When statutory interpretation has been studied somewhat, the research is largely limited to exploration of ideological voting, in disregard of legal principles or theories. The law is demonstrably significant in judicial decision making, though, and legal requirements must be integrated with political goals. So far, this empirical synthesis is largely lacking.

Professors of law have engaged in considerable historical research on statutory interpretation.[3] Unsurprisingly, they have disagreed over its implications. Those who favor a more active judicial role that uses matters of legislative history have demonstrated that this was the English legal practice at the time of the Constitution. Those who favor textualism have argued that the Constitution was meant to alter this practice. All agree, however, that judicial interpretive practices have changed over time.

During this nation's first century, the methods of statutory interpretation were not much analyzed, but some argue that the law "usually eschewed reference to extrinsic legislative materials in statutory interpretation before 1892."[4] Of course, the materials of legislative history were much less developed then and, during this time, the justices were influenced by other extratextual factors, such as the perpetuation of common law principles, perhaps a pragmatic approach to interpretation. The history is not perfectly clear and uncontested, however. Justices White and Scalia engaged in a debate over whether Chief Justice Marshall would have considered legislative history in statutory interpretation.[5] White cited cases indicating Justice Marshall's reliance on legislative intent, while Scalia claimed that he would be shocked by contemporary uses of legislative history for interpretation. The

Marshall Court's statutory interpretation has seen one close review, which found that its touchstone was legislative intent, though it relied significantly on text to evince that intent.[6] In the early days of our history, there was distinct evidence of judicial pragmatism in statutory interpretation. The Court considered the equities of the case and applied "judicial reason" in the interpretation of statutes.[7] This analysis concluded that the Marshall Court was pluralist and believed in "using differing interpretive techniques in different cases"[8] and that "the judiciary had the inherent discretion to decide how to interpret statutes."[9]

As the nineteenth century progressed, though, "the courts generally refused to consider legislative debate."[10] Thus, one Supreme Court opinion held that the Court "cannot, in any degree, be influenced by the construction placed upon [the statute] by individual members of Congress in the debate which took place on its passage, nor by the motives or reasons assigned by them for supporting or opposing amendments that were offered."[11] The courts of this era rejected legislative history, and associated purposivism, as a guide to statutory interpretation.

The twentieth century saw primary devotion to purposivism as an interpretive technique, with considerable use of legislative history.[12] The canons fell out of favor in this era as unduly formalist.[13] In the mid-1930s, the use of legislative history became an extensive practice in court opinions. The absolute number of references to the materials of legislative history grew dramatically in this period.[14] The era prominently saw a substantial theoretical defense of an interpretive methodology, culminating in the legal process school of Hart and Sacks. In the context of statutory interpretation, the legal process theorists were strong purposivists; they first sought to decide the purpose of the statute and then to interpret the words to best carry out that purpose.[15] They essentially placed fulfillment of purpose ahead of adherence to text. The Warren Court often embraced this approach to give effect to statutory purposes.

The end of the century, though, saw an apparently dramatic shift to textualism as governing interpretation. The rise of textualism may in part have been due to excesses of purposivism and legislative history, but it was generally propounded by conservative judges and justices, and surely reflected their views of the law more broadly. This era saw a much greater reliance on the use of dictionaries for statutory interpretation.[16] At least superficially, textualism seemed less judicially activist and more rule-like. In part for this reason, Justice Scalia has vigorously argued that strict textualism is the appropriate method for statutory interpretation.

The 1980s and 1990s evidenced the swing back to textualism in interpretation, and there is now a widespread belief that textualism is ascendant. One sign of this was the tripling of the rate of reference to dictionaries in interpretation.[17] The trend was so strong it was sometimes referred to as "hypertextualism." Although its command was not universal, Professor Manning suggests that even the purposivists on today's Court are more likely to ground their opinions in text and rely less on purpose than in the past.[18] However, this has been attributed at least in part to an evolution of textualism itself that has moved the theory toward a moderate position that incorporates intentionalism.[19] Indeed, Charles Tiefer argues that 1995 saw a renaissance of new "institutional legislative history" in response to the textualist push.[20]

While there has been much discussion about trends in statutory interpretation methodologies over time, a more reliable source is empirical research. The existing research has focused heavily upon the rate of use of legislative history in statutory interpretation. An early study of the 1950–1972 Court opinions found that legislative history or other intentionalist tools were used in the majority of cases.[21] The researcher found considerable differences among the use of the tools by the different justices, though, and also great differences in usage among different statutes.

Judge Patricia Wald performed another summary of the use of legislative history.[22] Her review found that the Court used legislative history in nearly every statutory interpretation case in the 1981–1982 term, a rate that declined to about 75% for the 1988–1989 term. An update of this research for the 1992–1993 term found that use of legislative history had fallen to 18%.[23] At this rate, legislative history appeared to be going the way of the dinosaurs.

A more recent empirical analysis, though, identified some "resurgence" of legislative history in statutory interpretation in the Supreme Court's 1996 term.[24] More than forty of the eighty decisions rendered in that term clearly involved statutory interpretation. Professor Schacter found that notions of legislative intent were found in 53% of these decisions. Legislative history was expressly used in 49% of the decisions. By contrast, dictionaries were used as interpretive aids in only 18% of the cases. Legislative history was not at its apex, but it apparently remains widely used.

The most recent research traced the Court's use of legislative history over a more extended period in cases involving workplace law (including discrimination disputes).[25] It found that legislative history was used in 40% to 50% of the majority opinions from 1969 until 1986. After this point, the use of legislative history then dropped to a frequency of around 25%, until rising to nearly 40% in 2002–2004. The researchers found the decline was in part due to the opinion writing of Justices Scalia and Thomas but also due to reduced use of legislative history by other justices, as the Burger Court became the Rehnquist Court.

One must be cautious about comparing the percentages in these various studies. Their precise criteria for counting legislative intent references were not necessarily identical, and we have seen inconsistencies in the reported results. Thus, it appears that legislative history went from being commonplace to being rare but bounced back to being a relatively significant interpretive tool. One shortcoming of much of this past research was its consideration of only a single Court term. This provides a relatively small sample, so that the variation might possibly be attributable to an artifact of the particular statutory disputes that came before the Court in the single year studied.

From the studies, one may tentatively conclude that reliance on legislative history has declined somewhat but is far from extinct. Unfortunately, much of the research has examined the relative frequency of only legislative history and not other interpretive tools. A seminal study, conducted by Nicholas Zeppos, was somewhat broader in examining the sources used in statutory interpretation by the Court, since the 1890s.[26] It found that text was the most common resource used by the Court (in 84.1% of the cases) but that reliance on legislative history was common (congressional reports used in 32% of the cases, debates in 16.9% of the cases, and material from hearings in 12.6% of the cases).[27] References to executive branch resources were rare. The research also concluded that considerations of the practical consequences of interpretation were consistent occurrences over a long period of time.[28] The research is somewhat dated now, but Zeppos concludes that "the Court has not adopted textualism as its methodology for deciding statutory cases."[29] He concluded that the Court was trending away from textualism and toward a more dynamic approach to statutory interpretation.

A detailed more recent study focused upon cases interpreting the Internal Revenue Code over an extended period of time.[30] This research created a series of criteria for textualist analysis and found a dramatic jump in the use of this method in the 1978–1983 period, even before Scalia joined the Court. The level of textualist use then declined somewhat but remained higher than the historic average. The study also found a relatively high level of intentionalist interpretation in recent years, in around half of all cases, but this may be due to the coding of interpretation of related statutes as intentionalist, though this is generally regarded as a textualist method of interpretation.

Professor Eskridge has performed a slightly more sophisticated analysis of the use of legislative history for a recent six-year period.[31] He assessed not only the mention of legislative history in Supreme Court opinions but also the significance of its usage. Some suggest that legislative history is used in three distinct ways: to reinforce the plain meaning of text, to answer ambiguities, and to confirm that the legislature did not intend an apparently absurd textual result. He found that the most common use of legislative history was to confirm what the Court found to be the plain meaning of a statute. His study showed a possible decline in the use of legislative history to escape apparent meaning, but the number of cases with this usage was very small (peaking at seven and averaging about two and one-half times per year). The rise of textualism may have been exaggerated. Philip Frickey notes that despite "nearly two decades of textualist assault, a longstanding cluster of eclectic interpretive practices—a balancing of textual, institutional, and purposive considerations—seems to have remained largely intact."[32]

The Expressed Views of the Current Justices

Before engaging in my own empirical analysis of statutory interpretation in the Rehnquist Court, I consider the positions formally taken by the justices of that Court. Some of these justices have addressed the relevant questions more straightforwardly than any others in history and more directly than many commentators. I begin with Justice Scalia, who has prominently discussed statutory interpretation and who is often given credit for the textualist revival. Some have suggested that he deserves nearly exclusive credit for the move to textualism.[33]

Justice Scalia has provided considerable evidence of his views on statutory interpretation, in publications as well as opinions, some of which have been referenced in prior chapters.[34] He is a devout supporter of textualism as an interpretive approach and a persistent critic of any reliance on legislative history, as I have discussed intermittently in prior chapters. While Scalia has suggested that legislative history is ideologically manipulable, he has rejected its use even when he concedes that it provides clear directions to the courts.[35] Justice Scalia's interpretive preferences are so well known and significant that they have been extensively analyzed by commentators.[36]

While Justice Scalia's devotion to text is evident, it is supplemented by the "aggressive" use of linguistic and substantive canons that may "carry him far afield from any plain meaning or ordinary usage that an ordinary reader, or even a member of Congress voting on the statute, might glean from the text."[37] Justice Scalia has occasionally been called a "fallen textualist" who fails to practice the theory "sincerely and consistently."[38] This might be evidenced by a decision in which he calls for an "interpretation of the statute" that is "faithful to its apparent purpose."[39] Scalia has also written that the pragmatic "consideration of policy consequences" of a decision is "part of the traditional judicial tool-kit."[40] Of course, his defenders would contest these criticisms, and Scalia's opinions typically rely centrally on the principles of textualism.

A strong underlying motivation for Scalia's position is the ideological influence on judicial choice. Justice Scalia has long criticized judicial activism, as found in the justices adopting constitutional or statutory rulings to suit their personal policy preferences. He argues that "under the guise or even the self-delusion of pursuing unexpressed legislative intents, common law judges will in fact pursue their own objectives and desires, extending their lawmaking proclivities."[41] Textualism, he maintains, can constrain this tendency of judges to act ideologically.

After Justice Scalia, the justice who has most clearly expressed views on statutory interpretation is Justice Breyer. His views were in part grounded in his experience as a congressional staffer. He urged that Congress "is a bureaucratic organization with twenty thousand employees, working full time, generating legislation through complicated, but organized, processes of interaction with other institutions."[42] Because it is a system, the legislative committees and their staffs perform an important role, as the full body delegates them various tasks. Breyer notes, for example, that a "legislator may vote for technical language that the legislator does not understand, knowing that committee members believe . . . that it has a proper function."[43] The content of legislative history is potentially important to Breyer as evidence of the true content of the congressional action in adopting the statute. Some have suggested, though, that legislative history is simply a tool by which Justice Breyer (and Justice Stevens) may "implement their pragmatic sensibilities."[44]

The other justices have not so clearly set forth their theories for statutory interpretation. Some clues may be found in both their academic writing and their judicial opinions. John Manning has argued that Stevens is the "most vocal" and "ablest defender" of the view that judges should interpret statutes "to implement the legislative purpose, even if doing so requires some deviation from the semantic detail of the enacted text."[45] Justice Stevens has embraced the delegation theory, writing that in matters of statutory interpretation, "Congress is the master."[46] He believes that the text is the paramount source of interpretation but that "we should never permit a narrow focus on text to obscure a commonsense appraisal of . . . additional evidence."[47] Stevens endorses Breyer's theory, stressing that legislators are "busy" and thus "endorse" the views of congressional committees in their statutory judgments.[48] Justice Souter has also endorsed this theory, holding that the meaning of a statute "cannot be gained by confining inquiry within its four corners" and that discerning the meaning requires consideration of its historic legislative process.[49] Justice Ginsburg has no "highly visible position" on such matters.[50]

Justice Kennedy has offered some criticism of reliance on legislative history, and in particular expressed a concern that it may be too easily manipulated to suit a judge's predilections. In one decision, he wrote that "[i]t does not foster a democratic exegesis for this Court to rummage through unauthoritative materials to consult the spirit of the legislation in order to discover an alternative interpretation of the statute with which the Court is more comfortable."[51] This caution might be read as an argument against the misuse of legislative history, though, rather than a proscription on its consideration.

While he initially appeared to be an ally of Justice Scalia, he has sometimes relied heavily on legislative history to reach a decision.[52] Justice O'Connor has not taken a clear interpretive decision but "has relied on legislative history in many cases."[53]

Justice Thomas is generally regarded as an ally of Justice Scalia, on interpretive method as well as other issues. While he has not so publicly and categorically rejected consideration of legislative history, Justice Thomas has generally shared Justice Scalia's approach. He has refused to join opinions because of their reliance on legislative history.[54] While perhaps not so adamant in his textualism, Justice Thomas has been characterized as a "faithful ally" of Justice Scalia's general theory of interpretation.[55]

The Schacter study of the 1996 term sheds some light on the particular justices and their use of legislative history. She found that Justices O'Connor, Souter, and Rehnquist each used legislative history in 60% or more of their statutory interpretation decisions.[56] The study of Supreme Court workplace decisions found lesser usage by these justices when they authored opinions (26% to 44%) and the most frequent use of legislative history by Justices Marshall, Burger, and Brennan. Use of legislative history by Justices Thomas and Scalia was extremely rare. The results of the past empirical research are at least roughly consistent with the expressed positions of the justices.

The extensive study of labor law opinions at the Court examined the justices' use of the canons of construction and found that this usage had increased over time. Justices Scalia, Thomas, and Stevens were by far the most likely to invoke such canons in the set of cases examined, though the authors found some difference in the manner in which they used the canons.[57] Justice White appeared especially loath to rely on such canons. The differences in the views of the justices may have been exaggerated, though, as pluralism is generally evident. Thus, "[j]udges show surprising agreement over the theory of interpretation applicable to a given case and, in reaching such agreement, every judge at least occasionally departs from his favored theories."[58]

Empirical Examination of Interpretive Use in the Recent Court

This section reports empirical findings of my own, in a study involving Supreme Court decisions involving statutory interpretation between the years 1994 and 2002, inclusive. The time period roughly captures the natural court following Stephen Breyer's appointment. Cases were initially screened through use of West's key number system, for cases with a headnote on "statutes." These cases were then screened further for decisions using one of the interpretive methods studied. Over 120 cases were sampled, providing over one thousand separate justice-votes for analysis. The vote of each justice is the basic unit of analysis for this study.

My analysis made several modifications in the methods used in past research. First, the justice's vote was associated with the use of an interpretive method, whether the justice authored the opinion using that method or simply joined the opinion using the method. It also includes usage in dissents and concurrences. Second, I recognized negative references to an interpretive methodology. When an opinion criticized the application of a particular interpretive method in the case, it was coded with a negative number. Previous studies have run the risk of coding such criticism as a positive treatment of the methodology, because of its mere mention in an opinion. These negative references were not infrequent, appearing in over 25% of the justice opinions of the database. Hence, their recognition is important. Third, I sought to measure all the methods and broke down the coding of the methods into more precise tools. Thus, I separately coded for different sources of legislative history and different aspects of textualism (e.g., plain meaning or the whole act rule).

To establish broader measures for particular interpretive theories, I created new variables that combined the justices' use of several variables. For this purpose, I broke the interpretive methodologies into four categories: textualism, legislative intent, canons, and pragmatism. Textualism (TEXT) is a new variable created from the combination of textualism, use of the plain meaning rule, use of dictionaries, use of common understanding of textual words, and use of the whole act rule. Legislative intent (LEGINT) is created from the combination of reference to legislative history, an explicit finding of ambiguity in statutory text, reliance on congressional inaction in response to a prior decision, or reliance on congressional reenactment in interpretation. CANON is a combination of reliance on several of the canons. For each theory, each justice is given a score that indicates his or her use of that theory. I also created a variable for pragmatic interpretation (PRAGMA) as a combination of reliance on the absurdity doctrine and reliance on deference to the executive branch, as under the *Chevron* doctrine.

Coding for pragmatism in interpretation is more difficult, because the theory is not so directly associated with the particular interpretive methodologies invoked by courts. Nor does it have clear "markers" of usage, such as reliance on materials of legislative history. Some have argued that nearly all the principles of statutory interpretation are consistent with a pragmatic approach to decision making.[59] Such a broad claim, though, is unhelpful in differentiating the effect of pragmatism. The absurdity rule, concerned as it is with consequences of interpretation, is an obvious candidate for coding pragmatism. *Chevron* deference is also included because it is easily understood as a delegation of interpretive authority to those who are better suited to promoting the effective functioning of a statute as discussed in Chapter 5.

From these uses, I calculated scores for each case in the database. For example, each time that a justice joined an opinion that referenced both the plain meaning rule and the whole act rule, that would produce a positive score of 2 for TEXT. By contrast, if a justice joined an opinion that made no positive references to the textualism variables but criticized one of them, the TEXT score would be -1. By using individual justice scores, the measures are weighted for greater consensus on the Court. Thus, a unanimous opinion with a 2 score for TEXT would receive nine measures of this score, while a 6-3 opinion would receive six measures, with the remaining three coded for the content of the concurring or dissenting opinions. Figure 6.1 displays the absolute frequency of opinions for each score for references to legislative intent for the period covered by the database, which includes much of the Rehnquist Court era.

Contrary to the existing research, it appears that legislative intent remains a significant source for statutory interpretation in the Supreme Court. A majority of cases make some positive use of some tool of legislative intent, though not necessarily the statute's legislative history. The frequency of the Court's use of legislative intent, though, is less than at some prior historical periods, as identified in prior research, so use may have declined slightly.

The type of legislative history cited in the opinions is also of some import. According to theory, certain sources are deemed more reliable and

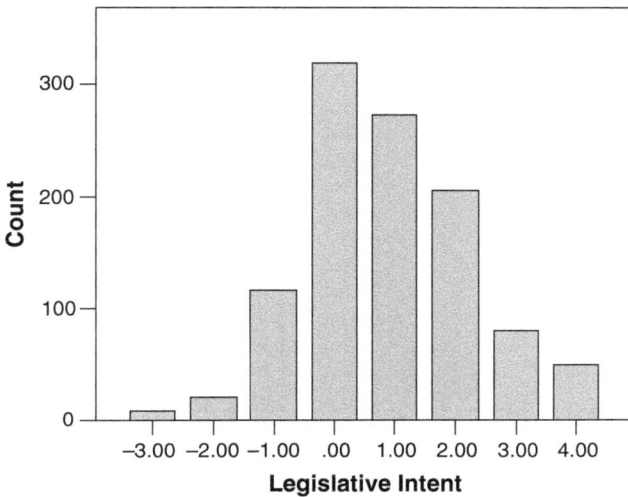

Figure 6.1   Legislative Intent Score Frequencies

should be used more often. If this were not the case, we would have additional information that the practice of reliance on legislative history is a manipulative one. One past study of the era when legislative history was most used (1938–1979) found that about half the references involved committee reports and about 20% involved floor debates.[60] In the data used for my analysis, some legislative history was used in 42% of the justices' opinions and committee reports were used in 23.8% of those opinions. Some post-enactment legislative history was used in a surprisingly material 8.5%. These results are roughly consistent with the study of the Internal Revenue Code, which found committee reports cited in around 28% of cases and post-enactment history in 9%.[61]

The following discussion contains similar analysis for other interpretive approaches. Figure 6.2 replicates this process of frequency counts, using the textualism scale.

Textualism is used somewhat more frequently than legislative intent, but not so much more often as might be presumed. A substantial minority of Supreme Court opinions makes no reference to principles of textualism or even makes a negative reference to one of the tenets of textualism. Brudney

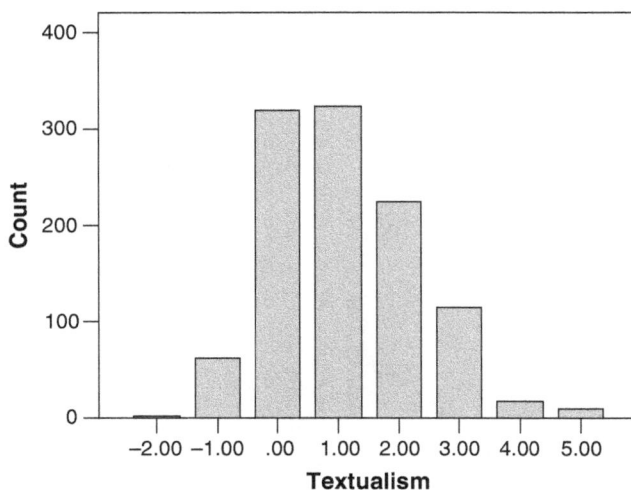

Figure 6.2   Textualism Score Frequencies

and Ditslear's study of workplace law decisions likewise found that explicit references to textual meaning interpretation were absent from many cases.[62] Claims of an overwhelming contemporary commitment to textualist interpretation are unsupported by this research.

Of the references, the clear majority of cases made direct reference to the content of the statutory text. Around 20% of the justices' opinions stated that this text had a plain meaning and used it. Twenty-five percent of those involved some use of a dictionary. The whole act rule was especially useful and employed in over 43% of the justices' opinions. The latter finding represents much greater use than was found in the Internal Revenue Code study, where use of the whole act rule was an order of magnitude less.[63] Textualism is clearly an important interpretive tool at the Court but by no means dominates all other tools.

Next, the quantitative measurement turns to the canons. Figure 6.3 displays the frequency of references to a canon of statutory construction.

Reference to the canons is much less common than use of textualism or legislative history, but they are used positively in over 10% of the opinions of the period.[64] Some have suggested that the use of the canons has seen a renaissance in the Rehnquist Court, but their use remains relatively rare.

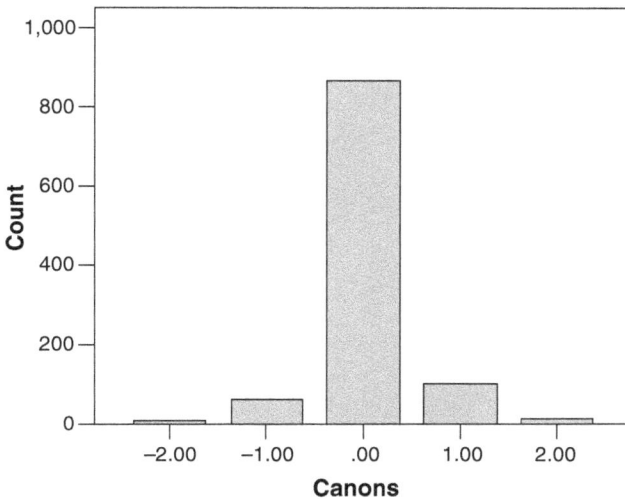

Figure 6.3   Canon Score Frequencies

Interestingly, a proportionally high number of references to the canons are negative ones. The net positive use of canons is quite low, which dispels suggestions that they have seen a renaissance in the current Court. None of the canons were much used, but the rule of lenity was the most common, and it appeared in but 3.5% of the justices' opinions. This usage rate is far lower than in the study of labor law cases.[65] The study also found significant use of the substantive canons, with Justices Souter and O'Connor the most likely to employ this interpretive device.[66] The difference may in part be due to the different set of cases but is probably largely ascribable to their far broader definition of canons, which included tools that I classified as textualism.

Figure 6.4 displays the frequency of references to my measure of principles of pragmatism.

Pragmatism is invoked much less frequently than textualism or legislative intent, but more than are the canons. Because it is somewhat more difficult to code for use of pragmatism, this figure may understate the Supreme Court's references to its role, both positive and negative. Even from the figure, though, it is clear that pragmatism is an important factor in a material minority of statutory interpretation cases heard by the Court. The Internal

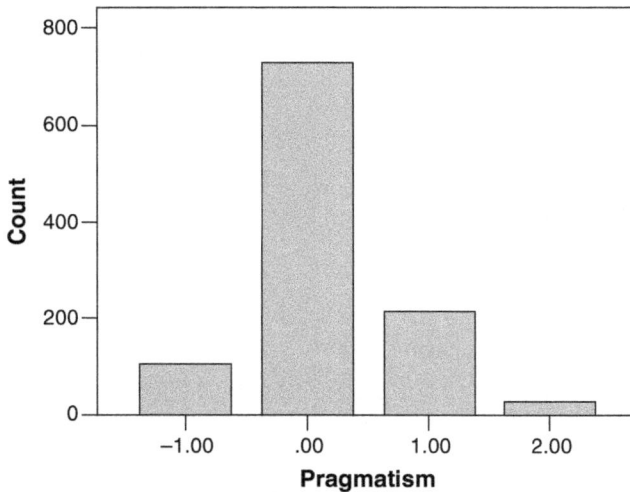

Figure 6.4   Pragmatism Score Frequencies

Revenue Code study found that the "presumption that Congress did not in-tend irrational or unjust applications of the law," a pragmatic standard, was used in about 9% of cases, consistent with the above results.[67] The justices in this study of tax cases were extremely reluctant to consider economic im-plications of their decisions, however.[68]

Justices and Use of Interpretive Methodologies

This section considers the relative usage of the methodology by individual justices in the period studied. The above figures presented cumulative data, and individual justices may vary in their use of interpretive theories. As dis-cussed above, Scalia is known for a devotion to textualism, while Breyer is publicly dedicated to the theory of legislative intent. Reputedly "Scalia is suf-ficiently committed to his views about legal method that he often declines to join other Justice's opinions that employ improper methods."[69] Indeed, Scalia has on occasion concurred and simply declined to join a portion of an opinion relying on legislative history.[70] However, he has also been called a "fallen tex-tualist," who fails to practice the theory "sincerely and consistently." Both these claims are based only on anecdotal examples, though, as relatively little empirical analysis has examined the extent to which the justices consistently adhere to particular approaches.

To provide some empirical evidence on the question, I provide average scores for each of the justices for their reliance on particular interpretive theories. Table 6.1 presents the mean score, by justice, for their reliance on particular interpretive theories.[71]

These results are at least roughly consistent with expectations and the justices' own pronouncements of their interpretive theories. Breyer and Stevens are most likely to use legislative intent, while Scalia and Thomas are the least likely to do so.[72] Some might be surprised that Scalia has a positive association with legislative intent, but this is attributable to the fact that my measure for legislative intent involves more than simple reliance on legislative history and the fact that Scalia joined a few opinions that used legislative history, though he authored no opinions with such reliance in my database.[73] All the justices rely relatively heavily on tools of textualism, and none make much use of the canons. Pragmatism shows the most significant disparity in usage among the justices, with Breyer and Stevens invoking the theory about five times as much as Scalia or Thomas. Nevertheless, there is plainly interpretive pluralism on the Court, as every justice had a positive association with every interpretive methodology.

Table 6.1 reported only averages and not the relative diversity of judicial approaches. To capture the latter, Figure 6.5 reports a chart with the mean

TABLE 6.1
Justices' Use of Interpretive Theories

	Legislative Intent	Textualism	Canons	Pragmatism
Breyer	1.21	1.05	.02	.28
Ginsburg	1.18	1.21	.04	.25
Kennedy	1.03	1.30	.04	.13
O'Connor	.76	1.34	.03	.18
Rehnquist	.89	1.37	.03	.10
Scalia	.45	1.44	.03	.06
Souter	1.20	1.18	.02	.22
Stevens	1.41	1.09	.03	.28
Thomas	.57	1.44	.02	.05

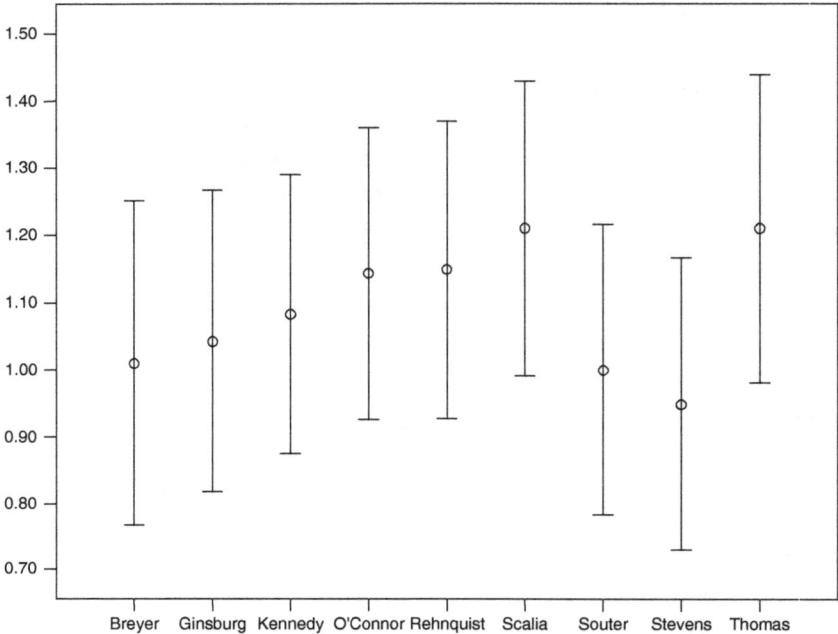

Figure 6.5 Error Bar Chart of Textualism Use

use of textualism of the justices, with error bars representing the 95% confidence intervals for their use of this method.

Figure 6.5 depicts the mean use of textualism with a circle and error bars representing 95% confidence intervals around the mean. While the median varies somewhat among the justices, the size of the error bars is relatively equal for all of the justices. While Justice Scalia is plainly somewhat more of a textualist than is Justice Stevens, both varied in their relative reliance on the method. The overlapping error bars mean that there was no statistically significant variation for this measure. Figure 6.6 replicates this chart for use of legislative intent.

Again, all of the justices display roughly the same standard deviation among cases, though this revolves around very different average usages for legislative intent. There are some plain differences among the justices,

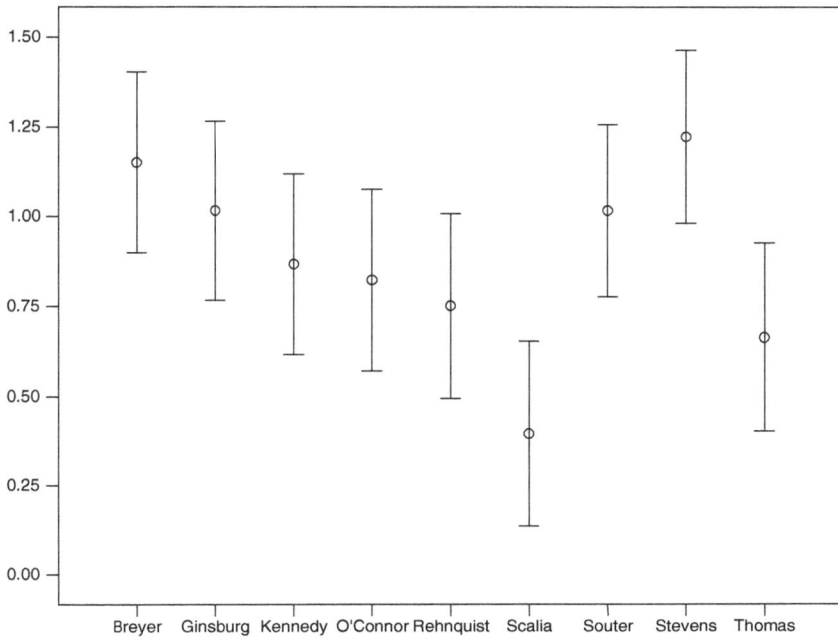

Figure 6.6   Error Bar Chart of Legislative Intent Use

as Scalia's upper ninety-fifth percentile use remains below several justices' lower ninety-fifth percentile usage, showing statistically significant differences for some pairs of justices. Thomas does not appear quite so averse to use of legislative intent as does Scalia. Figure 6.7 provides the same error bar chart, except for the justices' use of pragmatism in statutory interpretation.

Again we see roughly similar standard deviations of use of the method, and the relative use of pragmatism appears to correspond roughly to the justices' reliance on tools of legislative intent. The more conservative and textualist justices appear much less inclined to use pragmatism. The interaction of these methods of interpretation is discussed in the following section, which considers the combined use of methods by individual cases rather than just broad usage patterns.

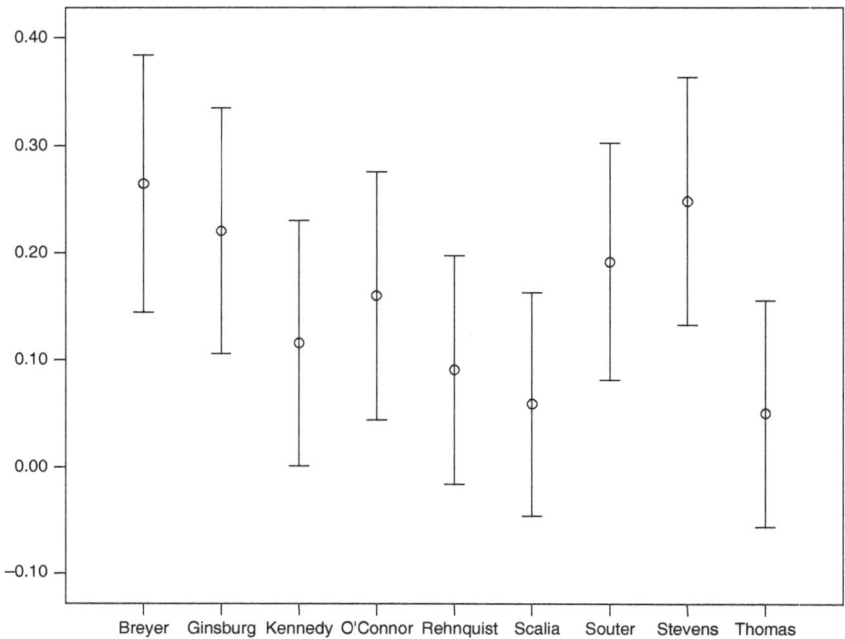

Figure 6.7 Error Bar Chart of Pragmatism Use

Interaction of Interpretive Methodologies

One issue of statutory interpretation that has gone largely unexplored is the interaction of the various methodologies. The justices often attempt to make the strongest case for their opinion's outcome by citing numerous bases for their result. Consequently, an opinion might well suggest that both textualism and the legislative history supported that result. Use of a combination of methodologies would be associated with a pluralist view of the various interpretive methods. Conversely, a justice might affirmatively disapprove of legislative history and reject it or simply disregard it and perhaps use other sources to supplant reliance on sources of legislative intent.[74] The latter approach is associated with Justice Scalia, who has gone so far as to write concurrences agreeing with the majority decision and stating nothing beyond his disagreement with the majority's reliance on legislative history. Professor Eskridge examined this in one context and found that numerous references to legislative history in his five-year study were used for the purpose of confirming the apparent plain meaning of the statutory text.[75] Zeppos found that historically greater use of textualism was accompanied by greater use of legislative history.[76]

The summary statistics reported above do not fully capture the degree to which justices relied on particular methodologies in particular cases and thus do not fully capture the potential conflict. I analyze the degree to which greater reliance on one given theory produces lesser reliance on other interpretive methodologies. This is performed through a regression using my cumulative scores for interpretive methodologies. Thus, I analyze whether a greater reliance on one approach, such as TEXT, produces a lesser reliance on another approach, such as LEGINT. This is the first analysis, with the LEGINT score as the dependent variable and scores for the other three interpretive methodologies as independent variables. The coefficient and t-scores for each independent variable are reported in Table 6.2.

The results show that textualism and legislative intent references are not significantly conflicting, though neither are they especially complementary. The negatively signed relationship does not approach statistical significance. Nor is there any statistically significant association between relying on the canons and legislative history, as sometimes suggested. While there are individual cases that use canons to override apparently clear legislative history,[77] these do not appear to be common. By contrast, legislative history and pragmatism appear to go hand in hand. There is a very strong positive association between grounding a decision both in legislative history and in pragmatism. Table 6.3 follows the same approach, except with pragmatism as the dependent variable.

TABLE 6.2

Effect of Alternative Methodologies
on Legislative History

	Legislative Intent	T-scores
Textualism	−.016	.55
Canons	−.031	1.04
Pragmatism	.245***	8.20

Note: *** = .01

TABLE 6.3
*Effect of Alternative Methodologies
on Pragmatism*

	Pragmatism	T-scores
Textualism	.020	.675
Canons	.038	1.26
Legislative Intent	.245***	8.20

Note: *** = .01

TABLE 6.4
Effect of Alternative Methodologies on Canons

	Canons	T-scores
Textualism	.049	1.59
Pragmatism	.040	1.26
Legislative Intent	−.033	1.04

In addition to the earlier finding that pragmatism accompanies legislative history, the theory also appears to be perfectly consistent with textualism and the canons of construction, though not significantly correlated in usage. To complete the test, Table 6.4 reports the same analysis, with use of canons as the dependent variable.

In this table, we see little conflict or synergy between canons and all the other interpretive methods. Although canons are often viewed as companions of textualism, there is but a mild association of their mutual use in Supreme Court opinions. The study of employment decisions found that there was a significant association between use of linguistic canons and textualism, but this study had a broader definition of what qualified as a canon and included theories that I classified as part of textualism.[78] There were no statistically significant relationships between other methods and use of the canons. The canons appear to serve as a gap filler, perhaps as they were initially intended.

One must be cautious in the interpretation of these results. Supreme Court opinions justify decisions, and justices may be inclined to cite all plausible supporting bases for their results. Consequently, one might expect to see positive associations between interpretive methodologies, as a justice would argue that both the text and the legislative history support his or her resolution of the case. This would be the traditional "kitchen sink" theory of argument. The use of different sources may provide a decision with "a more balanced and safer 'portfolio.' "[79] If true, this finding would still be a theoretically significant one, as it implies that the justices are more committed to the outcome of the decision than the interpretive methodology by which it is reached.

Despite this caveat, we can draw some conclusions about the interaction of the interpretive methodologies. In general, the justices appear to be pluralist in their statutory interpretations, frequently supporting their decisions with multiple interpretive theories.[80] The conflict between reliance on textualism and on legislative history, commonly propounded in research, does not appear in the results. One can also conclude that pragmatism is not inconsistent with other interpretive theories. All its associations are positive, and the association is a strong and statistically significant one with respect to reliance on legislative history. This finding would seem to dispel the concern that pragmatism unleashes the justices to do whatever they wish, unhinged from statutory text, legislative history, or traditional canons of construction.

Interpretive Methods and Court Consensus

Another tool for assessing the interpretive methodologies would be their ability to command a greater consensus of the Court. If a given approach produced greater consensus among justices with diverse preferences, this could suggest that it provided greater clarity and less susceptibility to ideological manipulation. Professor Vermeule laments the lack of evidence "whether judicial disagreement increases or decreases as sources are added beyond the statutory provisions at hand," and this section provides some of that evidence.[81]

The above discussion covered the frequency with which the interpretive methodologies were used overall and in tandem, but these numbers covered a variety of very different opinions. In some cases the Court was divided, while in others it was unanimous in its result (though perhaps with concurring opinions). The most frequent outcome in the dataset was a unanimous opinion, occurring in 39.7% of the cases. The second most frequent outcome, though, was a minimum winning 5-4 coalition, which occurred in 26.4% of the cases. This section considers whether certain interpretive methodologies can produce more consensus among the justices. For example, one might expect less consensus from the greater use of legislative intent, which is controversial. By contrast, reliance on the "ordinary meaning" of text itself supposedly enables diverse ideologies to reach consensus.[82]

The association of interpretive methodologies and consensus is easily tested in a regression in which the dependent variable is the vote in the case. Vote is captured as the percentage of justices in the majority (e.g., a 6-3 decision would be scored as .67). The degrees of reliance on the four cumulative interpretive methodology scores were used as independent variables. Table 6.5 displays the results of this analysis.

Only pragmatism showed a statistically significant effect on consensus, and its association was quite strong. This interpretive theory, when applicable, seems to command support across the spectrum of justices and suggests it was not so ideologically manipulable as some suggest. The associations for textualism and legislative intent do not approach statistical or substantive significance in their effect. The only existing research to examine this question is the labor law study of the canons of construction, where their usage was greatest in unanimous and close cases.[83]

The significance of the consensus association is unclear, however. The unanimous decisions may simply be the ones of little interest to the Court. Pragmatism may correlate with larger majorities simply because it is not a helpful methodology for resolving the sorts of close cases that produce 5-4

TABLE 6.5
Interpretive Theories and Court Consensus

	Vote	T-scores
Textualism	.010	.321
Pragmatism	.095***	3.014
Legislative Intent	−.019	.556
Canons	.032	1.047

Note: *** = .01

decisions. Thus, it may not be the methodology that produces consensus but the methodology's usefulness in particular types of cases. In addition, the regression methodology assumed a linear relationship between the variables and the vote in the case, which may not be accurate. For example, an examination of the legislative intent score shows some interesting nonlinear results. The data below breaks down the relative use of legislative history, using the mean score, by the size of the Supreme Court majority.

Vote	Legislative Intent
5-4	0.94
6-3	0.55
7-2	0.36
8-1	0.80
9-0	0.67

The legislative intent scores were highest in those cases decided through the minimum winning coalition, and this score included references in dissenting opinions as well. The scores were also relatively high in unanimous or near unanimous decisions and lower in those decided by 6-3 or 7-2 margins. This creates a possible inference that legislative history is especially useful, or necessary, for a case's resolution, in close decisions. The increased use of legislative intent methodologies in greater Court majorities might reflect the fact that these were clear cases in which the result found greater support in all interpretive methods, with the opinion providing the "kitchen sink" justification for an outcome. None of the other interpretive methodologies displayed this sort of quadratic association with the Court's vote in the case, and the textualism scores were very close to linear.[84]

These results are consistent with interpretive pluralism. The justices are more likely to use legislative history in different contexts, rather than being wedded to particular interpretive methodologies. The use of such history in the unanimous or 8-1 cases may have been attributable simply to an effort to confirm textual plain meaning. The greater use in close cases, though, presumably involved the more ambiguous statutes being interpreted. Thus, the findings on relative consensus associated with particular methods do not have conclusive implications. Nevertheless, the strong association of pragmatism with consensus is at least suggestive of some effect.

Conclusion

This survey of the Rehnquist Court illustrates the relative use of interpretive methodologies by its justices. The pattern of such use is largely consistent with that observed by outside commentators and with the comments of the justices themselves. Thus, Justice Scalia is relatively devoted to textualism, while Justice Breyer is among the greatest users of legislative intent and pragmatism in statutory interpretation. As a general matter, most justices show pluralist tendencies, though, and legislative intent remains a significant feature of Court decision making, even in this period when textualism was purportedly ascendant.

There is a clear association between interpretive methods and justice ideology. The most textualist justices are the conservatives: Scalia, Thomas, and Rehnquist. Conversely, more liberal justices, such as Stevens, Breyer, Souter, and Ginsburg, are the most likely to rely upon sources of legislative intent and pragmatism. Hence, the effect of ideology may appear as a legal choice of interpretive methods, even more profoundly than in outcomes, though the latter effect is explored further in the following chapter.

The findings on judicial consensus are necessarily tentative. The positive influence of pragmatism may in part be due to case characteristics that cannot be controlled in my study. Nevertheless, the association is an intriguing one. My measures of pragmatism are unavoidably incomplete, but the tools I employ appear structurally to contribute to more agreement among the justices. Plainly, pragmatism does not entirely overcome ideological divisions, though, as I will show in Chapter 7.

Ideology and the Practice of Statutory Interpretation

Perhaps the central dispute in statutory interpretation has involved the amenability of theories to ideological manipulation by the judiciary. This is not the only dispute; there are several theoretical arguments about the legitimacy of reliance on extratextual materials (discussed in Chapter 2) or the value of using legislative history (addressed in Chapter 3). I have argued that these theoretical arguments are inconclusive and often inapplicable under the delegation theory. Indeed, even the advocates of various approaches seem to realize that the dispute largely reduces to the question of whether a theory conduces to willful or ideological judicial decision making.

Defenders of textualism have argued, as a central contention, that alternative interpretive approaches are insufficiently constraining and empower ideological judicial decision making. Legislative history is dismissed as a tool for reaching the ideologically preferred result ("looking over the crowd"). Others have countered that textualism has this very effect of enabling ideological decision making. Still others maintain that it is the pluralism of interpretive approaches itself that yields ideological decision making, as judges may pick and choose the approach that best suits their preferred outcome. Pragmatism is often criticized as allowing undue judicial flexibility that enables individual ideological preferences to prevail. Hence, the prevention of willful judging is a key issue, but the commentators have not settled on what theories most enable such judging.

Ideological Decision Making

A major concern about judicial decision making is the fear that judges are simply imposing their personal ideological preferences on the resolution of a dispute, rather than applying the law. This theory has historic grounding in the legal realists, who claimed that the law did not dictate court outcomes. More recently, it is pursued by social scientists as something called the "attitudinal model" often associated with the seminal work of Jeffrey Segal and Harold Spaeth.[1] They have claimed that the widespread belief that justices follow the law is simply proof that "large numbers of otherwise rational people refuse to be confused by facts."[2]

There is in fact a great deal of empirical research demonstrating that judges have ideological patterns in their decisions. Segal and Spaeth reported a substantively strong and statistically significant association between the ideological preferences of members of the Warren and Burger Courts and whether their decisions reached liberal or conservative results.[3] The authors are not alone in reaching this conclusion. Over one hundred studies have empirically examined the link between judges' political party affiliations and their decisions.[4] Most of these studies "depict a Court driven by single-minded seekers of legal policy" who "wish to etch into the law their personal views."[5] The magnitude of this effect is especially great at the Supreme Court level and especially in controversial constitutional matters, such as civil liberties cases. Although the evidence of an ideological association is compelling, its extent has been overstated by some researchers; the data in no way indicates that ideology is the only factor driving judicial outcomes.[6]

The considerable evidence associating judicial ideology with judicial outcomes has given little attention to the role of the law, however. The association might be purely artifactual, if certain legal philosophies were co-extensive with ideologies. Thus, if textualism were indeed intrinsically conservative, a justice's conservative results could be explained by his or her dedication to a particular legal interpretive approach, not personal ideological preferences. Some argue that the disagreements between Justices Brennan and Rehnquist simply reflected "deep-felt convictions about the nature of federalism, the degree to which the Constitution protects individual rights, and so forth."[7] In addition, even if one accepts that judicial ideology is significant and the law does not inevitably determine outcomes, different types of legal rules may sometimes do so. Some laws or interpretive standards may constrain ideological proclivities. It is often suggested, for example, that rules are more constraining than are standards.

The data in this study of methods of statutory interpretation permit some integration of legal variables into the ideological research. I can consider the degree to which certain interpretive methods have an intrinsic ideological effect. I can also consider the degree to which different methods are more or less constraining on the justices' ideological preferences. Before embarking on this analysis, though, I review the limited existing research on the topic.

Existing Research on the Ideology of Statutory Interpretation

While the ideological implications of differing methods of statutory interpretation have been extensively debated, they have seen little empirical analysis of judicial practice. As I have repeatedly emphasized, such research is absolutely vital to drawing conclusions about the arguments. Much of the justification for particular approaches involves their constraint on judicial ideology. Indeed, the entire longstanding debate over interpretive methodologies becomes rather trivial if it were to appear that they are merely manipulable tools to reach results that were politically predetermined by individual justices.

Notwithstanding the significance of the intersection of interpretative method and ideology, it has seen relatively little study. James Brudney and Corey Ditslear have recently completed an empirical analysis of the

Supreme Court's use of canons of statutory interpretation.[8] They examined this use in 632 cases decided between 1969 and 2003 in various case categories, encompassing both the Burger and Rehnquist courts. The study found a pronounced increase in reliance on the canons in the Rehnquist era, as opposed to the Burger Court, and that canons tended to see greater use in close cases, where the Court was divided, rather than in unanimous cases. More saliently, the authors found that the canons did not appear neutral in their application. Liberal justices typically used the canons to reach liberal decisional outcomes, while conservative justices used the canons to reach conservative results. The "language canon reliance in majority opinions by both conservative Justices and liberal Justices has produced results remarkably consistent with their respective ideological preferences."[9]

This empirical finding on Supreme Court opinions clearly supports Llewellyn's legal realist critique of reliance on interpretive canons. The study even went beyond Llewellyn's hypothesis and found that individual canons were indeterminate, so that no parry was needed for a given thrust. When the majority invoked a given canon in support of its conclusion, the dissent was likely to invoke the very same canon in support of its contrary conclusion.[10]

Brudney and Ditslear considered canons in the very broad sense of any decision rules. Thus, it considered principles such as the whole act rule to be canonical. While this is a perfectly plausible broad interpretation of canons, I consider such a principle to be textualist in nature. There is value in assessing the impact of the traditional linguistic canons and the substantive canons, independent of decision rules created to implement a textualist approach. Indeed, the reliance on legislative history could itself be considered a canon of sorts, but to do so would obscure rather than illuminate the fundamental controversies about statutory interpretation.

The Brudney and Ditslear research also sheds some light on alternative approaches to statutory interpretation, beyond the canons, though this is not its focus. For example, it treated the plain meaning rule as a canon. This research is important and provides much insight, but it is limited in scope to workplace decisions and its methodology was focused on the canons and not designed to measure all the interpretive tools.

The Ideology of Interpretation

The typical ideological critique of interpretive methods lies in their purported malleability. This approach assumes that law can be constraining on the justices but that different legal approaches yield different levels of constraint. In one common view, justices strive to achieve their ideological preferences within the law and seek less certain legal tools in order to achieve those preferences. This view often suggests that reliance on legislative history enables ideological decision making, because of the magnitude and diversity of legislative history. The critique might be even more strongly applied to pluralism, which enables justices to pick and choose their theories, or to pragmatism, which allows judges to consider the policy consequences of their interpretations.

The common critique may be entirely incorrect, however. If one ascribes a higher level of sincerity to the justices, additional interpretive materials or methods might actually limit ideological decision making. Suppose that justices revert to their ideological preferences only when the legal materials are highly indeterminate. Arguably, reliance on fewer materials increases the likelihood of such indeterminacy that enables ideological choice. If so, use of more different interpretive sources could actually have the effect of reducing ideological decision making. Yet if one rejects such sincerity, it is unclear why any interpretive methodology would restrain ideologically oriented judges.

Some have taken a different line of reasoning and argued that interpretive theories have their own associated ideologies, so that the choice of a theory is not neutral but is itself ideologically tainted. Thus, Eskridge and Frickey contend that emphasis on textualism is a "cover for the injection of conservative values into statutes."[11] As discussed in Chapter 2, Judge Easterbrook's theory of statutes' domains tends to constrict the scope of statutes, which arguably has a systematically conservative ideological direction. This effect does not necessarily make it a "cover," as a sincerely held theory may have ideological consequences, but it raises the possibility. The prospect that method is an ideological beard is suggested by the relative affinity of particular justices' ideological preferences with their attitude toward textualism, as shown in Chapter 6. This association is clearer with respect to some of the canons. The rule of lenity would be expected to produce more liberal results, by introducing a preference for defendants. By contrast, the canon against retroactivity is explicit in its limitation of statutory domains and should therefore yield conservative results, under the Eskridge and Frickey theory.

Testing the Ideology of Interpretation

With this backdrop, it is possible to design tests of the ideological effects of different interpretive methodologies. Consider textualism. If Eskridge and Frickey are correct that this method is intrinsically a conservative one, we would see that decisions that make greater use of textualism would produce more conservative results, regardless of the ideology of the justices rendering the opinions. If this were incorrect, though, the decisions would reveal a different pattern. If textualism more effectively constrained ideological manipulation, we would see that decisions grounded in textualism would produce results that diverged from the justices' ideologies. Thus, liberal justices using textualism would produce more conservative outcomes than they might prefer, and conservative justices employing the method would yield outcomes more liberal than would be expected by their ideological proclivities. One study has used such an approach to show that reliance on originalism as an interpretive theory for constitutional decisions did not appear to affect the ideological direction of outcomes in those cases.[12]

This chapter tests these theories using the data described in the preceding chapter. The constraining effect of a given interpretive methodology can be examined by comparing cases where it is employed with those where it is inapplicable. As a benchmark measure for judicial ideological preferences, I use cases that raise constitutional civil liberties questions. These cases have been extensively studied and they form the core of the evidence on ideological decision making by the Court. Ample research has shown that Supreme Court decisions on such civil liberties questions have a substantial ideological component.[13] By comparing statutory interpretation decisions with the civil liberties outcomes, one might find evidence of the constraining effect of interpretive methodologies.

I begin by considering whether use of the plain meaning rule appeared to influence the opinions of the justices and produce consensus. The plain meaning rule, which lies at the heart of textualism, would seem to provide a decision standard that should be plain and ideologically neutral, if in fact interpretive methodologies determine decisions. Perhaps the justices could at least agree when statutory meaning was plain. For each justice, I examined the ideological direction of the opinion in those cases in which they invoked the plain meaning rule in support of their outcome. I compare these rates with decisions in a separate area of the law involving constitutional civil liberties. This approach was recently used in a study of criminal cases that did not examine particular theories but found that the justices showed no difference in the outcomes of their constitutional and statutory cases.[14]

Table 7.1 reports the percentage of conservative votes by justices in constitutional civil liberties cases,[15] the percentage of conservative votes in cases in this database in which they relied on the plain meaning rule in statutory interpretation, and the number of cases in which they invoked that rule.

All the justices used the plain meaning rule in a comparable number of opinions that they joined. Although the votes were cast *in the same cases*, it seems quite clear that plain meaning was not at all plain, as the justices differed considerably over the application of the standard in these same cases. The conservatism of plain meaning decisions varied wildly among the justices and roughly paralleled that of their decisions in constitutional civil liberties decisions. The probability of conservative votes from a justice using the plain meaning rule conforms pretty closely to their overall ideological preferences. There is a hint of a small effect for some justices, though in

TABLE 7.1
Plain Meaning Rule and Ideological Outcomes

	Civil Liberties (%)	Plain Meaning (%)	Number
Breyer	39.8	39.6	23
Ginsburg	35.4	39.8	23
Kennedy	63.4	63.3	21
O'Connor	64.3	76.5	26
Rehnquist	78.2	68.9	27
Scalia	71.6	71.4	29
Souter	39.2	45.8	27
Stevens	35.5	27.4	23
Thomas	74.9	76.5	24

opposite ideological directions. Justice O'Connor's difference was the only one with a statistically significant difference in outcomes.

Overall, the plain meaning standard seems ideologically manipulable and incapable of constraining preferences to provide greater consensus. This is contrary to the theory that textualism is intrinsically conservative, though, by showing that liberal justices were quite capable of using the plain meaning theory to reach liberal results, about as often as was the case for conservative justices, save for the possible Justice O'Connor effect, where plain meaning was associated with more conservative outcomes than she hypothetically might prefer.

Brudney and Ditslear found a similar result for the justices' use of canons of interpretation. They broke the justices down into the binary categories of liberal and conservative. They found that the liberal justices tended to reach liberal outcomes in cases where they used a canon (58.5%), while the conservative justices were much less likely to reach liberal results in cases in which they relied on a canon (30.7%).[16] The effect remained for both linguistic and substantive canons, though the substantive canons yielded slightly more ideologically oriented results. This finding suggests that the canons are ideologically manipulable, though it may be distorted by the categorization of the plain meaning rule as a canon, and it did not consider other methodologies used in cases to supplement the canons.

Some of the Brudney & Ditslear results for these analyses support the hypotheses of intrinsic effects of some of the interpretive theories. For example, the rule of lenity had a statistically significant liberal effect on outcomes, regardless of justice ideology. The same was true of the presumption against the retroactive application of statutes, which had a statistically significant conservative effect on outcomes. This is unsurprising, as these canons are openly directional in their effect. The results do suggest the important finding, though, that doctrinal law may sometimes be constraining on the justices and drive justices to depart from their preferred ideological outcomes.

One must be cautious in the interpretation of some of these findings, however. The *noscitur* canon showed a statistically significant liberal effect on outcomes in the cases studied. It is highly unlikely that this canon is intrinsically liberal, though, and this directional finding is likely an artifact of the particular statutes involved in the relatively few cases in which the canon was helpful to the justices. Again, this finding suggests that a clear doctrine expressed in a canon may have some constraining effect, as conservative justices may have reached a liberal outcome due to its applicability.

I next consider the association of the use of textualism for interpretation with the ideologies of the justices in my sample cases. This requires a measure of ideology for each justice, and I use the widely accepted Segal-Cover scores.[17] These scores were created to provide such an ideological measure that does not depend on voting patterns and avoids the risk of circularity. The scores were based on the assessment of a nominee's ideology at the time of his or her appointment, as reflected by press analyses in major newspapers.

Figure 7.1 shows the relative use of textualism as associated with justices' ideology, with liberal to conservative ideology depicted from left to right in the figure. The mean is represented by a circle with 95% confidence error bars surrounding it.

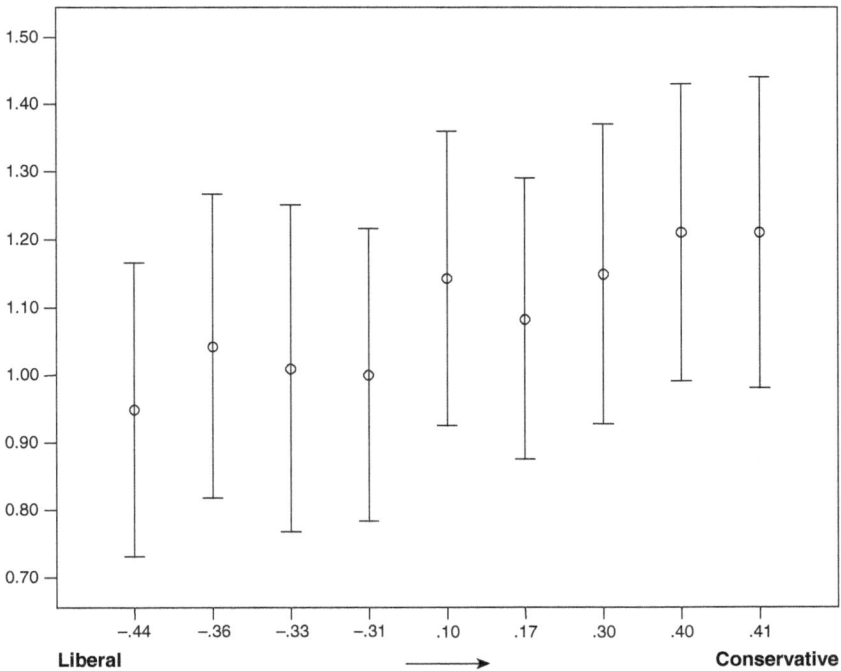

Figure 7.1 Relative Use of Textualism by Justice Ideology

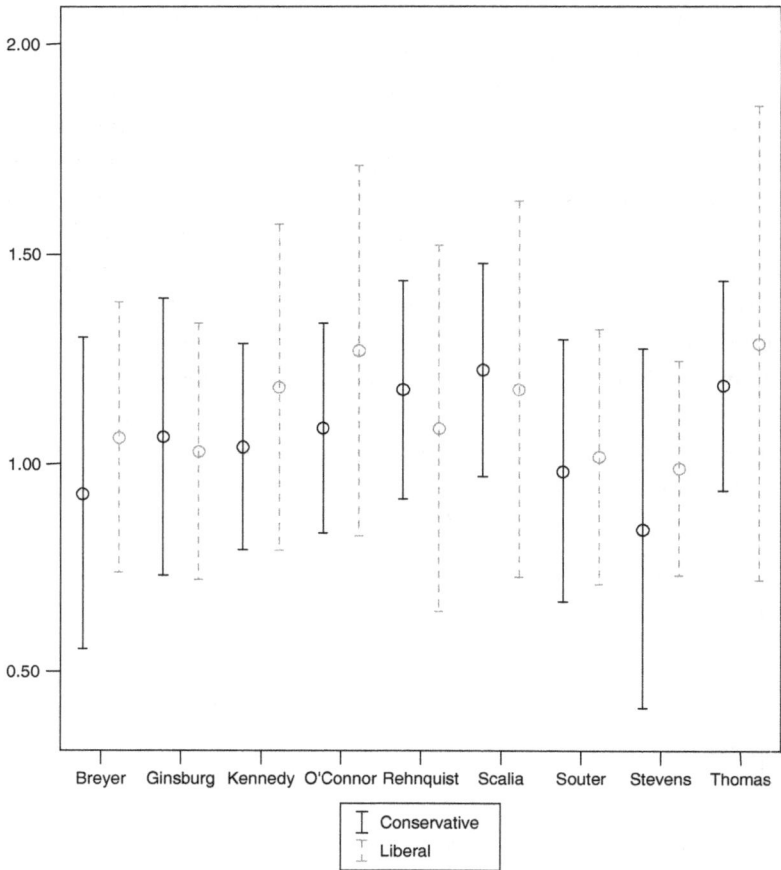

Figure 7.2   Use of Textualism by Ideological Outcome

   Examination of the mean use of textualism shows a steady, if imperfect, increase in reliance on textualism as justices become more conservative, though the error bars overlap preventing any claims of overall statistical significance. While conservative justices tend to make greater use of textualism, the difference is not great. This affinity is somewhat consistent with theories that textualism may be an intrinsically conservative theory of statutory interpretation. However, this figure shows all cases without regard to outcome. If textualism were authentically conservative by nature, one would expect to see more conservative outcomes with greater use of textualism. Figure 7.2 makes this comparison. For each of the justices, the figure shows the relative use of textualism in cases with liberal outcomes first and then the use of textualism in cases with conservative outcomes.

The results do not support the hypothesis that textualism is intrinsically conservative in direction. For six of the nine justices, reliance on textualism is greater in cases with liberal outcomes than those with conservative outcomes. For only Justices Ginsburg, Rehnquist, and Scalia was greater use of textualism associated with more conservatism of case outcome. Moreover, all of the differences were quite small.

The next analysis considers the use of the methods of legislative intent. There is no clear reason why using such intent should produce results of a particular ideological direction. The main argument about such intent is that it enables a justice to reach whatever ideological outcome the justice prefers. Figure 7.3 uses the same comparison of conservative and liberal outcomes as in Figure 7.2, except for relative use of legislative intent.

These results are more consistent. For every justice, greater use of legislative intent yielded more liberal outcomes, though in significantly varying degrees. This suggests that it may be reliance upon legislative intent that has an ideological effect (though the difference is not so great and the overlapping error bars make this effect an uncertain one). Of course, there is no objective baseline about the proper use of legislative intent, so it may be the rejection of legislative intent that is conservative in direction. The primary principle of textualism is the rejection of legislative history, so it might be that it is this rejection that is intrinsically ideological. These results might evidence the Easterbrookian theory of statutory domains, indicating that the use of legislative intent expands those domains and is generally liberal in ideological direction.

The findings that legislative intent has a relatively liberal effect for all justices is contrary to the theory that it is especially ideologically manipulable as a tool, unlike the findings for plain meaning reported above in Table 7.1. The theory of ideological use of legislative history suggests that the justices can pick and choose among its materials to reach desired outcomes. This may be contrasted with the apparently neutral hierarchy of legislative history sources. If legislative history were so ideologically manipulable, one might expect to find greater use of the less reliable sources in decisions that were ideologically amenable for particular justices. One might hypothesize

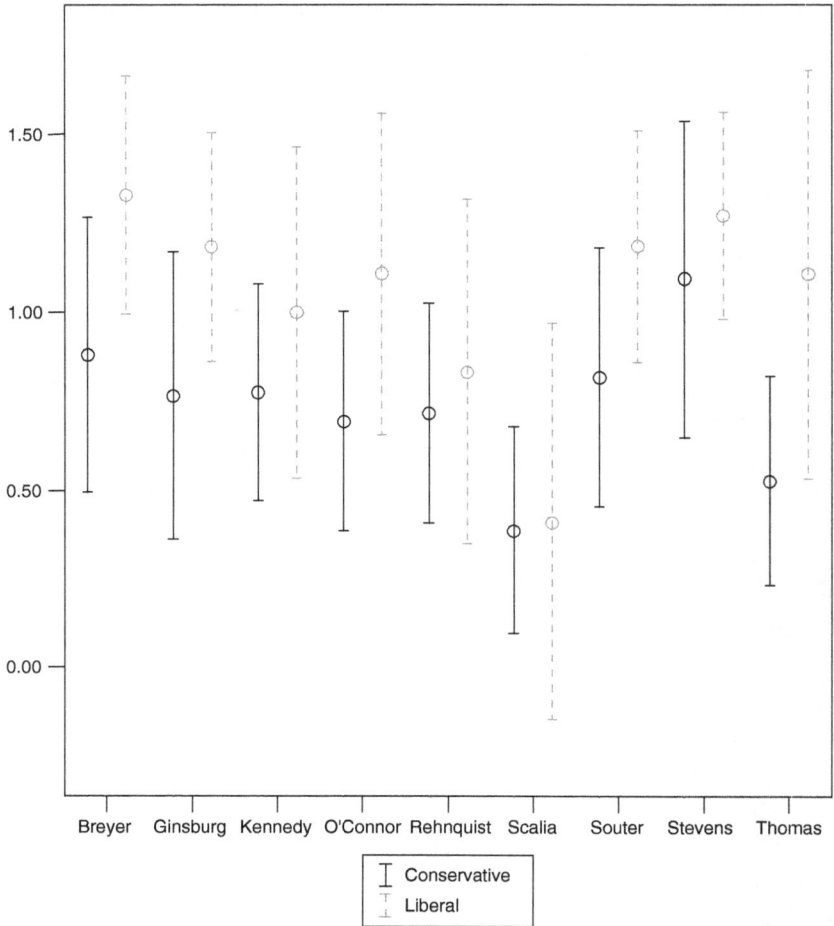

Figure 7.3   Use of Legislative Intent by Ideological Outcome

that liberals in Congress were more effective in seeding the legislative history with favorable content, though this seems unlikely, as conservative legislators should presumably have the same incentive. The results provide
some support for the notion that legislative history may be sincerely used by
the justices, especially insofar as it pulls Justice Thomas, for example, to
reach more liberal results. Indeed, these results may explain some of the
conservative antipathy for use of legislative intent.

As noted in Chapter 3, there is a hierarchy of authority for the value of different types of legislative history. The manipulation of such legislative history might appear in the sources chosen by the justices. If legislative history were indeed so manipulable, with justices choosing ideologically appealing materials, one might expect to see some effect from the sources used by the justices. Thus, one would expect to see a greater ideological effect when justices use the less reliable sources of legislative history. For example, one might expect a liberal justice to make greater use of less reliable sources when necessary to support a liberal outcome. I test this by examining the sources of legislative history use by the more liberal justices and the degree to which particular sources yield more liberal results.

Table 7.2 reports a regression analysis of the ideological direction of outcomes based upon reliance on different types of legislative history for the liberal justices (Breyer, Ginsburg, Souter, and Stevens). These are broken down into reliance on conference committee reports, committee reports, sponsor statements, and all other sources of legislative history. The latter would be considered more dubious and their use might suggest ideological manipulation. A positive coefficient suggests that the source was associated with more liberal outcomes, which these justices presumably favor.

These results show no evidence of ideological manipulation. The only source that shows any effect nearing statistical significance is committee reports, which are considered a relatively reliable indicator of legislative intent. It does not appear that liberal justices are deploying the relatively less reliable sources of legislative history in order to reach liberal results. Of course, all the legislative history sources are associated with slightly more liberal outcomes for the justices, so it might be that they are selectively pick-

TABLE 7.2
Liberal Justices and Sources of Legislative History

	Coefficient	Significance
Conference Committee	.075	.254
Committee	.103	.060
Sponsor	.108	.542
Other	.066	.346

ing and choosing ideologically amenable evidence from committee reports. The practical effect for the overall findings are quite low (.009), however, so any effect would be a very weak one. The selective use might also be found in conservative justices, so Table 7.3 repeats the analysis for the Court's conservative justices.

Once again, the relative use of these sources of legislative history is associated with more liberal case outcomes (except for sponsor statements), with a high level of statistical significance for committee reports. When even conservative justices use legislative history, it is more often supportive of liberal results. They help negate the theory that the liberal justices were selectively using liberal materials in conference reports to reach their desired outcomes. The practical effect for these regressions is actually somewhat greater than for liberal justices (.022) but still quite small. Again, these results are more consistent with the statutory domains theory of ideological effect than with ideological manipulability. These results are not conclusive, because they do not consider the relative frequency of the justices' relative use of the materials of legislative history or use of other interpretive methods in the same cases, but they are inconsistent with the ideological manipulability hypothesis.

There is a possible explanation for these results that is consistent with the critique of the use of legislative history. Suppose that the committees that were in charge of the legislation reviewed by the Supreme Court were controlled by Democrats. Given Democratic control of Congress for most of the twentieth century, this is a plausible assumption. Next, suppose that the members of the committees were unable to get bills passed with liberal content and consequently "rigged" the Committee Report in an attempt to try

TABLE 7.3
*Conservative Justices and Sources
of Legislative History*

	Coefficient	Significance
Conference Committee	.129	.063
Committee	.171	.001
Sponsor	−.141	.166
Other	.002	.973

to gain in judicial interpretation what they could not gain in the legislature. If so, the committee reports arguably served as an improper tool for creating statutory meaning not found in the law.

This hypothesis is intriguing but cannot carry much weight. The effect was quite small and actually more powerful for the conservative justices. The theory assumes a considerable degree of naivete by the conservative justices in their amenability to the hypothesized committee manipulation. In addition, the theory assumes an unrealistic view of the legislative process. As discussed in Chapter 3, legislators are probably as familiar with the content of committee reports as they are familiar with the precise statutory language. It is by no means clear that the committee reports are more ideologically manipulable than is the language itself. Nevertheless, it appears that committee reports produce slightly more liberal decisions than other sources, perhaps because they are used to expand statutes' domains.

The same detail of analysis is not so useful for pragmatic and canonical uses at the Supreme Court, because their relative usage is much less common. Table 7.4 shows the relative use of pragmatism by each of the justices, in their liberal and conservative opinions.

A caution in interpreting these numbers is required: they reflect the relative reliance on pragmatism in cases in which the justice addressed the pragmatism standard. Thus, Justice Rehnquist's usages of pragmatism were greater in his liberal opinions, but he considered pragmatism more often in his conservative opinions (26 vs. 11). However, the findings are still mean-

TABLE 7.4
Pragmatism Use by Ideology

Justice	Conservative	Liberal
Breyer	0.60	0.83
Ginsburg	0.50	0.81
Kennedy	0.10	0.65
O'Connor	0.15	1.00
Rehnquist	0.19	0.55
Scalia	0.07	0.57
Souter	0.44	0.67
Stevens	0.71	0.78
Thomas	0.04	0.56

ingful. Justice Rehnquist rejected the pragmatism standard in eleven of his conservative opinions but only in three of his liberal opinions.

These findings suggest that pragmatism is not so ideologically manipulable. The justices most likely to find that pragmatism supported a conservative result were the more *liberal* justices and by a fairly broad margin. The use of pragmatism in conservative opinions was relatively infrequent when one looks at the more conservative justices, in part because many of those conservative opinions by conservative justices had to reject or distinguish away the pragmatism standard to support their outcome. However, when the conservative justices reached a liberal outcome, they relied on pragmatism to nearly the degree as did the more liberal justices.

The results for the absurdity standard did not show quite the same effect, though the relative infrequency of its use means that the results are only tentative. Justices Thomas, Scalia, and Rehnquist were far more likely to find a liberal interpretation absurd than a conservative one. By contrast, Justices Stevens and Breyer were much more likely to find a conservative interpretation to be the absurd one. Hence, this pragmatism standard did appear to be a more ideologically manipulable one.

The executive deference standard, by contrast, showed somewhat less manipulability. Justice Rehnquist, for example, voted liberal in most of the cases in which he used the doctrine. Justices Scalia and Thomas voted liberal in nearly half these cases. However, the application of this doctrine also allowed significant ideological flexibility. This effect is illustrated by Table 7.5, which shows the rate at which the justices invoked the *Chevron* doctrine to defer to an agency decision, or distinguished the *Chevron* doctrine to avoid deference, depending on the direction of the agency decision being reviewed.

Plainly, the *Chevron* doctrine did not wash out the ideological voting tendencies of the justices. The ideological effect is starkest for Justices Thomas and Scalia, who found conservative agency decisions quite worthy of *Chevron* deference but deferred to liberal agency decisions only a minority of the time. Nearly as dramatic was the favoritism to liberal agency decisions shown by Justices Stevens and Breyer.

While *Chevron* obviously did not receive a neutral application from the justices, there is still some evidence of its anti-ideological effect. For example, Justice Rehnquist voted 50% of the time for liberal agency decisions, in deference to the *Chevron* rule, and Justice Stevens voted 50% of the time for

TABLE 7.5

Deference by Agency Decision Ideology

Justice	Conservative Agency Decision (%)	Liberal Agency Decision (%)
Breyer	55	95
Ginsburg	67	85
Kennedy	60	57
O'Connor	77	62
Rehnquist	70	50
Scalia	87	33
Souter	67	80
Stevens	50	96
Thomas	80	33

conservative agency decisions. Justice Souter's 67% affirmance rate for conservative agency decisions is nearly twice his conservative voting rate in constitutional civil liberties matters. The *Chevron* doctrine appears to have some teeth in providing a legal constraint on judicial ideology.

The lesser use of the canons was not particularly ideological, but neither was it very significant. Three justices, Rehnquist, Scalia, and Thomas, were most likely to invoke the canons for conservative results, but this effect was largely attributable to reliance on the substantive canons with innate conservative direction, such as the retroactivity and federalism canons. The substantive canons on federalism tended to produce conservative results, as the lenity canon tends to produce liberal results. For Justices Breyer and Ginsburg, the relative usage of canons, and distinguishing of canons, was roughly similar in both conservative and liberal judgments of the Court, but their overall usage was sufficiently rare that it is difficult to draw any confident conclusions about the ideological effect of the canons.

Comprehensive Analysis of Interpretive Methods

The above analyses evidence the relative ideological or constraining effect of the various interpretive methods. However, they do so in isolation, with separate measures for each tool. In many cases, various methods are available for use, and as discussed in the preceding chapter, the justices' use of different interpretive methods may overlap in individual cases. This section considers the effect of all the approaches in the cases studied.

To conduct this analysis, I incorporate the ideological variable with the various interpretive variables in a regression analysis. The dependent variable is the ideological direction of the case outcome. This is an imperfect test for the constraining effect of the methods. For example, if a given method produces conservative results and liberal results in an equal number of cases, it will not appear to have an effect in this study, though it in fact had a constraining effect. Nevertheless, the analysis may reveal whether certain methods pull certain justices away from their personal ideological preferences. It can also reveal if certain methods tend themselves to have an ideological directional effect. The independent variables are the individual justices' ideology measures and the four interpretive categories. The data below show the results with the significance levels of coefficients in parentheses. A positive association is correlated with a liberal outcome and a negative association is correlated with a conservative outcome.

Ideology	.166 (.000)
Legislative Intent	.105 (.001)
Textualism	−.009 (.763)
Canons	.049 (.101)
Pragmatism	.121 (.000)

The justice ideology measure is a highly significant determinant of the ideology of the voting outcome. If votes were purely ideological, though, one would expect to find no statistical significance for any of the legal variables. When a legal variable has significance over and above the effect of ideology, that finding provides some evidence that its use causes justices to depart from their preferred ideology, implying that it constitutes a legal constraint. The use of textualism showed no such constraining effect, contrary to frequent suppositions, but reliance on legislative intent and pragmatism was independently significant, both pushing results in a liberal direction.

Because the table included a control variable for justice ideology, the liberal direction of these interpretive methods primarily indicates their effect on relatively more conservative justices. While these justices were not legally compelled to consult the legislative materials that would draw them in a liberal direction, they did so. Apparently, they were persuaded by the legislative history that Congress intended a result more liberal than the justices themselves might prefer. Statistical analyses cannot reveal the internal thought processes of the justices, but a plausible inference is that relatively determinate legislative history persuaded conservative justices that the correct statutory interpretation of a case was the more liberal one.

The relatively liberal effect of pragmatism was largely an effect of the use of the *Chevron* deference doctrine. The agency decisions reviewed by the Court were more often than not liberal in direction, so a deference rule would tend to yield more liberal decisions by the Court. Table 7.5 shows that the doctrine did not have much anti-ideological effect on the decisions of Justices Thomas and Scalia, but its effect on Justices Rehnquist, Kennedy, and O'Connor was obviously enough to produce statistical significance.

The findings of this analysis are necessarily tentative. Both the choice of interpretive methods and outcome were within the control of the justices for each of the cases at issue. It is possible that a conservative judge might sometimes prefer to reach a liberal result and would use legislative history to reach that outcome. The justices were plainly pluralist in their choice of interpretive methods in the cases studied and may have selected whatever method achieved their desired ends. The clearest finding is that the use of textualism does not constrain willful judging, as seemed apparent by the application of the plain meaning doctrine displayed above in Table 7.1.

Nor does it appear that pluralism necessarily conduces to ideological judging. Table 6.1 demonstrates that only two justices consistently reject pluralism—Justices Scalia and Thomas. Yet a regression of these two justices on outcome shows a highly statistically significant association with ideological outcome judging. Thus, the avoidance of pluralism does not avert ideological judging.

Conclusion

The empirical findings of this chapter cannot resolve the contested issues of statutory interpretation or prove that one method or another is preferable.

Nor do they even attempt to address the purely theoretical disputes. The results do help resolve one central issue, though, involving the constraining effect of methods. The interpretive plan for such constraint has been called the "obsessive desire" of the new textualists.[18] Yet this effort appears to be in vain. Reliance on textualism shows no constraining effect, in contrast to other methods.

One of the most important principles in the debate over methodologies of statutory interpretation has been the need to cabin judicial discretion with law. The theory that textualism constrains may be the conventional wisdom, but it is utterly lacking in empirical support and contrary to the results of my study at the Supreme Court level. It is possible that none of the methodologies is truly constraining, and that the choice of theories is simply another front of the ideological battle.

The findings of this chapter require consideration of the ideological consequences of doctrinal choices. Interpretive regimes may have a sort of meta-ideological effect. If legislative history systematically tends to yield more liberal results, that might explain ideological choices of legislative history. In this pattern, the debate over apparently legal theories is in fact an ideological battle. Were there this association of theory and outcome, the legal battles could be the most important. A decision in a case resolves only the outcome of the dispute between the parties, while an opinion using a particular interpretive method sets a precedent available in future decisions.

The findings of this chapter and the prior one show that the justices are interpretive pluralists, to a greater or lesser degree. They choose to use different interpretive approaches in different cases. In an ideal world, this might suggest sincere judging in good faith, where the justices select the method most appropriate to the facts of the case. My findings are somewhat gloomier, however. The justices' decisions are significantly influenced by their ideological preferences, so they may be choosing the method that best supports the conclusion they wish to reach for ideological purposes.

At face value, these results might suggest that the justices were faithless agents, failing to pursue the legislature's objectives. Yet Congress seems relatively untroubled by this fact and has failed to take action to correct the situation. Perhaps this is because Congress realizes the inevitability of such ideological decision making at the Supreme Court level and the fact that pure textualism cannot constrain. Indeed, ideological decisions by the

Court may not reflect much faithless agency after all. The Court takes very few cases per year and only the most legally difficult. These close cases are not representative of legal disputes.[19] They may be cases involving background delegation where there simply is no clear legal answer, regardless of the legal methodology employed by the Court. If so, Congress has no effective means of controlling judicial ideology in such unforeseen, close cases.

Of course, this conclusion assumes that the cases are indeed unforeseen and close. Perhaps the judges are aggrandizing their power and imposing their ideologies even in cases that have a neutral legal resolution. The latter behavior is generally considered illegitimate in the U.S. political system. Unfortunately, it does not appear that the standards of statutory interpretation, even strict plain meaning textualism, are highly effective at restraining this tendency.

CHAPTER 8

Statutory Interpretation in the Lower Federal Courts

Up to this point, my analysis has focused on the Supreme Court's rulings on statutory interpretation. The Supreme Court, of course, sets the rules for the courts below, but the lower courts produce the vast preponderance of decisions. Arguably, the most important level of the federal judicial hierarchy is the circuit courts of appeals. They finally resolve thousands of cases annually and produce opinions that set the legal standard for future decisions within the circuit. Although their decisions may be appealed to the Supreme Court, the Court currently takes less than one hundred cases for review annually, leaving the circuit courts the final word on the vast majority of cases. Their opinions also establish the law for most issues of statutory interpretation, which never reach the Supreme Court for its resolution.

Understanding the law of statutory interpretation requires consideration of these lower courts. Unfortunately, the same level of detailed data is not available as for the smaller number of cases decided in the Supreme Court.

Nevertheless, this chapter embarks on a limited study of lower federal court practices relating to statutory interpretation theories. I focus on the interaction of the Supreme Court and lower federal courts in their statutory interpretation practices.

After reviewing the nature of the federal judicial hierarchy and association of different levels, I consider the practice of statutory interpretation in circuit courts over recent years. The first section of the chapter examines the relative use of different interpretive methodologies in the circuit courts. I examine the relative reliance on the primary interpretive methodologies over the past thirty years at this level of the judiciary.

The second major section of the chapter deals with subsequent treatment of the Supreme Court opinions using the different interpretive methodologies. I take the cases analyzed in the prior two chapters and examine how they have been cited in subsequent decisions. These cases are analyzed for the number of citations that a decision receives and the number of negative citations received, and each can be correlated with the interpretive methodologies used by the decisions.

The Federal Judicial Hierarchy and Statutory Interpretation

The Supreme Court sits at the apex of the federal judicial hierarchy and establishes the rules for lower courts. It has the final word on the interpretation of federal statutes. Circuit courts commonly reach conflicting interpretations of statutes, and the Supreme Court resolves the conflict. In doing so, it establishes the law for the entire nation. Subsequent circuit court decisions must follow the Supreme Court's interpretation, not their own prior decision that was reversed.

In theory, the Supreme Court could also create rules of statutory interpretation that circuit courts must follow. For example, the Supreme Court has created substantive canons of construction that are applied by lower federal courts. In theory, the Court could declare, for example, that legislative history is not to be used in statutory interpretation. This would set a precedent, directing lower courts not to consider legislative history in future disputes over the interpretation of any statute. If the lower courts did not attend to the precedent, their decisions could be reversed.

While statutory interpretive methodologies have not been studied, there is a wealth of research on the adherence of lower courts to Supreme Court decisions. A study of search and seizure decisions found a very high correspondence between Supreme Court doctrines and circuit court decisions.[1] Studies of different categories of Supreme Court precedent and subsequent circuit applications have reached the same conclusion.[2] The research has demonstrated that "after the Supreme Court made a major shift in policy, the decisional trends of the courts of appeals moved in the same direction to a statistically significant degree."[3] The studies have involved constitutional decisions of the Court, but there is no reason to believe statutory interpretation rulings would differ.

As noted in preceding chapters, the Supreme Court has largely taken a pluralist approach to means of statutory interpretation. Consequently, it has not given clear directives to lower federal courts on proper interpretive methods. Nevertheless, various justices have emphasized different approaches and the relative balance of Court reliance on different tools of interpretation has varied over time. Lower federal courts may take indirect cues from Supreme Court practice and adapt their own interpretive methods accordingly. The widespread belief that the Rehnquist Court disapproved of reliance on legislative history (though not entirely accurate) could cause lower courts to eschew reliance on the materials of legislative history.

Although this reaction need not be an explicit one, the circuit courts have in dozens of cases quoted Scalia's separate opinions that reject reliance on legislative history to interpret statutes. These decisions have not embraced a position that consideration of legislative history is never appropriate, and some have gone on to consider it. However, they do suggest that the circuit courts are "looking over their shoulders" at Justice Scalia when interpreting statutes. The Fifth Circuit has written that it was "mindful, at the outset, of Justice Scalia's recent reference to the use of legislative history as oftentimes being 'the equivalent of entering a crowded cocktail party and looking over the heads of the guests for one's friends'."[4] In another case, the Third Circuit opinion explicitly "recognize[d] that Justice Scalia has expressed disapproval of judicial inquiry into legislative history" but found it was necessary under the criteria for determining whether a statute creates a private right of action (a use Justice Scalia finds acceptable).[5] This surely suggests some influence of Justice Scalia's theories, as the court felt the need to find a special justification for analyzing legislative history.

Justice Scalia is but a single justice, though, and this surely tempers his effect on lower-court decisions. A recent opinion wrote that the "Supreme Court has given less emphasis to legislative history in recent years, recognizing that it is frequently an unreliable indicator of congressional intent," though it also noted that only Justice Scalia rejected its consideration outright.[6] A perceived disapproval of legislative history by the Court more broadly may have a greater impact. One can find some examples of this apparent influence. For example, the Ninth Circuit has explained that the "case law of the Supreme Court" established that "legislative history, untethered to text in an enacted statute, has no compulsive legal effect."[7] A Third Circuit ruling noted some years ago that the "Supreme Court of the United States appears increasingly reluctant to rely on legislative history."[8] A perception of this reluctance might well affect the circuit courts' willingness to use legislative history.

Such an effect on the lower courts is not clear, as one can readily find references to use of the legislative history in circuit court opinions. A First Circuit opinion recently declared that "this court and the Supreme court have checked a sense of a statute's plain meaning against undisputed legislative history as a guide against judicial error."[9] Another opinion lamented that the role of legislative history in the review of administrative decisions "has been the subject of mixed messages from the Supreme Court."[10] Thus, the Supreme Court's signals on the use of legislative history may not be so clear as to control its use at the circuit court level. Anecdotal cases cannot capture the true overall picture, so some empirical analysis is necessary, as provided in the following discussion. Such research has been limited to date, but one study of lower-court tax decisions found very significant use of pragmatism ("practical reasoning") in their interpretations of the Tax Code.[11]

Use of Legislative Intent in Circuit Courts

This section embarks on a study of the frequency of circuit courts' use of legislative history in statutory interpretation over time. Given the huge number of circuit court cases on statutory interpretation (over one thousand per year), judge-by-judge analysis is unrealistic as is careful opinion reading. To overcome this problem, I use case databases to search for terms that serve as a proxy for the use of legislative intent. I searched Westlaw for the use of the term "legislative history" over the past thirty years and counted the annual number of cases employing the phrase. This has some inevitable inaccuracy; a case that affirmatively dismissed legislative history as unreliable could appear in the search. The review of a subset of the cases, though, indicated that the distortion is a very small one. Only about 1% of the references to "legislative history" in circuit court opinions were negative. Thus, the simple count should pick up any gross changes in use of legislative history over time. There are surely numerous times when the courts use legislative history but not the phrase, which would yield an underestimate of its use, so the numbers should not be viewed as absolute numbers of its use in circuit court cases. This difference should only be random noise, though, and would not obscure trends over time. The frequency of such references in the circuit courts from 1976 to 2005 is displayed in Figure 8.1, as a simple count. Because the overall circuit court caseload has increased somewhat over the time period, perfect neutrality over the time period would appear as a slowly increasing straight line.

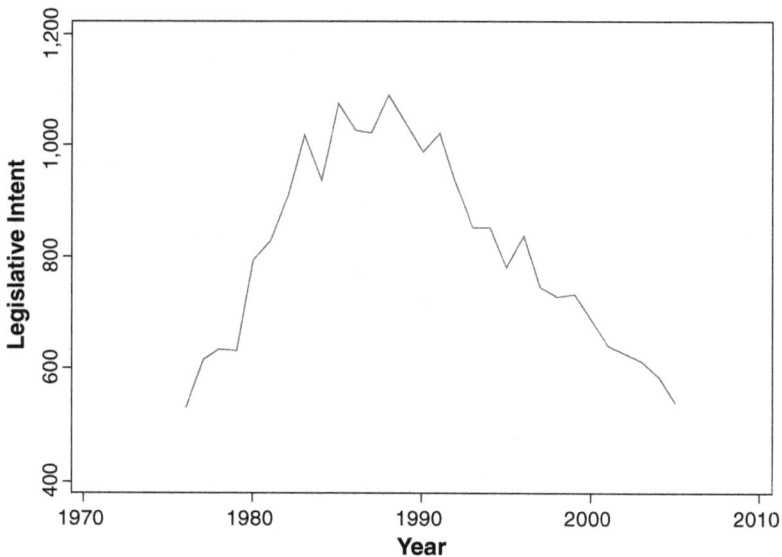

Figure 8.1   Circuit Court "Legislative History" References

Changes in the use of legislative history over the period are quite strik-ing. The 1970s and early 1980s are often regarded as the "heyday" of leg-islative history, but the circuit courts in the late 1970s referred to it only around 600 times per year. The 1980s saw a dramatic increase and from 1983–1992, the courts referred to legislative history an average of more than one thousand times per year. Since that time, references have seen a steady decline to a level similar to that of the late 1970s. The Rehnquist Court, and Justice Scalia's service on the Court, began in 1986. The shift in circuit court usage begins about six years later. One might reasonably expect a certain lag time for circuit courts to receive and appreciate a message about methods of statutory interpretation, so these results are consistent with a hypothesis that the Rehnquist Court effectively discouraged the use of legislative history by lower courts.

The decline in the use of legislative history might not be across the board. Rather, the circuit courts may have disavowed some sources of leg-islative history as less reliable, while continuing to rely upon the more author-itative sources. I used a similar method to check for references to "Conference Committee" reports during the same time period. This may not capture every reference to Conference Committees but should illustrate a trend over time. Such reports are clearly the most reliable source of legislative history, as discussed previously. Figure 8.2 presents the number of those references per year.

The results are inconsistent with any shift to "more reliable" sources of legislative history. References to conference committee reports have steadily declined over the time period. Their numbers exceeded 10% of the "legisla-tive history" references in the 1970s, but they have represented less than 5% of those references in the 2000s. The reason for this is murky, but the re-sults are contrary to any theory suggesting a shift to more reliable sources of legislative history.

The "death of legislative history" as an interpretive tool is much more profound in the circuit courts than in the Supreme Court. One possible ex-planation for this effect would be found in the composition of the circuit courts. If use of legislative history were associated with liberalism, the de-cline in use of this method might be due to more conservatives on the cir-cuit courts. The relative ideology of circuit court judges can be measured with "judicial common space" (JCS) scores. These ascribe an ideological

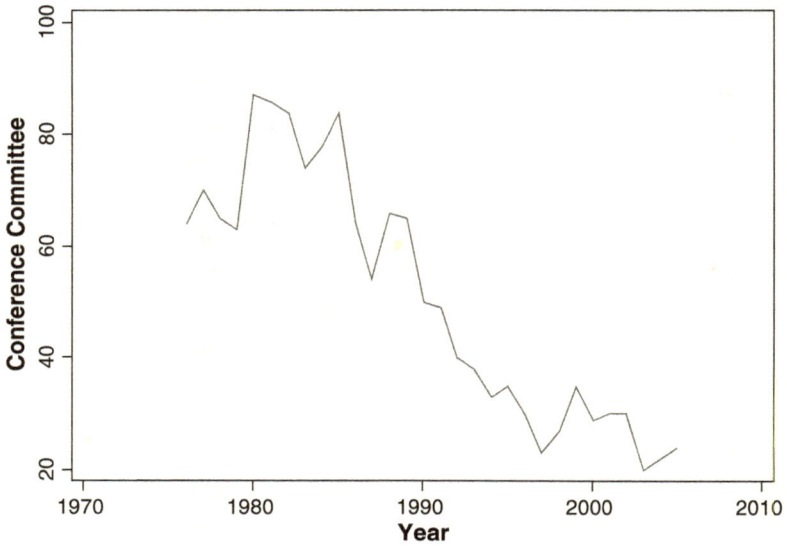

Figure 8.2   Circuit Court "Conference Committee" References

position to each circuit court judge, based on the ideology of the appointing president and the in-state influence of the local senator.[12] Annualized median JCS scores for the various circuits are available for a portion of the time period in question. The apex of liberalism for the circuit courts occurred around 1980. After this time, the courts became dramatically more conservative, until Clinton's election in 1992, after which the courts became somewhat more liberal, though still relatively conservative. This pattern does not map closely on the use of legislative history. The dramatic increase in usage of legislative intent occurred precisely as the circuit courts became more conservative, and reliance on legislative history peaked at around the same time as conservatism peaked. Its use declined in the 1990s, as the circuit courts became more liberal in orientation.

Thus, it does not appear that the dramatic reduction in the use of legislative history is attributable to a changed ideological composition of the circuit courts. The most likely explanation is that either the courts themselves, or perhaps the litigants appearing before those courts, believe that legislative history is a less appropriate means of statutory interpretation. This may be due to the "conventional wisdom" associated with the Supreme Court's perceived preferences. Justice Scalia's campaign against the use of legislative history may thus have had an effect on the circuit courts generally, even as it has seen only limited power on the Supreme Court itself. The lower courts may perceive a "major policy shift" for statutory interpretation methods at the Supreme Court level during the Rehnquist era, though it has not demonstrably occurred.

Use of Textualism in Circuit Courts

Textualism's use is somewhat more difficult to measure than is the apparent use of legislative history in statutory interpretation. Judges nearly always make some reference to the text of the interpreted statute, and there is no phrase like "legislative history" or "Conference Committee" that will capture most textualist reliance. The number of cases at the circuit court level is too great to read and code individual opinions, as in the Supreme Court research.

Use of textualism might be approximately measured through the Westlaw Keynumber system. The service codes cases for their legal rulings. Some of its codes for statutory interpretation may be used to measure frequency of textualist reliance. The Keynumber 361k187, described as "meaning of language," captures various textualist principles such as the use of "literal and grammatical interpretation" of statutes. The Keynumber 361k204, described as "statute as a whole, and intrinsic aids to construction," captures textualist principles such as the whole act rule. I combine cases coded with these two key numbers for my measure of the use of textualism.

This measure is somewhat under-inclusive and over-inclusive. It is under-inclusive because it seems Westlaw limits its coding to fairly explicit references to the interpretive approach, while nearly every case probably employs a modest degree of textual analysis. It is over-inclusive, because the coding contains some cases where the method is found inapplicable, that is, the text is analyzed and found to be too ambiguous to resolve the case. A review of a sample of cases, though, suggested that this is relatively uncommon in the coding. In addition, the Keynumbers include some measures that I categorized as canons, and some cases may be double counted, because they fall within both Keynumbers. Hence, the absolute count may not be a reliable measure of textualism's use. However, the measure should roughly capture its relative importance over time, as the inaccuracies would not be systematic and should represent only random noise from year to year. Figure 8.3 displays the frequency of such use over the same time period as for my legislative history analysis.

The results reveal a very pronounced increase in the use of textualism around 1990. The increase was as much as fivefold up to around 2000, when textualism usage peaked and leveled off. Once again, this cannot be ascribed to circuit court ideology, because 1992 was the era when conservatism on the courts peaked, and they became steadily more liberal during the great increase in reliance on textualism.

The great rising trend in use of textualism apparently coincided with the dramatic decrease in references to legislative history. This corresponds to the public debate, which views the two interpretive methods as opposed. Chapter 6 showed that this opposition was not so great at the Supreme Court level, but the circuit court results may be different. Indeed, it is ironic

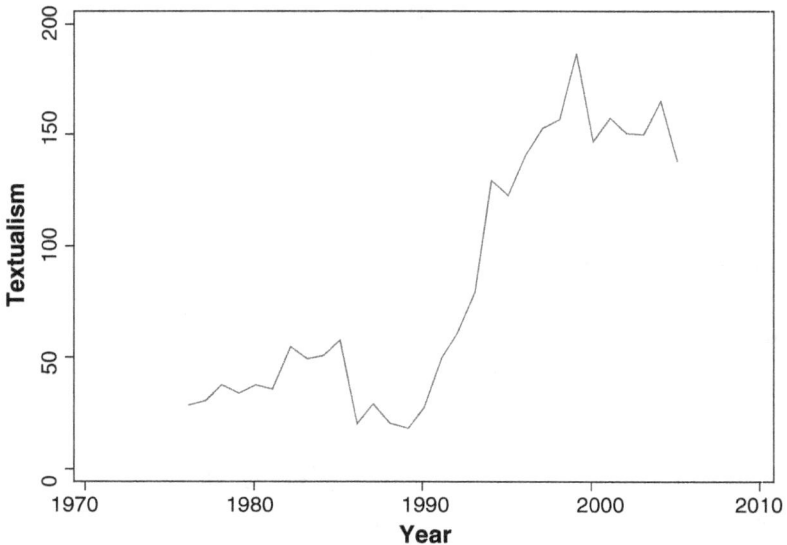

Figure 8.3   Circuit Court Textualism References

that the circuit courts have shifted away from reliance on legislative history at roughly the same time that the Supreme Court apparently swung toward greater reliance on legislative history.[13] This provides more confirmation of a possible effect for Justice Scalia's aggressive advocacy for textualism in statutory interpretation. However, this effect is not a transcendent one. The absolute numbers for textualism references are lower than references to legislative history in every year. The direct comparison of such numbers is not a reliable comparison of influence, though, for reasons discussed above. The fact that hundreds of circuit court cases every year refer to legislative history indicates that the method has not been extinguished as an important interpretive tool.

Use of Pragmatism in Circuit Courts

Chapter 6 addressed the difficulties of identifying pragmatism as a tool of judicial decision making, in the Supreme Court context. Without the ability to scrutinize opinion language, the task is even more difficult. The Westlaw Keynumber system can be used for at least a rough measure of pragmatism. The Westlaw "key" 361k181(2), labeled "effects and consequences," roughly corresponds to use of the absurdity doctrine in statutory interpretation, though it appears to be slightly broader in its coding. Again, the measure is a crude one, as it includes a small number of cases dismissing the absurdity doctrine but should serve as a rough proxy for its usage. Figure 8.4 shows the number of cases coded with this key number over the time period of the previous figures.

These data show a dramatic increase in references to pragmatism by circuit court opinions, beginning in the mid-1990s and continuing to the present. The absolute number of such references is quite small, far less than references to legislative history or textual tools for statutory interpretation. As observed in Chapter 6, however, this type of tool for finding the role of pragmatism captures only the tip of the iceberg of its usage. While the absolute significance of pragmatism in statutory interpretation is uncertain, the results suggest that its use has seen a dramatic increase in the most recent decade. Pragmatism may be becoming more acceptable as an interpretive tool for the judiciary, though its absolute frequency is uncertain.

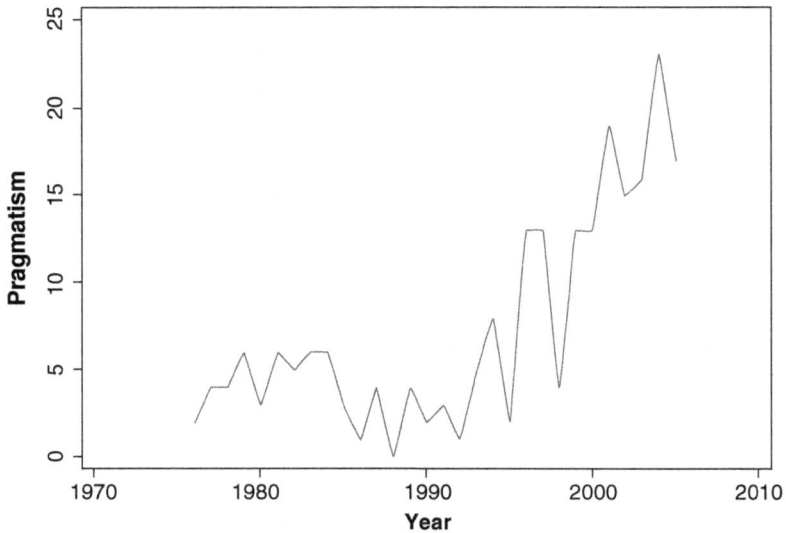

Figure 8.4   Circuit Court Pragmatism References

Use of Canons in Circuit Courts

The relative use of linguistic canons in the courts is easy to study, as they are affixed to Latin terms otherwise unused by judges. My analysis for canon use simply searched for the terms: *noscitur a socii* ("known by its associates"), *ejusdem generis* ("of the same kind"), and *expressio unius* ("the express mention of one thing excludes all others") over the time period. The same caveats apply to the word search, and a scan of the cases indicated that it was not uncommon that a court might use these terms in finding them *inapplicable*, unlike the case of use of legislative history. However, most uses were positive, and distinguishing the applicability of the canons to a particular case is a plain recognition of the significance of the interpretive methodology. Figure 8.5 shows relative use of the canons over the period.

The results show a distinct increase in the usage of canons beginning around 1990 and lasting until 2000, when the increase halted. This roughly parallels the time period in which the use of legislative history was declining and textualism references were growing.

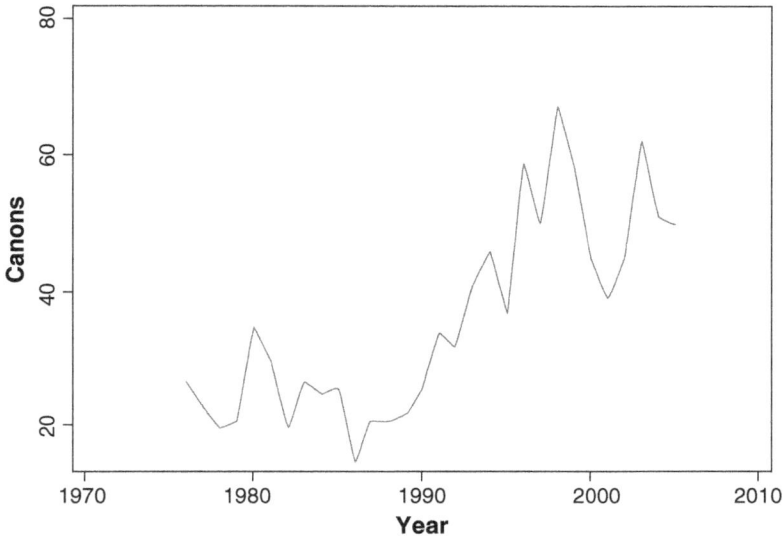

Figure 8.5   Circuit Court Canon References

Much has been written about trends in statutory interpretation. It is commonly suggested that textualism became ascendant over legislative history and that textualism was associated with use of the linguistic canons. Chapter 6 showed that this conventional wisdom was not a terribly accurate description of Supreme Court practice. The data in this chapter suggest that the conventional wisdom is more accurate with respect to circuit court practice. Whether this is a cause or an effect of the conventional wisdom is indeterminate. Nevertheless, the circuit courts remain pluralist, making great use of legislative history, though at a lower rate than in past time periods.

Precedential Effect of Supreme Court Decisions

This book is primarily about statutory interpretation in the Supreme Court, and the influence of Supreme Court decisions is felt primarily in their precedential power. A particular decision formally resolves only the dispute between the two parties; the societal effect of the decision arises from the power of the ruling as a precedent for future decisions, most of them in lower courts. It is this precedential effect that has "more far-reaching consequences by altering the existing state of legal policy and thus helping to shape the outcomes of future disputes."[14] This section considers whether different sources of interpretation yield different precedential effects.

The precedents set by the Supreme Court may involve appropriate interpretive methodologies, but they more commonly involve the application of the particular statute interpreted by the Supreme Court. Thus, if the Supreme Court declares that a particular statute has a particular meaning, future courts must grapple with that interpretation in subsequent disputes arising under the statute. Thus, the Supreme Court held in *Central Bank* that the Securities Exchange Act, which prohibits securities fraud with a private right of enforcement action, does not contain any prohibition on "aiding and abetting" such a fraud in such private actions.[15] The decision in *Central Bank* was grounded centrally in textualism, though it considered contrary arguments about congressional intent (though it cited no legislative history). The decision was a highly contested 5-4 vote, and the opinion was written by Justice Kennedy.

The *Central Bank* ruling had to be followed and applied by lower courts, many of which had previously recognized a cause of action for aiding and abetting securities fraud. A Supreme Court precedent, though, cannot resolve all contested questions in its language, any more than a statute can do so. Thus, a Supreme Court opinion delegates interpretive authority to lower courts. In the wake of the decision, courts have struggled over which parties are primarily liable as direct committers of fraud and which defendants are merely aiders and abettors and therefore not liable.

I explore whether different interpretive methods for statutes yield different precedential effects. Evidence discussed in Chapter 3 indicates that decisions grounded in textualism are more likely to be overturned by subsequent Congresses. The meaning of this finding is not precisely clear, but it contains a suggestion that such decisions were wrong or pragmatically unworkable. This section considers the fate of such decisions in future court rulings.

To conduct this analysis, I again turn to services provided by Westlaw in its KeyCite system. This database takes each Supreme Court decision and lists how many cases have cited that opinion. It also distinguishes, to some degree, the characteristics of that citation. Some citations are negative and undermine the authority of the cited case. At the extreme, these would involve an overruling, which is signified by a red flag. Because we are analyzing Supreme Court decisions, this would have to involve a Supreme Court overruling, which are quite rare. Lesser negative treatment could involve a decision limiting the scope of the Supreme Court holding, distinguishing the opinion from the decision below, or criticizing its application to that case such as "not followed," which is signified by a yellow flag on Westlaw. These are generally regarded as negative treatments of a precedent.

Westlaw also cumulates positive treatments of precedent. Any citation of a case might be considered a positive treatment of that opinion, but the mere presence of a citation, perhaps in a string citation, does not suggest significant precedential effect. Westlaw distinguishes among the positive citations to indicate the depth of treatment by the applying court. A "four star" citation, called "examined" by the service, indicates that the citing case contains an extensive discussion of the precedent, often representing a full page of text in the citing case. These would be considered substantial positive citations, or cases where the precedent had a powerful effect on the later application.[16] I also calculated all positive citations, which were those categorized by Westlaw as being "two star" or higher.[17]

For each of the cases in my database, I totaled the number of overall positive citations, substantial positive citations, and negative citations for each of the cases. The descriptive statistics for these categories are presented in Table 8.1.

This reveals a very large variation in citation frequency for the cases in my database. Some cases have received zero citations. While the average case received about sixty-eight citations, the standard deviation was very large. Negative citations are, as would be expected, less common but by no means rare. The average case received nine negative citations of some sort. The distribution of cases is not a normal one and has a heavy right tail of highly cited cases. For statistical analysis, I converted the numbers to a log scale to better normalize the distribution. The log scales for the treatment as positive, substantial positive, or negative are used as dependent variables.

As noted above, the *Central Bank* opinion saw considerable application by lower courts. As of this writing, it had many hundreds of positive citations. However, a significant amount of its treatment was categorized as negative

TABLE 8.1
Descriptive Statistics on Precedent Variables

	Minimum	Maximum	Mean	Standard Deviation
All Positive	0	1013	67.9	130.4
Substantial Positive	0	444	23.7	56.9
All Negative	0	85	9.1	14.2

by the KeyCite service. Six cases found an application of *Central Bank* superseded by statutory modifications, one case declined to follow it on state law grounds, two cases recognized disagreement, eight cases declined to extend its holding, and twenty-three cases distinguished the opinion from the case before the court. This illustrates a common tendency: the cases receiving the most positive citations tend also to receive the most negative citations, probably because they deal with an important issue area, with many more subsequent lower-court applications.

The data on citations enables a test for the effect of interpretive methodologies on subsequent precedential applications. Earlier cases obviously have more opportunities to be cited, so I must account for the year in which the decision is rendered, as a control variable. In addition, the size of the Court's majority coalition may affect citation rates.[18] Perhaps a larger majority provides a stronger decision, with more citations, or conversely a larger majority may simply be an artifact of less-important facts or law that might produce fewer citations. Of course, the size of the majority coalition is also somewhat influenced by the opinion's choice of statutory interpretive methods, according to my findings in Chapter 7, so this is not a purely exogenous control variable. Yet another factor which might affect citation rates is the ideological direction of the opinion. Perhaps liberal and conservative opinions are cited at different rates because of the ideological composition of lower courts or some other reason. Each of these was entered into the multiple regression as control variables for year, vote, and ideology. Table 8.2 presents the results of this study on the total positive citations received by the cases in my data, using the variables for interpretive methodology as in the preceding chapters.

The association for the variable for year is negative as expected, meaning that cases decided earlier received more citations. The association for vote was also negative, meaning that cases decided by a smaller margin receive

TABLE 8.2
Interpretive Theories and Total Positive Citations

	Citations	T-score
Year	−.183***	5.869
Vote	−.186***	5.975
Ideology	−.015	.487
Textualism	.106***	3.426
Legislative Intent	.016	.512
Pragmatism	.033	.312
Canons	−.053*	1.719

Note: *** = .01; * = .10

TABLE 8.3
Interpretive Theories and Substantial
Positive Citations

	Citations	T-score
Year	−.008	.249
Vote	−.175***	5.231
Ideology	−.052	1.532
Textualism	.071**	2.122
Legislative Intent	.039	1.133
Pragmatism	.078**	2.263
Canons	−.126***	3.770

Note: *** = .01; ** = .05

more citations, perhaps because they are the more significant ones. For our interpretive methodologies, textualism had a pronounced positive effect. Opinions that made more use of textualism in statutory interpretation subsequently received more total positive citations. The next analysis, reported in Table 8.3, uses the same methodology but for the dependent variable of substantial positive citations, which may be the best measure for precedential impact.

The year of the decision is surprisingly insignificant, though the negative association with vote remains. Perhaps the significant citations tend to occur soon after the Court's ruling. Both textualism and pragmatism have a significant association here. This might be interpreted as evidence that these methods are most "useful" to later court interpretations. The association with use of the canons is quite significant and negative, perhaps meaning that statutory decisions resolved by canons are less useful, or simply less important, interpretations.

There is a possibility of some reverse causality in this finding. The opinions that receive the most citations may simply be those regarding statutes in the most important issue areas. If the justices were consistent in their dedication to particular interpretive methods, this would not be true, but we have seen that the justices are generally pluralists. Hence, it may be that justices invoke the canons on cases of less concern to them but use textualism or pragmatism on high-profile cases. This would be an interesting and important finding in its own right, if the causality indeed ran in this direction. These results further dispel the hypothesis that reliance on legislative intent is ideologically manipulable. If that were true, the justices would be more likely to use legislative intent in cases that were most salient to them and which would receive more citations. My results show that this is not the case.

The next analysis considers negative citations to Supreme Court opinions, again using the same approach and reported in Table 8.4.

The control variables are significant, including ideology. Liberal statutory interpretation decisions receive significantly more negative citations than conservatism. This may speak to the quality of the opinions but may merely reflect the relatively conservative makeup of the lower court judici-

TABLE 8.4
*Interpretive Theories and Total
Negative Citations*

	Citations	T-score
Year	−.073**	2.255
Vote	−.233***	7.265
Ideology	.07**	2.144
Textualism	.146***	4.569
Legislative Intent	.027	.823
Pragmatism	.075**	2.258
Canons	−.006	.182

Note: *** = .01; ** = .05

ary during the relevant time period. Textualism and pragmatism were associated with more negative treatment at a statistically significant rate.

The positive associations with negative citations for textualism and pragmatism may in part simply be due to the fact that they involve significant
cases, as found in the associations for substantial positive citations. However,
the size of the correlation coefficients is informative. A one unit change in the
textualism score produces a 7.1% increase in substantial positive citations but
a 14.6% increase in negative citations. The highest possible textualism score
would project to more than 50% more negative citations. The approach produces an increase in negative citations much larger than the increase in positive ones. Pragmatism results in higher substantial positive citations and more
negative citations at about the same rate.

These results provide no evidence that textualist interpretations are more
useful or clearer. A statutory interpretation grounded in textualism is likely
to receive more negative treatment, relative to positive treatment. The same
is true to a degree for decisions grounded in the canons. They produce
many fewer substantial positive citations but no fewer negative citations
than decisions grounded in other sources. Greater use of legislative intent
and pragmatism does not produce this net negative treatment effect.

Cases decided according to textualist principles have great precedential
use, significantly more than those using legislative intent. They produce
more positive citations but are even more strongly associated with negative
citations. The reason for this greater use is unclear. As noted above, it might
be that justices reserve their greatest textualist emphasis for the decisions of
greatest significance to them. Those significant cases would arise more frequently and receive more citations. This would not explain the relatively
greater number of negative citations, however.

There is an alternative explanation for the greater citation to textualist
precedents. Decisions that produce greater uncertainty are more likely to
result in more litigation to resolve that uncertainty.[19] When a decision is
clear in its implications, such litigation is unnecessary and wasteful, as the
case outcome will be clear. The greater citation of textualist decisions, the
product of greater litigation, indicates that such opinions may be relatively
unclear. This is contrary to the conventional wisdom, which associates textualism with "rules" that have greater certainty in application.[20] Justice
Scalia has argued that use of legislative history in statutory interpretation

was "more likely to confuse than clarify."[21] Yet these citation results suggest the contrary—that the greater use of textualism produces greater uncertainty in the law. The relatively higher number of negative citations furthers this conclusion, as numerous lower courts found the need to distinguish or otherwise limit the use of the textualist opinions of the Supreme Court.

Future Research on Lower-Court Decision Making

The study of citations is yet at a nascent stage of empirical analysis. More fine-grained analyses would be very beneficial. For example, researchers could examine a smaller sample of cases and assess the particular nature of the citations. Precedent may, of course, be manipulated. Strong legal realists believe it is infinitely manipulable. Judge Easterbrook of the Seventh Circuit has declared that "precedent doesn't govern" cases.[22] Some have said that the "Supreme Court has generated so much precedent that it is usually possible to find support for any conclusion."[23]

Such extreme realism is excessive and refuted by the above-cited studies showing circuit responses to Supreme Court doctrines. Similarly we have seen that the supposedly conservative method of textualism grew even as the circuit courts became more liberal. Nevertheless, it plainly has a measure of truth. More liberal circuit court justices tend to render more liberal decisions, even with the same body of governing precedent. Judicial ideology is an important determinant of circuit court decisions.[24] A recent study examined ideological decision-making patterns in various areas of statutory interpretation, including the National Environmental Protection Act, labor law, environmental law, and civil rights law, and found pronounced differences in decision outcomes depending on whether the panel consisted primarily of judges appointed by Democrats or Republicans.[25]

The studies on the effect of ideological decision making have not considered judicial interpretive methods, however. One pathbreaking study has looked at the effect of judicial interpretive methods on the Seventh Circuit, including standards such as reliance on legislative history and textualism (measured by reliance on dictionaries for interpretation).[26] The study found that judges with similar interpretive methods were no more likely to agree on decisions than those with differing methods. The study did not incorporate more recent findings on panel effects, however.[27] Nevertheless, it establishes a template for future research on the effect of such methods.

Conclusion

The study of precedential effects of Supreme Court rulings on lower courts is very important. This chapter's analysis has only scratched the surface of this research. The study of circuit court use of interpretive methodologies could be connected more closely with individual judicial ideologies. Variation in practice across different types of statutes would also be an interesting field to study. This chapter simply shows the trends in time in circuit court practice and the precedential fate of Supreme Court opinions grounded in different approaches to statutory interpretation.

The meaning of the findings on precedential use of opinions with different interpretative methodologies is not plain. The direction of the causality is not certain, and the relative meaning of having more or fewer citations is also somewhat murky. One can conclude that the results provide no support for the conventional textualist claim that the method produces clear rulings that are transparent in meaning to the public and easy in application by lower courts. If that were the case, we would expect to see fewer citations and fewer negative citations for textualist opinions. In reality, textualism is associated with more of both.

It has been suggested that "when normative discussions are at an impasse, empirical findings may provide the only basis for reaching agreement."[28] While this may be an ambitious goal, empirical research can surely inform the normative debate. The case for various interpretive methodologies, such as textualism, is often defended in terms of their professed ability to achieve beneficial consequences. Such claims can and should be tested.[29] If the empirical tests support the claimed benefits of textualism, its defenders will have a powerful sword in support of their normative position. However, this book suggests that some of the consequential claims about textualism are not supported. While no single study is conclusive, my results indicate that the case for textualism is much weaker than commonly claimed.

It is clear from the findings that pluralism rules the day in judicial statutory interpretation. Interpretive methods vary by justice and by time period, but all remain in play for statutory interpretation cases. The judiciary has considerable discretion in determining the proper interpretation of a statute in a given set of factual circumstances. This is the result of a delegation of authority from Congress, which apparently wishes to take advantage of judicial expertise in the application of statutes to cases. Although the legislature arguably could command a particular interpretive methodology, it has left the question to the judgment of the judges. It may influence this judgment on individual statutes, through its choice of textual clarity or the materials of legislative history, but the ultimate decision is one of the judiciary's interpretive discretion. Presumably, this reflects a history of sagacious use of such discretion. While my results do not demonstrate the best interpretive method or exercise of case-by-case discretion, I do believe that pragmatism is a more defensible judicial practice than sometimes recognized. Once one recognizes that the legislature is delegating discretion to the judiciary, judges should not be shy about applying their common sense pragmatic wisdom to the resolution of cases.

Notes

NOTES TO PREFACE

1. Muscarello v. United States, 524 U.S. 125 (1998).
2. *Id.* at 140.
3. Smith v. United States, 508 U.S. 223 (1993).

NOTES TO CHAPTER 1

1. Einer Elhauge, "Preference-Eliciting Statutory Default Rules," 102 *Columbia Law Review* 2027, 2070 (2002).
2. Adrian Vermeule, *Judging under Uncertainty: An Institutional Theory of Legal Interpretation* 31 (2006).
3. Abner S. Greene, "The Missing Step of Textualism," 74 *Fordham Law Review* 1913, 1915 (2006).
4. William Eskridge, *Dynamic Statutory Interpretation* 131 (1994).
5. Matthew C. Stephenson, "Legislative Allocation of Delegated Power: Uncertainty, Risk, and the Choice Between Agencies and Courts," 119 *Harvard Law Review* 1036 (2006).
6. John D. Huber & Charles R. Shipan, *Deliberate Discretion?: The Institutional Foundations of Bureaucratic Autonomy* 1 (2002).
7. *Id.* at 33.
8. David B. Spence & Frank B. Cross, "A Public Choice Case for the Administrative State," 89 *Georgetown Law Journal* 97 (2000).
9. David Epstein & Sharyn O'Halloran, *Delegating Powers: A Transaction Cost Politics Approach to Policy Making under Separate Powers* 27 (1999).
10. H. L. A. Hart, *The Concept of Law* 124–136 (2nd ed. 1995).
11. Friedrich v. City of Chicago, 888 F.2d 511, 514 (7th Cir. 1989).
12. The Federalist No. 37 (James Madison) (Isaac Kramnick ed. 1987).
13. *See* Robert Katzmann, *Courts and Congress* 61 (1997) (noting that "ambiguity is a deliberate strategy to secure a majority coalition in support of the legislation").

14. Landgraf v. USI Film Productions, 511 U.S. 244, 262–263 (1994).

15. James J. Brudney, "Congressional Commentary on Judicial Interpretations of Statutes: Idle Chatter or Telling Response?," 94 *Michigan Law Review* 1, 10 (1994).

16. George I. Lovell, *Legislative Deferrals: Statutory Ambiguity, Judicial Power, and American Democracy* (2003).

17. *Id.* at xviii.

18. Joseph A. Grundfest & A. C. Pritchard, "Statutes with Multiple Personality Disorders: The Value of Ambiguity in Statutory Design and Interpretation," 54 *Stanford Law Review* 627 (2002).

19. Richard J. Pierce, Jr., "Political Accountability and Delegated Power: A Response to Professor Lowi," 36 *American University Law Review* 391, 398–401 (1987).

20. Schooner Paulina's Cargo v. United States, II U.S. (7 Cranch) 52, 60 (1812) (Marshall, C. J.).

21. John F. Manning, "Textualism and Legislative Intent," 93 *Virginia Law Review* 419, 419 (2005) (referring to the rational as the "touchstone of federal statutory interpretation" for this era).

22. Richard A. Posner, "Statutory Interpretation—in the Classroom and in the Courtroom," 50 *University of Chicago Law Review* 800, 817 (1983)

23. Archibald Cox, "Judge Learned Hand and the Interpretation of Statutes," 60 *Harvard Law Review* 370 (1947).

24. Karl M. Llewellyn, "Remarks on the Theory of Appellate Decision and the Rules or Canons about How Statutes Are to Be Construed," 3 *Vanderbilt Law Review* 395, 401 (1950).

25. General Accounting Office, *Principles of Federal Appropriations Law* 2–59 (1991).

26. *Id.* at 2–60.

27. *Id.*

28. William N. Eskridge, *Dynamic Statutory Interpretation* 16 (1994).

29. Frank Easterbrook, "The Role of Original Intent in Statutory Construction," 11 *Harvard Journal of Law and Public Policy* 61 (1988).

30. Thomas W. Merrill, "Textualism and the Future of the *Chevron* Doctrine," 72 *Washington University Law Quarterly* 351, 353 (1994).

31. John F. Manning, "What Divides Textualists from Purposivists?," 106 *Columbia Law Review* 70, 98 (2006).

32. *Id.* at 70, 107.

33. Daniel A. Farber & Philip P. Frickey, "Practical Reason and the First Amendment," 34 *UCLA Law Review* 1615, 1636 (1987).

34. I *Holmes-Laski Letters* 249 (M. Howe ed. 1953).

35. Martin Redish, "Federal Common Law and American Political Theory: A Response to Professor Weinberg," 83 *Northwestern University Law Review* 853, 857 (1989).

36. Martin Shapiro, *The Supreme Court and Administrative Agencies* 19–29 (1968).

37. "Statutory Interpretation" *supra* note 22 at 800, 811.

38. T. Alexander Aleinikoff, "Updating Statutory Interpretation," 87 *Michigan Law Review* 20, 21 (1988).

39. *Judging under Uncertainty, supra* note 2 at 42.

40. Nicholas S. Zeppos, "The Use of Authority in Statutory Interpretation," 70 *Texas Law Review* 1073, 1100 (1992).

41. Daniel A. Farber & Brett H. McDonnell, " 'Is There a Text in this Class?': The Conflict Between Textualism and Antitrust," 14 *Journal of Contemporary Legal Issues* 619, 620 (2005).

42. William Baxter, "Separation of Powers, Prosecutorial Discretion, and the 'Common Law' Nature of Antitrust Law," 60 *Texas Law Review* 661, 663 (1982).

43. Martin H. Redish, "Federal Common Law and American Political Theory: A Response to Professor Weinberg," 83 *Northwestern University Law Review* 853, 857 (1989).

44. Robert E. Scott & George G. Triantis, "Anticipating Litigation in Contract Design," 115 *Yale Law Journal* 814 (2006).

45. *Delegating Powers, supra* note 9, at 37.

46. *Deliberate Discretion?, supra* note 6, at 9.

47. *See* Einer Elhauge, *Statutory Default Rules* (forthcoming Harvard University Press).

48. United States v. Jin Fuey Moy, 241 U.S. 394, 402 (1916).

49. Beth M. Henschen, "Judicial Use of Legislative History and Intent in Statutory Interpretation," 10 *Legislative Studies Quarterly* 353 (1985).

50. Victoria F. Nourse & Jane S. Schacter, "The Politics of Legislative Drafting: A Congressional Case Study," 77 *New York University Law Review* 575, 617 (2002).

51. William N. Eskridge, Jr. & John Ferejohn, *Superstatutes: The New American Constitutionalism* (forthcoming).

52. Nicholas Quinn Rosenkranz, "Federal Rules of Statutory Interpretation," 115 *Harvard Law Review* 2085, 2086 (2002).

53. *Id.* at 2088.

54. Morell E. Mullins, Sr., "Tools, Not Rules: The Heuristic Nature of Statutory Interpretation," 30 *Journal of Legislation* 1, 4 (2003).

55. Jeffrey A. Segal & Harold J. Spaeth, *The Supreme Court and the Attitudinal Model* (1993); Jeffrey A. Segal & Harold J. Spaeth, *The Supreme Court and the Attitudinal Model Revisited* (2002).

56. *The Supreme Court and the Attitudinal Model, supra* note 55, at 259–260.

57. Lawrence S. Wrightsman, *Judicial Decision Making: Is Psychology Relevant?* 55–56 (1999).

58. Mark J. Richards & Herbert M. Kritzer, "Jurisprudential Regimes in Supreme Court Decision Making," 96 *American Political Science Review* 305 (2002).

59. Frank Cross, *Decision Making in the U.S. Courts of Appeals* 178–200 (2007).

60. *See* Lawrence Baum, *Judges and Their Audiences* (2006).

61. *See* Terri Jennings Peretti, *In Defense of a Political Court* (1999).

62. *See Legislative Deferrals, supra* note 16.

63. Adrian Vermeule, *Judging under Uncertainty: An Institutional Theory of Legal Interpretation* 77 (2006).

64. Adrian Vermeule, "Interpretive Choice," 75 *New York University Law Review* 74, 77 (2000).

NOTES TO CHAPTER 2

1. John F. Manning, "Textualism and the Equity of the Statute," 101 *Columbia Law Review* 1, 18 (2001).

2. John F. Manning, "Textualism and Legislative Intent," 91 *Virginia Law Review* 419, 420 (2005).

3. Morell E. Mullins, Sr., "Tools, Not Rules: The Heuristic Nature of Statutory Interpretation," 30 *Journal of Legislation* 1, 22 (2003).

4. H. G. Gadamer, *Truth and Method* (J. Weinsheimer & D. Marshall trans., 2nd rev. ed. 1989).

5. H. Hart & A. Sacks, *The Legal Process: Basic Problems in the Making and Application of Law* 1188 (W. Eskridge & P. Frickey eds. 1994).

6. Towne v. Eisner, 245 U.S. 418, 425 (1918).

7. Antonin Scalia, *A Matter of Interpretation* 23 (1997).

8. Caleb Nelson, "What Is Textualism?," 91 *Virginia Law Review* 347, 409 (2005).

9. In Erickson, 815 F.2d 1090, 1092 (7th Cir. 1987).

10. Business Electronics Corp. v. Sharp Electronics Corp, 485 U.S. 717, 731 (1988).

11. Nix v. Heddon, 149 U.S. 304 (1893).

12. MCI v. AT&T, 512 U.S. 218, 228 n.3 (1994).

13. *See* Rickie Sonpal, "Old Dictionaries and New Textualists," 71 *Fordham Law Review* 2177, 2180 (2003).

14. *Id.* at 2212–2213.

15. Ellen P. Aprill, "The Law of the Word: Dictionary Shopping in the Supreme Court," 30 *Arizona State Law Journal* 275 (1998).

16. Jason Weinstein, "Against Dictionaries: Using Analogical Reasoning to Achieve a More Restrained Textualism," 38 *University of Michigan Journal of Law Reform* 649, 657 (2005).

17. *See*, e.g., Buckhannon Board 7 Care Home, Inc. v. West Virginia Department of Health & Human Resources, 532 U.S. 598 (2001).

18. Aharon Barak, *Purposive Interpretation in the Law* 14 (2005).

19. James J. Brudney, "Congressional Commentary on Judicial Interpretations of Statutes: Idle Chatter or Telling Response?," 93 *Michigan Law Review* 1, 5 (1994).

20. United Savings Association v. Timbers of Inwood Forest Associations, 484 U.S. 365, 371 (1988).

21. Antonin Scalia, *A Matter of Interpretation* 17 (1997).

22. Kenneth A. Shepsle, "Congress Is a 'They,' Not an 'It': Legislative Intent as Oxymoron," 12 *International Review of Law and Economics* 239 (1992).

23. Frank H. Easterbrook, "Statutes' Domains," 50 *University of Chicago Law Review* 548 (1983).

24. Kenneth J. Arrow, *Social Choice and Individual Values* (2nd ed. 1963).

25. Daniel A. Faber & Philip P. Frickey, *Law and Public Choice* 48 (1991).

26. Richard H. Pildes & Elizabeth S. Anderson, "Slinging Arrows at Democracy: Social Choice Theory, Value Pluralism, and Democratic Politics," 90 *Columbia Law Review* 2121, 2141 (1990).

27. William H. Riker, *Liberalism Against Populism* 128 (1982).

28. Richard G. Niemi, "Majority Decision Making with Partial Unidimensionality," 63 *American Political Science Review* 488, 493 (1969).

29. Keith T. Poole & Howard Rosenthal, *Congress: A Political-Economic History of Roll Call Voting* 32 (1997).

30. Arthur Lupia & Matthew D. McCubbins, "Lost in Translation: Social Choice Theory Is Misapplied Against Legislative Intent," 14 *Journal of Contemporary Legal Issues* 585 (2005).

31. *See* "What Is Textualism?," *supra* note 8, at 370–371.

32. Herrmann v. Cencom Cable Associations, 978 F.2d 978, 982 (7th Cir. 1992).

33. 128 Congressional Record 16918–19 (1982).

34. Max Radin, "A Short Way with Statutes," 56 *Harvard Law Review* 388, 407 (1942).

35. John F. Manning, "What Divides Textualists from Purposivists?," 106 *Cloumbia Law Review* 97–98.

36. *A Matter of Interpretation*, *supra* note 7, at 17.

37. Nicholas Quinn Rosenkranz, "Federal Rules of Statutory Interpretation," 115 *Harvard Law Review* 2085, 2136 (2002).

38. Bank One Chicago, N.A. v. Midwest Bank & Trust Co., 516 U.S. 264, 276–277 (1996) (Stevens, J., concurring).

39. Lawrence M. Solan, "Private Language, Public Laws: The Central Role of Legislative Intent in Statutory Interpretation," 93 *Georgetown Law Journal*, 446–447 (2005).

40. John F. Manning, "Putting Legislative History to a Vote: A Response to Professor Siegel," 53 *Vanderbilt Law Review* 1529, 1534 (2000).

41. John F. Manning, "Competing Presumptions about Statutory Coherence," 74 *Fordham Law Review* 9, 2047–2048 (2006).

42. Jonathan R. Siegel, "The Use of Legislative History in a System of Separated Powers," 53 *Vanderbilt Law Review* 1457, 1474 (2000).

43. Abby Wright, "For All Intents and Purposes: What Collective Intention Tells Us about Congress and Statutory Interpretation," 154 *University of Pennsylvania Law Review* 983, 1011 (2006).

44. *See* David C. Jenson, "From Deference to Restraint: Using the *Chevron* Framework to Evaluate Presidential Signing Statements," 91 *Minnesota Law Review* 1908, 1918–1919 (2007).

45. Chevron U.S.A., Inc. v. Natural Resources Defense Council, 467 U.S. 837 (1984).

46. Thomas Merrill, "Textualism and the Future of the *Chevron* Doctrine," 72 *Washington University Law Quarterly* 351, 372 (1994).

47. Frank H. Easterbrook, "Text, History, and Structure in Statutory Interpretation," 17 *Harvard Journal of Law and Public Policy* 61, 68 (1994).

48. *See* Frank H. Easterbrook, "Judicial Discretion in Statutory Interpretation," 57 *Oklahoma Law Review* 1, 3–5 (2004).

49. *Id.* at 7.

50. Adrian Vermeule, *Judging under Uncertainty* (2005).

51. William N. Eskridge, Jr., "No Frills Textualism," 119 *Harvard Law Review* 2041, 206–265 (2006).

52. John F. Manning, "Putting Legislative History to a Vote: A Response to Professor Siegel," 53 *Vanderbilt Law Review* 1529, 1531 (2000).

53. *See,* e.g., Mathew McCubbins, *et al.*, "Congressional Oversight Overlooked: Police Patrols versus Fire Alarms," 28 *American Political Science Review* 165 (1984).

54. John Manning, "Textualism as a Nondelegation Doctrine," 97 *Columbia Law Review* 731 (1997).

55. William Eskridge, *Dynamic Statutory Interpretation* 34 (1994).

56. "What Is Textualism?," *supra* note 8, at 372.

57. Schwegmann Brothers v. Calvert Distillers Corp., 341 U.S. 384, 395 (1951) (Jackson, J. concurring).

58. Lon L. Fuller, *The Morality of Law* (rev. ed. 1969).

59. "What Is Textualism?," *supra* note 8, at 367.

60. Richard A. Posner, *The Problems of Jurisprudence* 48 (1990).

61. Beth M. Henschen, "Judicial Use of Legislative History and Intent in Statutory Interpretation," 10 *Legislative Studies Quarterly* 353, 355 (1985).

62. Abner J. Mikva, "A Reply to Judge Starr's Observations," 1987 *Duke Law Journal* 380, 381.

63. Joseph A. Grundfest & A. C. Pritchard, "Statutes with Multiple Personality Disorders: The Value of Ambiguity in Statutory Design and Interpretation," 54 *Stanford Law Review* 627–629 (2002).

64. Daniel A. Farber, "Do Theories of Statutory Interpretation Matter? A Case Study," 94 *Northwestern University Law Review* 1409, 1411 (2000).

65. Wis. Pub. Intervenor v. Mortier, 501 U.S. 597, 610 n.4 (1991).

66. United States v. Fisher 6 U.S. (2 Cranch) 358, 396 (1805).

67. United States v. American Trucking Associations, 310 U.S. 534, 543–544 (1940).

68. William D. Popkin, *Statutes in Court: The History and Theory of Statutory Interpretation* (1999).

69. Antonin Scalia, *A Matter of Interpretation* 36 (1997).

70. *See*, e.g., "What Is Textualism?," *supra* note 8, at 374–403.

71. Terri Jennings Peretti, *In Defense of a Political Court* (1999).

72. *Id.* at 243.

73. Richard A. Posner, *Overcoming Law* 131 (1995).

74. Felix Frankfurter, "Some Reflections on the Reading of Statutes," 2 *The Record of the Association of the Bar of the City of New York* 213–214 (1947).

75. Jules L. Coleman & Brian Leiter, "Determinacy, Objectivity, and Authority," 12 *University of Pennsylvania Law Review* 549, 571 (1993).

76. "Text, History, and Structure in Statutory Interpretation," *supra* note 47, at 68.

77. "What Divides Textualists from Purposivists?," *supra* note 35, at 106.

78. William T. Mayton, "Law among the Pleonasms: The Futility and Aconstitutionality of Legislative History in Statutory Interpretation," 41 *Emory Law Journal* 113, 123 (1992).

79. James J. Brudney & Corey Ditslear, "Canons of Construction and the Elusive Quest for Neutral Reasoning," 58 *Vanderbilt Law Review* 1, 104 (2005) (citing the Civil Rights Act, ERISA, and the ADEA as examples of such statutes).

80. Clark v. Martinez, 125 S.Ct. 716, 727 (2005).

81. *See* Jonathan R. Siegel, "The Polymorphic Principle and the Judicial Role in Statutory Interpretation," 84 *Texas Law Review* 339 (2005).

82. Robinson v. Shell Oil Co., 519 U.S. 337 (1997).

83. James J. Brudney & Corey Ditslear, "Canons of Construction and the Elusive Quest for Neutral Reasoning," 58 *Vanderbilt Law Review* 1, 97 n.395 (2005).

84. Asgrow Seed Co. v. Winterboer, 513 U.S. 179, 192 (1995).

85. W. David Slawson, "Legislative History and the Need to Bring Statutory Interpretation under the Rule of Law," 44 *Stanford Law Review* 383, 400 (1992).

86. George L. Priest & Benjamin Klein, "The Selection of Disputes for Litigation," 13 *Journal of Legal Studies* 1 (1984).

87. Daniel Kessler, *et al.*, "Explaining Deviations from the Fifty-Percent Rule: A Multimodal Approach to the Selection of Cases for Litigation," 25 *Journal of Legal Studies* 233 (1996).

88. Richard J. Pierce, "The Supreme Court's New Hypertextualism: An Invitation to Cacophony and Incoherence in the Administrative State," 95 *Columbia Law Review* 749, 752 (1995).

89. Frederick Schauer, "Statutory Construction and the Coordinating Function of Plain Meaning," 1990 *Supreme Court Review* 231.

90. "Do Theories of Statutory Interpretation Matter?" *supra* note 64.

91. Charles Jordan Tabb & Robert M. Lawless, "Commas, Gerunds, and Conjunctions," 42 *Syracuse Law Review* 823, 880–881 (1991).

92. Bradley C. Karkkainen, " 'Plain Meaning' ": Justice Scalia's Jurisprudence of Strict Statutory Construction," 17 *Harvard Journal of Law and Public Policy* 401, 474 (1994).

93. "Statutes' Domains," *supra* note 23, at 543.

94. Richard A. Posner, "The Institutional Dimension of Statutory and Constitutional Interpretation," 101 *Michigan Law Review* 952, 955 (2003).

95. "Congressional Commentary on Judicial Interpretations of Statutes," *supra* note 19, at 29.

96. Aharon Barak, *Purposive Interpretation in Law* 282 (2005).

97. *See* Jason Czarnezki & Sara Benesh, "The Ideology of Legal Interpretation" [presented at the 2006 annual meeting of the Midwest Political Science Association].

98. John F. Manning, "What Divides Textualists from Purposivists?," 106 *Columbia Law Review* 70, 87–88 (2006).

99. Morell E. Mullins, Sr., "Tools, Not Rules: The Heuristic Nature of Statutory Interpretation," 30 *Journal of Legislation* 1, 6 (2003).

100. *Judging under Uncertainty*, *supra* note 50 at 82.

NOTES TO CHAPTER 3

1. James Willard Hurst, *The Growth of American Law: The Law Makers* 187–189 (1950).

2. John F. Manning, "Textualism and Legislative Intent," 91 *Virginia Law Review* 419 (2005).

3. T. Grey, "The Constitution as Scripture," 37 *Stanford Law Review* 1 (1984).

4. Aharon Barak, *Purposive Interpretation in Law* 19 (2005).

5. Schooner Paulina's Cargo v. United States, II U.S. (7 Cranch) 52, 60 (1812).

6. United States v. American Trucking Association, 310 U.S. 534, 543 (1940).

7. *See* Henry M. Hart, Jr. & Albert M. Sacks, *The Legal Process: Basic Problems in the Making and Application of Law* (1958).

8. Universal Camera Corp. v. NLRB, 340 U.S. 474, 489 (1951).

9. St. Francis College v. Al-Khazraji, 481 U.S. 604 (1987).

10. Commissioner v. Acker, 361 U.S. 87, 95 (1958).

11. *Purposive Interpretation in Law*, *supra* note 4.

12. *Id.* at 88.

13. Richard A. Posner, "Statutory Interpretation—in the Classroom and in the Courtroom," 50 *University of Chicago Law Review* 800, 817 (1983).

14. Richard A. Posner, *The Problems of Jurisprudence* 276 (1990).

15. *Id.* at 277.

16. 475 U.S. 355 (1986).

17. *Purposive Interpretation in Law*, *supra* note 4, at 117.

18. Rodriguez v. United States, 480 U.S. 522, 525–526 (1987) (per curiam).

19. Frank H. Easterbrook, "The Role of Original Intent in Statutory Construction," 11 *Harvard Journal of Law and Public Policy* 59, 61 (1988).

20. Universal Camera Corp. v. NLRB, 340 U.S. 474 (1951).

21. Brown Shoe v. United States, 370 U.S. 294, 320 (1961).

22. Kent Greenawalt, *Statutory Interpretation: 20 Questions* 195 (1999).

23. General Accounting Office, *Principles of Federal Appropriations Law* 2–65 (1991).

24. Commissioner of Internal Revenue v. Acker, 361 U.S. 87, 94 (1959) (Frankfurter, Clark and Harlan dissenting).

25. William S. Blatt, "Interpretive Communities: The Missing Element in Statutory Interpretation," 95 *Northwestern University Law Review* 629, 669 (2001).

26. James M. Landis, "A Note on Statutory Interpretation," 43 *Harvard Law Review* 886, 889 (1930).

27. William L. Eskridge, *et al.*, *Legislation and Statutory Interpretation* 303 (2000).

28. North Haven Board of Education v. Bell, 456 U.S. 512, 530 (1982).

29. Red Lion Broadcasting Co. v. FCC, 395 U.S. 367, 380–381 (1969).

30. James J. Brudney, "Congressional Commentary on Judicial Interpretations of Statutes: Idle Chatter or Telling Response?," 94 *Michigan Law Review* 56 (1994).

31. *Id.* at 57.

32. Stephen Breyer, "On the Uses of Legislative History in Interpreting Statutes," 65 *Southern California Law Review* 845, 859–860 (1992).

33. "Congressional Commentary on Judicial Interpretations of Statutes," *supra* note 30, at 74.

34. "On the Uses of Legislative History in Interpreting Statutes," *supra* note 32, at 866.

35. Bank One Chicago v. Midwest Bank & Trust Co., 516 U.S. 264, 280 (Scalia, J. concurring).

36. Einer Elhauge, *Statutory Default Rules* (forthcoming).

37. Jeremy Waldron, "Legislators' Intentions and Unintentional Legislation," in *Essays in Legal Philosophy* 329 (A. Marmor ed. 1995).

38. "Congressional Commentary on Judicial Interpretations of Statutes," *supra* note 30 at 1.

39. *Id.* at 32.

40. Thomas Gilligan & Keith Krehbiel, "Organization of Informative Committees by a Rational Legislature," 34 *American Journal of Political Science* 531 (1990), Keith Krehbiel, *Information and Legislative Organization* 95 (1991).

41. Charles Tiefer, "The Reconceptualization of Legislative History in the Supreme Court," 2000 *Wisconsin Law Review* 205, 266–267.

42. Einer R. Elhauge, "Does Interest Group Theory Justify More Intrusive Judicial Review?," 101 *Yale Law Journal* 31, 42 (1991).

43. William T. Bianco, "Reliable Source or Usual Suspects? Cue-Taking, Information Transmission, and Legislative Committees," 59 *Journal of Politics* 913 (1997).

44. *Id.* at 916.

45. Vijay Krishna & John Morgan, "Asymmetric Information and Legislative Rules: Some Amendments," 95 *American Political Science Review* 435 (2001).

46. Frank H. Easterbrook, "Statutes' Domains," 50 *University of Chicago Law Review* 548 (1983).

47. Michael D. Gilbert, "Single Subject Rules and the Legislative Process," 67 *University of Pittsburgh Law Review* 803, 855 (2006).

48. Patricia M. Wald, "The Sizzling Sleeper: The Use of Legislative History in Construing Statutes in the 1988–89 Term of the United States Supreme Court," 39 *American University Law Review* 277, 285 (1990).

49. Caleb Nelson, "What Is Textualism?," 91 *Virginia Law Review* 347, 362–363 (2005).

50. W. David Slawson, "Legislative History and the Need to Bring Statutory Interpretation under the Rule of Law," 44 *Stanford Law Review* 398 (1992).

51. *Statutory Interpretation: 20 Questions, supra* note 22, at 182.

52. "What Is Textualism?," *supra* note 49, at 363.

53. Adrian Vermeule, "Legislative History and the Limits of Judicial Competence: The Untold Story of Holy Trinity Church," 50 *Stanford Law Review* 1833, 1937 (1998).

54. Adrian Vermeule, *Judging under Uncertainty: An Institutional Theory of Legal Interpretation* 112 (2006).

55. "Congressional Commentary on Judicial Interpretation of Statutes," *supra* note 30, at 70.

56. Antonin Scalia, *A Matter of Interpretation* 32 (1997).

57. "Legislative History and the Need to Bring Statutory Interpretation under the Rule of Law," *supra* note 50, at 403.

58. Pierce v. Underwood, 487 U.S. 552, 567 (1988).

59. Joan Biskupic, "Scalia Takes a Narrow View in Seeking Congress' Will," 48 *Congressional Quarterly* 913, 917 (1990).

60. "Congressional Commentary on Judicial Interpretations of Statutes," *supra* note 30, at 28 n.105.

61. *A Matter of Interpretation, supra* note 56, at 34.

62. "Congressional Commentary on Judicial Interpretation of Statutes," *supra* note 30, at 27.

63. *Id.* at 28 (emphasis added).

64. *Id.* at 53.

65. "Legislative History and the Need to Bring Statutory Interpretation under the Rule of Law," *supra* note 50, at 405.

66. *A Matter of Interpretation, supra* note 56, at 35.

67. Adrian Vermeule, *Judging under Uncertainty: An Institutional Theory of Legal Interpretation* 2–3 (2006).

68. William N. Eskridge, *Dynamic Statutory Interpretation* 22 (1994).

69. Nicholas S. Zeppos, "Legislative History and the Interpretation of Statutes: Toward a Fact-Finding Model of Statutory Interpretation," 76 *Virginia Law Review* 1295, 1323 (1990).

70. Maxwell O. Chibundu, "Structure and Structuralism in the Interpretation of Statutes," 62 *University of Cincinnati Law Review* 1439, 1526 (1994).

71. Nicholas S. Zeppos, "The Use of Authority in Statutory Interpretation: An Empirical Analysis," 70 *Texas Law Review* 1073, 1093 (1992).

72. Abner S. Greene, "The Missing Step of Textualism," 74 *Fordham Law Review* 1913, 1928 (2006).

73. Richard A. Posner, *The Federal Courts: Crisis and Reform* 287 (1985).

74. John F. Manning, "Competing Presumptions about Statutory Coherence," 74 *Fordham Law Review* 2009, 2028 (2006).

75. Martin H. Redish & Theodore T. Chung, "Democratic Theory and the Legislative Process: Mourning the Death of Originalism in Statutory Interpretation," 68 *Tulane Law Review* 865 (1994).

76. Frank H. Easterbrook, "The Role of Original Intent in Statutory Construction," 11 *Harvard Journal of Law and Public Policy* 59, 62 (1988).

77. Frank H. Easterbrook, "Legal Interpretation and the Power of the Judiciary," 7 *Harvard Journal of Law and Public Policy* 87, 92 (1984).

78. Jonathan Molot, "Ambivalence about Formalism," 93 *Virginia Law Review* 1, 9 (2007).

79. "Democratic Theory and the Legislative Process," *supra* note 75, at 803, 819.

80. Michael E. Solimine & James L. Walker, "The Next Word: Congressional Response to Supreme Court Statutory Decisions," 65 *Temple Law Review* 425 (1992).

81. William N. Eskridge, Jr., "Overriding Supreme Court Statutory Interpretation Decisions," 101 *Yale Law Journal* 331, 350 tbl.8 (1991).

82. Daniel J. Bussel, "Textualism's Failures: A Study of Overruled Bankruptcy Decisions," 53 *Vanderbilt Law Review* 887 (2000).

83. West Virginia Univ. Hospitals, Inc. v. Casey, 499 U.S. 83, 113–115 (Stevens, J., dissenting).

84. "The Next Word," *supra* note 80, at 381.

85. Joseph Ignagni, *et al.*, "Statutory Construction and Congressional Response," 26 *American Politics Research Quarterly* 459, 473–477 (1998).

NOTES TO CHAPTER 4

1. Varsity Corp. v. Howe, 516 U.S. 489, 511 (1996).

2. Hammoc v. Loan and Trust Co., 105 U.S. (15 Otto) 77, 84–85 (1881).

3. Arcadia v. Ohio Power Co., 498 U.S. 73, 78 (1990).

4. Richard A. Posner, "Statutory Interpretation—in the Classroom and in the Courtroom," 50 *University of Chicago Law Review* 800, 812 (1983).

5. William N. Eskridge, Jr., Philip P. Frickey, & Elizabeth Garrett, *Cases and Materials on Legislation* 852 (3rd ed. 2001).

6. EEOC v. Arabian American Oil Co., 499 U.S. 244, 248 (1991).

7. Landsgraf v. USI Film Products, 511 U.S. 244 (1994).

8. Jonathan R. Siegel, "The Polymorphic Principle and the Judicial Role in Statutory Interpretation," 84 *Texas Law Review* 339, 381 (2005).

9. Gregory v. Ashcroft, 501 U.S. 452 (1991).

10. Karl L. Llewellyn, "Remarks on the Theory of Appellate Decisions and the Rules or Canons about How Statutes Are to Be Construed," 3 *Vanderbilt Law Review* 395 (1950).

11. *Id.* at 399.

12. Cass R. Sunstein, "Interpreting Statutes in the Regulatory State," 103 *Harvard Law Review* 405, 452 (1989).

13. David Shapiro, "Continuity and Change in Statutory Interpretation," 67 *New York University Law Review* 921, 925 (1992).

14. Jonathan R. Macey & Geoffrey P. Miller, "The Canons of Construction and Judicial Preferences," 45 *Vanderbilt Law Review* 647, 660 (1992).

15. James J. Brudney & Corey Ditslear, "Canons of Construction and the Elusive Quest for Neutral Reasoning," 58 *Vanderbilt Law Review* 1, 7 (2005).

16. William F. Eskridge, *Dynamic Statutory Interpretation* 280 (1994).

17. Richard A. Posner, "Statutory Interpretation—in the Classroom and in the Courtroom," 50 *University of Chicago Law Review* 800, 816–817 (1983).

18. Richard A. Posner, *The Problems of Jurisprudence* 279 (1990).

19. Cass R. Sunstein, "Interpreting Statutes in the Regulatory State," 103 *Harvard Law Review* 405, 455 (1989).

20. *The Problems of Jurisprudence, supra* note 18, at 281.

21. Barnhart v. Peabody Coal Co., 537 U.S. 149 (2003).

22. Max Radin, "Statutory Interpretation," 43 *Harvard Law Review* 863, 73 (1930).

23. Commonwealth v. Kelly, 58 N.E. 691 (Mass. 1900).

24. William N. Eskridge, *et al.*, *Legislation and Statutory Interpretation* 253–268 (2000).

25. Richard A. Posner, "Statutory Interpretation—in the Classroom and in the Courtroom," 50 *University of Chicago Law Review* 800, 806 (1983).

26. Matthew D. McCubbins & Daniel B. Rodriguez, "Canonical Construction and Statutory Revisionism: The Strange Case of the Appropriations Canon," 14 *Journal of Contemporary Legal Issues* 669, 671 (2005).

27. James J. Brudney & Corey Ditslear, "Canons of Construction and the Elusive Quest for Neutral Reasoning," 58 *Vanderbilt Law Review* 1, 13 (2005).

28. Antonin Scalia, *A Matter of Interpretation* 28 (1997).

29. Philip P. Frickey, "Interpretive-Regime Change," 38 *Loyola of Los Angeles Law Review* 1971, 1989 (2005).

30. "Continuity and Change in Statutory Interpretation," *supra* note 13, at 949.

31. Antonin Scalia, "Assorted Canards of Legal Analysis," 40 *Case Western Reserve Law Review* 581, 586 (1989–1990).

32. United States v. Gradwell, 243 U.S. 476, 485 (1917).

33. Rice v. Santa Fe Elevator Corp., 331 U.S. 218, 230 (1947).

34. Ernest A. Young, "The Rehnquist Court's Two Federalisms," 83 *Texas Law Review* 1 (2004).

35. Calvin Massey, "Federalism and the Rehnquist Court," 53 *Hastings Law Journal* 431, 508 (2002).

36. Michael Herz, "The Rehnquist Court and Administrative Law," 99 *Northwestern University Law Review* 297, 355 (2004).

37. *A Matter of Interpretation, supra* note 28, at 28–29.

38. William N. Eskridge, Jr. & Philip P. Frickey, "The Supreme Court, 1993 Term Foreword: Law as Equilibrium," 108 *Harvard Law Review* 26, 66–69 (1994).

39. "Canons of Construction and the Elusive Quest for Neutral Reasoning," *supra* note 27, at 73.

40. John F. Manning, "Legal Realism and the Canons' Revival," 5 *The Green Bag* 283, 285 (2002).

41. Victoria F. Nourse & Jane S. Schacter, "The Politics of Legislative Drafting: A Congressional Case Study," 77 *New York University Law Review* 575, 600–604 (2002).

42. Abner Mikva, "Reading and Writing Statutes," 48 *University of Pittsburgh Law Review* 627, 629 (1987).

43. Patricia M. Wald, "Some Observations on the Use of Legislative History in the 1981 Supreme Court Term," 68 *Iowa Law Review* 195, 208 (1983).

44. *A Matter of Interpretation, supra* note 28, at 28.

45. 491 U.S. 223 (1989).

46. William F. Eskridge, *Dynamic Statutory Interpretation* 283–285 (1994).

47. Blatchford v. Native Village of Noatak, 501 U.S. 775, 785 (1991).

48. Kent Greenawalt, *Statutory Interpretation: 20 Questions* 209–210 (1999).

49. "Canons of Construction and the Elusive Quest for Neutral Reasoning," *supra* note 27, at 42–43.

50. *Id.*

51. *Id.* at 6.

52. Richard A. Posner, "Statutory Interpretation—in the Classroom and in the Courtroom," 50 *University of Chicago Law Review* 800, 816 (1983).

53. "Canons of Construction and the Elusive Quest for Neutral Reasoning," *supra* note 27, at 6.

54. *Id.* at 97.

55. The Federalist no. 78 at 439 (Alexander Hamilton) (Isaac Kramnick ed. 1987).

NOTES TO CHAPTER 5

1. The Federalist no. 78 (Alexander Hamilton).

2. Richard A. Posner, *The Problems of Jurisprudence* 73–74 (1990).

3. Richard A. Posner, *Overcoming Law* 252 (1995).

4. *See The Problems of Jurisprudence, supra* note 2 at 291.

5. Richard A. Posner, *Law, Pragmatism, and Democracy* 3 (2003).

6. *Id.* at 12.

7. Daniel A. Farber, "The Inevitability of Practical Reason: Statutes, Formalism, and the Rule of Law," 45 *Vanderbilt Law Review* 533, 539 (1992).

8. Thomas W. Merrill, "Textualism and the Future of the *Chevron* Doctrine," 72 *Washington University Law Quarterly* 351 (1994).

9. Cass R. Sunstein, "Interpreting Statutes in the Regulatory State," 103 *Harvard Law Review* 405, 435 (1989).

10. Richard Rorty, "The Banality of Pragmatism," 63 *Southern California Law Review* 1811 (1990).

11. *See The Problems of Jurisprudence, supra* note 2, at 73.

12. *See* William D. Popkin, *Statutes in Court: The History and Theory of Statutory Interpretation* 210 (1999).

13. Karl N. Llewellyn, "Remarks on the Theory of Appellate Decision and the Rules or Canons about How Statutes Are to Be Construed," 3 *Vanderbilt Law Review* 395, 398–401 (1950).

14. *See* "Interpreting Statutes in the Regulatory State," *supra* note 9, at 479–480.

15. Cass R. Sunstein & Adrian Vermeule, "Interpretation and Institutions," 101 *Michigan Law Review* 885 (2003).

16. *Id.* at 893.

17. Walter B. Kennedy, "Pragmatism as a Philosophy of Law," 9 *Marquette Law Review*, 63, 72–73 (1924–1925).

18. Jeffrey A. Segal, "Separation-of-Powers Games in the Positive Theory of Congress and Courts," 91 *American Political Science Review* 28, 42 (1997).

19. Daniel J. Bussell, "Textualism's Failures: A Study of Overruled Bankruptcy Decisions," 53 *Vanderbilt Law Review* 887 (2000).

20. National Society of Professional Engineers v. United States, 435 U.S. 679, 687–688 (1978).

21. Lon L. Fuller, "The Case of the Speluncean Explorers," 62 *Harvard Law Review* 616, 625 (1949).

22. William T. Mayton, "Law among the Pleonasms: The Futility and Aconstitutionality of Legislative History in Statutory Interpretation," 41 *Emory Law Journal* 113, 128 (1992).

23. Veronica Dougherty, "Absurdity and the Limits of Literalism: Defining the Absurd Result Principle in Statutory Interpretation," 44 *American University Law Review* 127, 133 (1994).

24. W. David Slawson, "Legislative History and the Need to Bring Statutory Interpretation under the Rule of Law," 44 *Stanford Law Review* 383 (1992).

25. John F. Manning, "The Absurdity Doctrine," 116 *Harvard Law Review* 2387, 2390 (2003).

26. Adrian Vermeule, *Judging under Uncertainty: An Institutional Theory of Legal Interpretation* 57 (2006).

27. Cass R. Sunstein, "Law and Administration after *Chevron*," 90 *Columbia Law Review* 2071, 2087-2088 (1990).

28. *Judging under Uncertainty, supra* note 26, at 209.

29. William N. Eskridge, Jr., "Dynamic Interpretation of Economic Regulatory Legislation (Countervailing Duty Law)," 21 *Law and Policy in International Business* 663 (1990).

30. Jonathan Molot, "Ambivalence about Formalism," 93 *Virginia Law Review* 1, 39 (2007).

31. *Judging under Uncertainty, supra* note 26, at 225.

32. United States v. Mead Corp., 533 U.S. 218 (2001).

33. Matthew C. Stephenson, "The Strategic Substitution Effect: Textual Plausibility, Procedural Formality, and Judicial Review of Agency Statutory Interpretations," 120 *Harvard Law Review* 528 (2006).

34. Cass R. Sunstein, "Is Tobacco a Drug? Administrative Agencies as Common Law Courts," 47 *Duke Law Journal* 1013, 1060 (1998).

35. "Ambivalence about Formalism," *supra* note 30, at 93.

36. Conroy v. Aniskoff, 507 U.S. 511, 517 n.12 (1993).

37. *Law, Pragmatism, and Democracy, supra* note 5, at 94.

38. Martin H. Redish & Theodore T. Chung, "Democratic Theory and the Legislative Process: Mourning the Death of Originalism in Statutory Interpretation," 68 *Tulane Law Review* 803, 807 (1994).

39. Aharon Barak, *Purposive Interpretation in Law* 289 (2005).

40. "Democratic Theory and the Legislative Process," *supra* note 38.

41. *The Problems of Jurisprudence, supra* note 2, at 251.

42. *Law, Pragmatism, and Democracy, supra* note 5, at 351.

43. Daniel A. Farber, "Statutory Interpretation and Legislative Supremacy," 78 *Georgetown Law Journal* 281, 291 (1989).

44. *Purposive Interpretation in Law, supra* note 39, at 289-290.

45. William F. Eskridge, *Dynamic Statutory Interpretation* 65 (1994).

46. *Id.* at 69.

47. *Id.* at 287-288.

48. "The Inevitability of Practical Reason," *supra* note 7, at 539.

49. Stephen F. Ross, "The Location and Limits of Dynamic Statutory Interpretation in Modern Judicial Reasoning," 6 *Issues in Legal Scholarship* 1, 3 (2002).

50. *Law, Pragmatism, and Democracy, supra* note 5, at 96.

51. J. Braxton Craven, Jr., "Paean to Pragmatism," 50 *North Carolina Law Review* 977 (1972).

52. *Id.*

53. "Interpreting Statutes in the Regulatory State," *supra* note 9, at 440.

54. Richard A. Posner, "Pragmatic Adjudication," in *The Revival of Pragmatism: New Essays on Social Thought, Law, and Culture* 244 (Morris Dickstein ed. 1998).

55. Cass R. Sunstein & Adrian Vermeule, "Interpretation and Institutions," 101 *Michigan Law Review* 885, 892 (2003).

56. Donald Horowitz, *The Courts and Social Policy* (1977).

57. Stephen Breyer, "Judicial Review of Questions of Law and Policy," 38 *Administrative Law Review* 363, 389 (1986).

58. R. Shep Melnick, *Regulation and the Courts* (1983).

59. *Judging under Uncertainty*, *supra* note 26, at 38.

60. Richard A. Posner, *The Problematics of Moral and Legal Theory* 257–58 (1999).

61. *Judging under Uncertainty*, *supra* note 26, at 84.

62. Stefanie A. Lindquist & Frank B. Cross, "Empirically Testing Dworkin's Chain Novel Theory: Studying the Path of Precedent," 80 *New York University Law Review* 1156 (2005).

63. Adrian Vermeule, "The Judiciary Is a 'They,' Not an 'It': Interpretive Theory and the Fallacy of Division," 14 *Journal of Contemporary Legal Issues* 549 (2005).

64. Malcolm M. Feeley & Edward L. Rubin, *Judicial Policy Making and the Modern State* (1998).

65. *Id.* at 13.

66. *Id.*

67. *Id.* at 16.

68. *Id.* at 19.

69. Cass R. Sunstein & Adrian Vermeule, "Interpretation and Institutions," 101 *Michigan Law Review* 885, 893 (2003).

70. John Braithwaite, *Meta Risk Management and Responsive Governance*, at 3 [presented at the Risk Regulation, Accountability, and Development Conference] (June 2003).

71. Frank H. Easterbrook, "Foreword: The Court and the Economic System," 98 *Harvard Law Review* 4, 15 (1984).

72. Barnard Grofman, "Public Choice, Civic Republicanism, and American Politics: Perspectives of a 'Reasonable Choice' Modeler," 71 *Texas Law Review* 1541, 1543 (1993).

73. Herbert Jacob, *Law and Politics in the United States* 154–155 (2nd ed. 2005).

74. Frank B. Cross, "The Judiciary and Public Choice," 50 *Hastings Law Journal* 355 (1999).

75. Frank B. Cross, "In Praise of Irrational Plaintiffs," 86 *Cornell Law Review* 1 (2000).

76. *Judging under Uncertainty*, *supra* note 26, at 111.

77. Antonin Scalia, *A Matter of Interpretation* 13 (1997).

78. Paul G. Mahoney, "The Common Law and Economic Growth: Hayek Might Be Right," 30 *Journal of Legal Studies* 503 (2001).

79. Rafael La Porta, *et al*, "The Quality of Government," 15 *Journal of Law, Economics, and Organization* 222 (1999); Rafael La Porta, *et al.*, "Law and Finance," 106 *Journal of Political Economy* 1113 (1998); Rafael La Porta *et al.*, "Legal Determinants of External Finance," 52 *Journal of Finance* 1131 (1997). Similar results were reported by Ross Levine, "Law, Finance, and Economic Growth," 8 *Journal of Financial Intermediation* 8 (1999).

80. Rafael La Porta, *et al.*, "The Guarantees of Freedom," *NBER Working Paper* 8759 (February 2002).

81. *See* Thorsten Beck, Asli Demirguc-Kunt, & Ross Levine, "Law and Firms' Access to Finance," 7 *American Law and Economics Review* 211 (2005) (finding that common law systems better enable national financial systems); Thorsten Beck, Asli Demirguc-Kunt & Ross Levine, "Law and Finance: Why Does Legal Origin Matter," 31 *Journal of Comparative Economics* 653 (2003); Ross Levine, "The Legal Environment, Banks, and Long-Run Economic Growth," 30 *Journal of Money, Credit, and Banking* 596 (1998).

82. Daron Acemoglu & Simon Johnson, "Unbundling Institutions," *Journal of Political Economy* 113 (2005).

83. *See* Michael Smith, "Deterrence and Origin of Legal System: Evidence from 1950–1999," 7 *American Law and Economics Review* 350 (2005).

84. *Law, Pragmatism, and Democracy, supra* note 5, at 95.

85. John F. Manning, "Textualism and the Equity of the Statute," 101 *Columbia Law Review* 1, 85–102 (2001).

86. The Federalist No. 78 at 470 (Alexander Hamilton).

87. David F. Epstein, *Political Theory of the Federalist* 188–190 (1984).

88. *A Matter of Interpretation, supra* note 77, at 13.

89. *Judging under Uncertainty, supra* note 26, at 18.

90. 1 F. A. Hayek, *The Fatal Conceit: The Errors of Socialism* 37 (W.W. Bartley III ed. 1988).

91. *See, e.g.*, Friedrich A. von Hayek, "Economics and Knowledge," 4 *Economica* 33 (1937); Friedrich A. von Hayek, "The Use of Knowledge in Society," 35 *American Economics Review* 519 (1945).

92. Robert Boyd & Peter J. Richerson, "Why Does Culture Increase Human Adaptability," 16 *Ethology and Sociobiology* 125 (1995).

93. Peter J. Richerson & Robert Boyd, *Not by Genes Alone* (2005).

94. *Id.* at 67.

95. *Id.* at 113–115.

96. *Id.* at 69.

97. *See id.* at 116.

98. *Id.* at 125.

99. See Joseph Henrich and Richard McElreath, "The Evolution of Cultural Evolution," 12 *Evolutionary Anthropology* 123, 128 (2003).

100. Frank H. Easterbrook, "Stability and Reliability in Judicial Decisions," 73 *Cornell Law Review* 422, 423 (1988).

101. Friedrich A. von Hayek, *Rules and Order* 119 (1973).

102. *Statutes in Court, supra* note 12, at 208.

NOTES TO CHAPTER 6

1. Jane S. Schacter, "The Confounding Common Law Originalism in Recent Supreme Court Statutory Interpretation: Implications for the Legislative History Debate and Beyond," 51 *Stanford Law Review* 1, 2 (1998).

2. Jonathan Molot, "Ambivalence about Formalism," 93 *Virginia Law Review* 1, 11 (2007).

3. Some of this historical research is reviewed in Jonathan T. Molot, "The Rise and Fall of Textualism," 106 *Columbia Law Review* 1 (2006).

4. William F. Eskridge, *Dynamic Statutory Interpretation* 208 (1994).

5. *See* Wisconsin Public Intervenor v. Mortier, 501 U.S. 597 (1991).

6. John Choon Yoo, "Marshall's Plan: The Early Supreme Court and Statutory Interpretation," 101 *Yale Law Journal* 1607 (1992).

7. *Id.* at 1630.

8. *Id.* at 1617.

9. *Id.* at 1630.

10. William T. Mayton, "Law among the Pleonasms: The Futility and Aconstitutionality of Legislative History in Statutory Interpretation," 42 *Emory Law Journal* 113, 117 (1992).

11. Aldridge v. Williams, 44 U.S. (3 How.) 268, 269 (1844).

12. William D. Popkin, *Statutes in Court: The History and Theory of Statutory Interpretation* 118 (1999).

13. Charles Tiefer, "The Reconceptualization of Legislative History in the Supreme Court," 2000 *Wisconsin Law Review* 205, 214–215.

14. Jorge L. Carro & Andrew R. Brann, "The U.S. Supreme Court and the Use of Legislative Histories: A Statistical Analysis," 22 *Jurimetrics: The Journal of Law, Science, and Technology* 294 (1982).

15. *Id.* at 147.

16. *See* "Looking it Up: Dictionaries and Statutory Interpretation," 107 *Harvard Law Review* 1437, 1438 (1994).

17. Rickie Sonpal, "Old Dictionaries and New Textualists," 71 *Fordham Law Review* 2177, 2191 (2003).

18. John F. Manning, "Competing Presumptions about Statutory Coherence," 74 *Fordham Law Review* 2009, 2035 n. 116 (2006).

19. "The Rise and Fall of Textualism," *supra* note 3.

20. Charles Tiefer, "The Reconceptualization of Legislative History in the Supreme Court," 2000 *Wisconsin Law Review* 205.

21. Beth M. Henschen, "Judicial Use of Legislative History and Intent in Statutory Interpretation," 10 *Legislative Studies Quarterly* 353, 361 (1985).

22. Patricia M. Wald, "The Sizzling Sleeper: The Use of Legislative History in Construing Statutes in the 1988–89 Term of the United States Supreme Court," 39 *American University Law Review* 277 (1990).

23. Thomas Merrill, "Textualism and the Future of the *Chevron* Doctrine," 72 *Washington University Law Quarterly* 351, 355 (1994).

24. "The Confounding Common Law Originalism in Recent Supreme Court Statutory Interpretation," *supra* note 1, at 5.

25. James J. Brudney & Corey Ditslear, "The Decline and Fall of Legislative History? Patterns of Supreme Court Reliance in the Burger and Rehnquist Eras," 89 *Judicature* 220 (2006).

26. *See* Nicholas S. Zeppos, "The Use of Authority in Statutory Interpretation: An Empirical Analysis," 70 *Texas Law Review* 1073 (1992).

27. *Id.* at 1093.

28. *Id.* at 1097.

29. *Id.* at 1103.

30. Nancy Staudt, *et al.*, "Judging Statutes: Interpretive Regimes," 38 *Loyola of Los Angeles Law Review* 1909 (2005).

31. William F. Eskridge, *Dynamic Statutory Interpretation* 227 (1994).

32. Philip P. Frickey, "Interpretive-Regime Change," 38 *Loyola of Los Angeles Law Review* 1971, 1973–1974 (2005).

33. *See* Gregory E. Maggs, "The Secret Decline of Legislative History: Has Someone Heard a Voice Crying in the Wilderness?," 1994 *Public Interest Law Review* 57.

34. *See* Antonin Scalia, *A Matter of Interpretation* (1997).

35. *See*, e.g., Babbitt v. Sweet Home Chapter of Communities for a Greater Oregon, 515 U.S. 687, 703 (Scalia & Thomas, J. J. & Rehnquist, C. J., dissenting).

36. *See*, e.g., Bradley C. Karkkainen, " 'Plain Meaning': Justice Scalia's Jurisprudence of Strict Statutory Construction," 17 *Harvard Journal of Law and Public Policy* 401 (1994); Nicholas S. Zeppos, "Justice Scalia's Textualism: The 'New' New Legal Process," 12 *Cardozo Law Review* 1597 (1991).

37. " 'Plain Meaning,' " *supra* note 36, at 449.

38. "Justice Scalia's Textualism," *supra* note 36, at 1634.

39. Blanchard v. Bergeron, 489 U.S. 87, 100 (1989).

40. Antonin Scalia, "Judicial Deference to Administrative Interpretations of Law," 1989 *Duke Law Journal* 511, 515.

41. *A Matter of Interpretation*, *supra* note 34, at 17–18.

42. Stephen Breyer, "On the Use of Legislative History in Interpreting Statutes," 65 *Southern California Law Review* 845, 858 (1992).

43. *Id.* at 866.

44. Charles Tiefer, "The Reconceptualization of Legislative History in the Supreme Court," 2000 *Wisconsin Law Review* 205, 272.

45. John Manning, "Competing Presumptions about Statutory Coherence," 74 *Fordham Law Review* 2009 (2006).

46. W. Va. Univ. Hosps., Inc. v. Casey, 499 U.S. 83, 115 (1991) (Stevens, J., dissenting).

47. Barnhart v. Sigmon Coal Co., 534 U.S. 438, 472 (2002) (Stevens, J., dissenting).

48. Bank One of America National Trust & Savings Association v. 203 North LaSalle St. Partnership.

49. U.S. v. Thompson/Ctr. Arms Co. 504 U.S. 505, 517 (1992).

50. "The Reconceptualization of Legislative History in the Supreme Court," *supra* note 44, at 221 n.90.

51. Public Citizen v. United States Dep't of Justice, 491 U.S. 440, 473 (concurring) (1989).

52. *See*, e.g., Gustafson v. Alloyd Co., 513 U.S. 561 (1995).

53. "The Secret Decline of Legislative History," *supra* note 33, at 57.

54. U.S. v. Thompson/Arms Center Arms Company, 504 U.S. 505, 521 (1992).

55. R. Randall Kelso, "Statutory Interpretation Doctrine on the Modern Supreme Court and Four Doctrinal Approaches to Judicial Decision-Making," 25 *Pepperdine Law Review* 37, 39 (1997).

56. "The Confounding Common Law Originalism," *supra* note 1, at 17.

57. James J. Brudney & Corey Ditslear, "Canons of Construction and the Elusive Quest for Neutral Reasoning," 58 *Vanderbilt Law Review* 1, 45 (2005).

58. William S. Blatt, "Interpretive Communities: The Missing Element in Statutory Interpretation," 95 *Northwestern University Law Review* 629, 660 (2001).

59. *See* Geoffrey P. Miller, "Pragmatics and the Maxims of Interpretation," 1990 *Wisconsin Law Review* 1179.

60. "The U.S. Supreme Court and the Use of Legislative Histories," *supra* note 14, at 294, 304.

61. "Judging Statutes," *supra* note 30, at 1942.

62. *See* "Canons of Construction and the Elusive Quest for Neutral Reasoning," *supra* note 57, at 30.

63. "Judging Statutes," *supra* note 30, at 1935.

64. These numbers are much lower than found by Brudney & Ditslear's study of workplace law cases, "Canons of Construction and the Elusive Quest for Neutral Reasoning," *supra* note 57, at 34.

65. *Id.* at 45–50.

66. *Id.* at 50.

67. "Judging Statutes," *supra* note 30, at 1956–1957.

68. *Id.* at 1959.

69. "Textualism and the Future of the *Chevron* Doctrine," *supra* note 23, at 351.

70. *See*, e.g., Chickasaw Nation v. United States, 534 U.S. 84 (2001); Zedner v. United States, No. 05–5992 (June 5, 2006).

71. The score is simply the justice's mean use of that theory. For example, if a justice relied on legislative history in 60% of decisions but ignored legislative history in 40%, the justice's score would be 0.6 {1*.6 + 0*.4}. If a justice relied on legislative history 50% of the time, ignored legislative history 25% of the time, and affirmatively rejected reliance on legislative history 25% of the time, the justice's score would be 0.25 {1*.5 + 0*.25 + −1*.25}. Numbers can be greater than one, because a justice might refer to multiple aspects of legislative intent in an opinion.

72. These results are roughly consistent with the Brudney & Ditslear findings, though they had Stevens and Ginsburg as the justices who most frequently used legislative history. *See* "The Decline and Fall of Legislative History?" *supra* note 25, at 223.

73. This is confirmed by Michael H. Kolby, "The Supreme Court's Declining Reliance on Legislative History," 36 *Harvard Journal of Legislation* 395 n.100 (1999) (reporting that Scalia joined more than three opinions per year citing to legislative history between 1980 and 1998).

74. This association is briefly discussed in "The Decline and Fall of Legislative History?" *supra* note 25, at 225 (suggesting that in the workplace cases, the justices relied less on legislative history but did not replace it with other interpretive supports for their conclusion).

75. *Dynamic Statutory Interpretation*, *supra* note 4.

76. "The Use of Authority in Statutory Interpretation: An Empirical Analysis," *supra* note 26, at 1118.

77. *See*, e.g., Sutton v. United Air Lines, 527 U.S. 471 (1999).

78. "Canons of Construction," *supra* note 57, at 67.

79. "The Use of Authority in Statutory Interpretation: An Empirical Analysis," *supra* note 26, at 1135.

80. *See* Charles Tiefer, "The Reconceptualization of Legislative History in the Supreme Court," 2000 *Wisconsin Law Review* 205, 272 (contending that many justices take an "agnostic position" in the debate among theories of statutory interpretation).

81. Adrian Vermeule, *Judging under Uncertainty: An Institutional Theory of Legal Interpretation* 189 (2006).

82. *See*, e.g., Frederick Schauer, "Statutory Construction and the Coordinating Function of Plain Meaning," 1990 *Supreme Court Review* 231.

83. "Canons of Construction," *supra* note 57, at 52.

84. The research on workplace decisions found that use of canons was associated with close decisions. *See* "Canons of Construction," *supra* note 57, at 52–53. No such clear pattern appeared in this data.

NOTES TO CHAPTER 7

1. Jeffrey A. Segal & Harold J. Spaeth, *The Supreme Court and the Attitudinal Model* (1993).

2. *Id.* at 316.

3. *Id.* at 226–229.

4. Daniel R. Pinello, "Linking Party to Judicial Ideology in American Courts: A Meta-Analysis," 20 *Justice System Journal* 219 (1999).

5. Tracey E. George & Lee Epstein, "On the Nature of Supreme Court Decisionmaking," 86 *American Political Science Review* 323, 325 (1992).

6. Frank B. Cross, "Political Science and the New Legal Realism: A Case of Unfortunate Interdisciplinary Ignorance," 82 *Northwestern University Law Review* 251 (1997).

7. Patrick Wiseman, *Ethical Jurisprudence*, 40 *Loyola Law Review* 281, 288 n. 25 (1994).

8. James J. Brudney & Corey Ditslear, "Canons of Construction and the Elusive Quest for Neutral Reasoning," 58 *Vanderbilt Law Review* 1 (2005).

9. *Id.* at 103.

10. *Id.* at 104.

11. William N. Eskridge, Jr. & Philip P. Frickey, "Foreword: Law as Equilibrium," 108 *Harvard Law Review* 26, 77 (1994).

12. *See* Jeffrey A. Segal & Robert M. Howard, "An Original Look at Originalism," 36 *Law and Society Review* 113 (2002).

13. *See, e.g.,* Jeffrey A. Segal & Harold J. Spaeth, *The Supreme Court and the Attitudinal Model Revisited* 322 (2002).

14. Ward Farnsworth, "Signatures of Ideology: The Case of the Supreme Court's Criminal Docket," 104 *Michigan Law Review* 67 (2005).

15. The data for liberal votes in civil liberties cases comes from Lee Epstein *et al.*, *The Supreme Court Compendium: Data, Decisions, and Developments* 486–488 (3rd ed. 2003).

16. "Canons of Construction and the Elusive Quest for Neutral Reasoning," *supra* note 8, at 59.

17. Jeffrey A. Segal & Albert D. Cover, "Ideological Values and the Votes of U.S. Supreme Court Justices," 83 *American Political Science Review* 557 (1989).

18. Martin Redish & Theodore Chung, "Democratic Theory and the Legislative Process: Mourning the Death of Originalism in Statutory Interpretation," 68 *Tulane Law Review*, 803, 830 (1994).

19. *See* "Political Science and the New Legal Realism," *supra* note 6, at 284–289.

NOTES TO CHAPTER 8

1. Donald R. Songer & Reginald S. Sheehan, "Supreme Court Impact on Compliance and Outcomes: *Miranda* and *New York Times* in the United States Courts of Appeals," *Western Political Quarterly* 297 (1990).

2. *See*, e.g., Sara C. Benesh & Malia Reddick, "Overruled: An Event History Analysis of Lower Court Reaction to Supreme Court Alteration of Precedent," 64 *Journal of Policy* 534 (2002) (studying the *Miranda* opinion and the *New York Times* libel decision).

3. Donald R. Songer, "The Circuit Courts of Appeals," in *The American Courts: A Critical Assessment* 41 (John B. Gates & Charles A. Johnson eds. 1991).

4. Nalle v. C.I.R., 997 F.2d 1134 (1993).

5. American Trucking Association, Inc. v. Delaware River Joint Toll Bridge Commission, 458 F.3d 291, 298 (2006).

6. Minnesota Licensed Practical Nurses Association v. N.L.R.B., 406 F.3d 1020 (8th Cir. 2005).

7. Northwest Environmental Defense Center v. Bonneville Power Admin., 477 F.3d 668 (2007).

8. U.S. v. Contents of Accounts Nos. 3034504504 and 144-07143 at Merrill, Lynch, Pierce, Fenner and Smith, Inc., 971 F.2d 974, 982 (1992).

9. Phillips v. Pembroke Real Estate, Inc., 459 F.3d 128, 142 (2006).

10. Protection & Advocacy for Persons with Disabilities, Conn. v. Mental Health & Addiction Services, 448 F.3d 119 (2nd Cir. 2006).

11. Daniel M. Schneider, "Empirical Research on Judicial Reasoning: Statutory Interpretation in Federal Tax Cases," 31 *New Mexico Law Review* 325 (2001).

12. *See* Micheal W. Giles, *et al.*, "Picking Federal Judges: A Note on Policy and Partisan Selection Agendas," 54 *Political Research Quarterly* 623 (2001).

13. Charles Tiefer, "The Reconceptualization of Legislative History in the Supreme Court," 2000 *Wisconsin Law Review* 205, 221–232.

14. Thomas G. Hansford and James F. Spriggs, II, *The Politics of Precedent on the Supreme Court* 2–3 (2006).

15. Central Bank of Denver, N.A. v. First Interstate Bank of Denver, N.A., 511 U.S. 164 (1994).

16. Four-star citations may be negative in character; this is relatively uncommon and even in these cases they suggest that the decision was central to the outcome of the case, a measure of its importance.

17. I excluded "one-star" citations, because these are citations in an opinion that lack any textual exposition.

18. *See* Sara Benesh & Malia Reddick, "Overruled: An Event History Analysis of Lower Court Reaction to Supreme Court Alteration of Precedent," 64 *Journal of Policy* 534 (2002).

19. *See* Andrew F. Hanssen, "The Effect of Judicial Institutions on Uncertainty and the Rate of Litigation: The Election Versus Appointment of State Judges," 28 *Journal of Legal Studies* 205 (1999) (noting that "[m]odels of the litigation process suggest that litigation rates will be higher where uncertainty over court decisions is greater").

20. *See* Joseph A. Grundfest & A. C. Pritchard, "Statutes with Multiple Personality Disorders: The Value of Ambiguity in Statutory Design and Interpretation," 54

Stanford Law Review 627, 643 (2002) (noting that reliance on legislative history is criticized for increasing the "potential for confusion" in the law).

21. Conroy v. Aniskoff, 507 U.S. 511, 519 (Scalia, J., concurring).

22. Linda Greenhouse, "Precedent for Lower Courts, Tyrant or Teacher," *New York Times,* Jan. 29, 1988, at 12.

23. Lee Epstein & Thomas G. Walker, *Constitutional Law for a Changing America: Rights, Liberties, and Justice* 21 (1995).

24. Frank B. Cross, *Decision Making in the U.S. Courts of Appeals,* 11–38 (2007).

25. Cass R. Sinstein, *Are Judges Political?* 20–21 (2006).

26. Jason J. Czarnezki & William K. Ford, "The Phantom Philosophy? An Empirical Investigation of Legal Interpretation," 65 *Maryland Law Review* 841 (2006).

27. Joshua B. Fischman, "Decision-Making Under a Norm of Consensus: A Structural Analysis of Three-Judge Panels" [presented at the First Annual Conference on Empirical Legal Studies] (2006).

28. "The Phantom Philosophy?" *supra* note 26, at 845.

29. *See,* e.g., Cass R. Sunstein, "Must Formalism Be Defended Empirically?" 66 *University of Chicago Law Review* 636 (1999).

Index

absurdity doctrine, 108–10, 143–44, 174, 189

activism, 20; pragmatism and, 115, 117–19, 125, 132; Scalia on, 119, 140

Administrative Procedures Act, 4, 112

agency: administrative, committees *v.*, 38–39; *Chevron* deference to, 37–38, 110–12, 174–75, 177; delegation, 4–5, 8, 15–16, 38–40; textualism and, 33, 38–39

agents: courts as, 3, 18; "faithful," theory, 24; judges as, 3, 16, 19; principal/, relationship, 3, 11–12, 14, 16, 19, 76

Agriculture Committee, 39, 70

ambiguous language: CERCLA and, 62; delegation and, 5, 7, 44; substantive canons and, 88, 97; textualism on, 12, 26, 28–29, 36, 43–45, 47, 50–51, 54, 57, 81–82

amendments, 65, 67, 70, 73; Celler-Kefauver, 63–64; supermajority vote for, 107

amicus briefs, 120

antecedent, rule of last, 87

antitrust laws, 15, 27, 64, 81, 107–8, 122, 127

Armstrong, Senator, 33

Arrow, Kenneth, 31–32

attitudinal model, 160

authority, delegation of, 4, 8–9, 38–39, 67, 69, 71, 76, 94, 114, 116, 200

background delegation, 5–6, 8, 62; absurdity doctrine and, 109–10; ambiguous language and, 44;

legislative history, intentionalism and, 10, 78–79

bankruptcy decisions, overrides, 82, 106

Barak, Aharon: on legislative supremacy, 55; on pragmatism, 114, 117–18; on purposivism, 60–62, 118

Baum, Lawrence, 21

best policy, 2, 13, 15, 120–21

bicameralism/presentment argument, 12, 33, 37–38, 63

bills: advocates and opponents of, 65–66; amendments to, 65, 67, 70, 73; blocking, 77–78, 107; committee reports *v.*, reading, 75; floor debates on, 65; legislative history of, 75; parallel, passed by two houses of Congress, 70–71; passage of, 9, 44, 64–66, 70–71, 75–78

Blackmun, Harry, 98

Boyd, Robert, 129

Brennan, William J., 98, 142, 161

Breyer, Stephen, 143, 158; ideology and, 165, 168, 170, 173–75; on legislative history, 68, 74, 140–41; on legislative intent, 148–49, 151, 158; on pragmatism, 121, 158

Brown, Representative, 78

Brown Shoe, 63–64, 81

Brudney, James: on interpretive methods, 161–62, 166; on legislative history, 55, 74, 76; on textualism, 29, 145–46

Buckley, James, 75

Burger, Warren, 142

canons, 2, 9, 85–101; in circuit courts, 187, 190–91; common law and, 58, 86,

canons (*continued*)
88, 94–96; conservatism and, 87, 94,
96, 99, 162, 175; of constitutional
avoidance, 90; critique of, indeterminacy, 91–92, 97, 99; critique of, logical,
92–93; critiques of, answering, 96–99;
delegation and, 97–98, 100; federalism,
90, 95–96, 98; ideology and, 94, 96,
98–100, 163–64, 166–67, 175, 176;
labor laws and, 142, 147; legislative
drafting and, 87–88, 96–97, 99; of liberal interpretation of remedial statutes,
95–96; liberalism and, 96, 162; linguistic, 58, 85–88, 93, 98, 100–101, 190–91;
Posner on, 88, 92, 96, 100; pragmatic,
88; preemption, 95–96; research on,
143, 146–47, 149, 153–54, 156, 162;
study of, 99–100; substantive, 85–86,
88–90, 94–96, 97, 98, 100; temporal
instability of, 98–99; textualism and,
29, 85, 90
capital punishment, 47
case-by-case decisions, 45, 46; of
Easterbrook *v.* Posner, 53; pragmatism
and, 105, 109, 112; rule-following *v.*,
124; top-down determination through
rules *v.*, 5, 6, 112, 130
Celler-Kefauver Amendment, 63–64
Central Bank, 192–94
CERCLA (Comprehensive
Environmental Response
Compensation and Liability Act), 7,
29, 62, 73–74, 127
Chevron doctrine, 37–38, 110–12,
174–75, 177
Chung, Theodore T., 114
circuit courts, 180–91, 199; canons in,
187, 190–91; ideology in, 185–86,
194, 196, 198; legislative intent in,
183–87; pluralism of, 191; pragmatism
in, 189–90; textualism in, 187–89
circuit splits, 123
civil liberties cases, 164–65
Civil Rights Act, 6, 60, 78, 89
civil rights laws, 42, 89
Clayton Act, 7
Clinton, Bill, 186
closed rule voting, 70
collective intent, 32–33
committee hearings, 66, 80

committee reports: bills *v.*, reading, 75;
conference, 64, 70–71, 171; as
legislative history, 64–66, 67–68, 69,
71–72, 80, 171–73, 185–86; legislative
intent from, 77–79, 80
committees, congressional: administrative agency *v.*, 38–39; Agriculture, 39,
70; delegation and, 35, 36, 37, 39–40,
68; organization and structure of,
69–72, 75–77; oversight, 39; self-
delegation and, 36, 71
common law: canons and, 58, 86, 88,
94–96; economic value of, 126–27;
liabilities and, 7; pragmatism and, 107,
123, 126–28, 130, 133, 135; precedent,
126–27; rule of law *v.*, 42; statutory
law *v.*, 32
Comprehensive Environmental Response
Compensation and Liability Act
(CERCLA), 7, 29, 62, 73–74, 127
compromise, legislative, 32, 36, 43–44,
55, 61–63, 69, 95
conference committee reports, 64,
70–71, 171
congressional committees. *See* committees, congressional
congressional ideology, 69–70
consensus, judicial, 23, 155–57
consent by silence, 74–75
conservatism: canons and, 87, 94, 96,
99, 162, 175; ideology and, 20, 47, 53,
54–56, 79, 81, 83, 158, 160, 163–77,
185–86, 194, 196; originalism and,
56, 164; textualism and, 32, 67,
151, 161
Constitution: constitutional argument
for textualism, 33–40; delegation
and, 12; judicial power from, 1–4,
113–14
constitutional avoidance, canon of, 90
constitutionality, 89–90, 113
consumer protection laws, 53–54
context, textualism on, 26–28, 51, 74
contracts, 15–16, 31, 60, 85
courts: as agents, 3, 18; circuit, 180–91,
194, 196, 199; consensus, interpretive
methods and, 155–57; delegation to,
39–40, 109, 114, 116; lower federal,
180–200; mistrust of, 40; role of, 2–3,
9, 45

critical legal theory, 26
cultural evolution, 129–30
cycling, democratic and majoritarian, 31

delegation, 3–5; agency, 4–5, 8, 15–16, 38–40; ambiguous language and, 5, 7, 44; of authority, 4, 8–9, 38–39, 67, 69, 71, 76, 94, 114, 116, 200; background, 5–6, 8, 10, 43, 44, 62, 78–79, 109–10; canons and, 97–98, 100; committees and, 35, 36, 37, 39–40, 68; constitution and, 12; to courts, 39–40, 109, 114, 116; delegated power, 3–5; direct, 6–9; discretionary, 5, 11, 14, 17–19; intentionalism, legislative history and, 10, 68, 78–79; internal, 68, 78; of judicial power, 3–5; labor laws and, 7, 22; to legislative committee, disempowers president, 37; legislative history as, 67–69; legislative intent and, 10–11, 67, 68; pragmatism and, 9, 14–16, 107, 109–10; self-, 17, 35–36, 36, 40, 65, 67–68, 71; textualism and, 24; types of, 5–9
Dellmuth v. Muth, 98
Dewey, John, 102
dictionaries, 27–28, 34–36, 41, 54, 57, 136–37
dictionary shopping, 28, 54
direct delegation, 6–9
Dirksen, Senator, 78
discretion: with ideological judicial decision making, 19–22, 46–49, 53, 76–77, 82; pluralism and, 46–47; pragmatism and, 14–16, 102, 107, 118–19, 123
discretionary delegation, 5, 11, 14, 17–19
Ditslear, Corey, 146, 161–62, 166
Dworkin, Ronald, 115, 121–22
dynamic statutory interpretation, 66, 105–6, 111–13, 115; Eskridge on, 83, 103, 105, 117–18, 132; research on, 139; Segal on, 105–6

Easterbrook, Frank, 124; on domains of statutes, limiting, 55, 87, 163, 169; on legislative history, 30, 38; on legislative intent, 30, 43, 63; on pluralism, 81; on precedent, 130, 198; on textualism, 27, 33, 37–38, 53, 55

ejusdem generis ("of the same kind"), 87, 88, 190
Elhauge, Einer, 16
empirics, importance of, 22–23
Employment of the Handicapped Act, 98
environmental laws, 121
Epstein, David, 5
Erdman Act, 7
Eskridge, William: on agency, 110; on canons, 91, 96, 98; on Civil Rights Act, 78; on delegation, 4; on dynamic statutory interpretation, 83, 103, 105, 117–18, 132; on legislative history, 139, 152–53; on legislative intent, 11; on pluralism, 17; on textualism, 38, 82, 163–64
expressio unius est exclusio alterius ("the express mention of one thing excludes all others"), 87, 88, 92, 190
Exxon Corporation v. Hunt, 62

factions, 124
Farber, Daniel, 53
Federal Communications Commission, 8
federalism canons, 90, 95–96, 98
The Federalist, 127
federal judicial hierarchy, 181–83
Ferejohn, John, 17
filibusters, 77–78
floor debates, 65, 80
floor speakers, 77
formalism, 83, 104, 124, 127, 128, 130–31
Frankfurter, Felix: on intentionalism, 63; on purposivism, 60; on statutory text, 50
Frickey, Philip: on canons, 96; on textualism, 139, 163–64
Fuller, Lon, 41, 108
future circumstances, anticipation of, 5–6

Gadamer, Hanz-Georg, 26, 50, 93
General Accounting Office (GAO), 10
Ginsburg, Ruth Bader, 141, 158; ideology and, 165, 168, 169, 170, 173, 175
government: checks on power of, 48; scope of, limiting, 55
grammar rules, 35, 85, 86–87, 88, 93

grave doubt, about constitutionality, 89–90
group decision making, 31–33
Grundfest, Joseph A., 44

Hamilton, Alexander, 100, 103, 127
Hand, Learned, 10, 27, 61
Hart, A., 26
Hart, H. L. A., 6
Hart, H. M, 60, 136
Hayek, Friedrich, 123, 128–31
Helms, Jesse, 74
hermeneutics, 26, 50
Holmes, Oliver Wendell: on ambiguous language, 26; on pluralism, 17; on pragmatism, 13, 102–3
Horowitz, Donald, 121
House of Representatives: ideological differences between Supreme Court and, 83; pivotal voters in, 78
Hunt, 63

ideological judicial decision making, 140, 160–61; discretion with, 19–22, 46–49, 53, 76–77, 82; Posner on, 49, 55, 80; rule of law and, 21, 48, 49
ideological preferences, 48, 54, 83, 106
ideology, 159–79; canons and, 94, 96, 98–100, 163–64, 166–67, 175, 176; in circuit courts, 185–86, 194, 196, 198; congressional, 69–70; conscious v. subconscious, 21; faithless, 3; of interpretive methods, 158, 163–79; legislative history and, 79–84, 159, 169–72, 177, 178; legislative intent and, 79–81, 169–70, 176, 196; liberalism v. conservatism and, 20, 47, 53, 54–56, 79, 81, 83, 158, 160, 163–77, 185–86, 194, 196; plain meaning and, 164–66, 169, 179; pragmatism and, 115, 118, 124, 158, 173–74, 176; research on, 161–62; Supreme Court and, 20–21; textualism and, 47–56, 79–83, 159, 164–68, 176, 178–79
ideology of interpretation, 163–64; testing, 164–75
imaginative reconstruction, 10, 61
intent: collective, 32–33; objectified, 29–30
intentionalism, 59–64; with contracts, 31, 60; delegation, legislative history and,

10, 68, 78–79; legislative history and, 59–66, 69; pragmatism and, 116; purposivism v., 60–63; specific v. general, 63; statutory enactment process and, 61; textualism and, 28, 42, 63. *See also* legislative intent
interest groups, 124
internal delegation, 68, 78
Internal Revenue Code, 139, 145–48
interpretation: laws v., 34; liberal, of remedial statutes, canon of, 95–96; meaning of, 9, 50–52. *See also* statutory interpretation
interpretive methods: Brudney on, 161–62, 166; comprehensive analysis of, 175–77; court consensus and, 155–57; ideology of, 158, 163–79; interaction of, 152–55; justices' use of, 148–52; in lower federal courts, 181–82; positive and negative citations with, 193–98, 199
interpretive pluralism, 17–19

Jackson, Judge, 40–41
James, William, 102
JCS (judicial common space) scores, 185–86
Johnson, Lyndon, 78
judges: as agents, 3, 16, 19; errors of, 19, 23; mistrust/trust of, 19, 115–16, 132; as pragmatic partners, 14; as superlegislators, 48. *See also specific individuals*
judicial aptitude, 77, 93
judicial common space (JCS) scores, 185–86
judicial decision making, 128–31. *See also* ideological judicial decision making
judicial lawmaking, 112, 117
judicial power: from Constitution, 1–4, 113–14; delegation of, 3–5; pragmatism and, 112–19, 132
judicial practice, research on, 135–39
justices, 134–58; interpretive methods, use of, 148–52; research on judicial practice, 135–39; views of current, expressed, 139–42. *See also specific individuals*

Kennedy, Anthony: ideology and, 165, 168, 170, 173, 175, 177; on legislative history, 141–42

knowability, 11
Krehbiel, Keith, 69

labor laws, 7, 22, 142, 147
Landis, James, 65
LaPorta, Rafael, 126
laws: antitrust, 15, 27, 64, 81, 107–8, 122, 127; civil rights, 42, 89; consumer protection, 53–54; environmental, 121; extrinsic sources in statutory text as source of, 36; extrinsic sources in text as source of, 36; hypothetical, banning vehicles, 26; interpretation *v.*, 34; labor, 7, 22, 142, 147; neutral, 53, 77; securities, 80, 192; statutory, 32; workplace, 146. *See also* bills; common law; rule of law; statutes
legal pragmatism, 103–5
Legal Process school, 109, 136
legal realists, 91, 99, 160, 162, 198
legislating, policymaking as, 49
legislative compromise, 32, 36, 43–44, 55, 61–63, 69, 95
legislative drafting, 15, 35, 44–45, 63–65, 68, 76; canons and, 87–88, 96–97, 99
legislative history, 2, 58–84; of bills, 75; Breyer on, 68, 74, 140–41; of CERCLA, 7; committee reports as, 64–66, 67–68, 69, 71–72, 80, 171–73, 185–86; conference committee reports as, 64, 70–71, 171; as delegation, 67–69; errors from, 79; ideology and, 79–84, 159, 169–72, 177, 178; intentionalism and, 59–66, 69; intentionalism, delegation and, 10, 68, 78–79; Kennedy on, 141–42; legislative intent and, 22, 32, 67, 74, 77, 79, 84; legislative purpose and, 60, 69; lower federal courts and, 181–87, 189–91, 197–98; manipulation/manufacturing of, 72–74, 77, 79–81, 84; pluralism and, 17–18, 19; post-enactment, 66–67; purposivism and, 62–64, 68; reliability of, 72–79, 84; research on, 135–39, 144–46, 148–49, 152–54, 156–58; Scalia on, 68, 75, 77, 91, 135, 138, 140, 142, 149, 182–83, 185, 187, 197–98; self-delegation and, 35–36, 40, 65, 67–68, 71; sources of, 64–66, 68, 80, 171–73; sponsor statements as, 66, 72, 171, 172; state statutes and, 68; textualism *v.*, 25,
27, 30, 33–36, 38–43, 54–57, 58–59, 67, 69, 73–74, 134; tools and standards of, 64–67; validity of, 69–72
legislative intent, 2, 9, 10–11; Breyer on, 148–49, 151, 158; in circuit courts, 183–87; from committee reports, 77–79, 80; delegation and, 10–11, 67, 68; Easterbrook on, 30, 43, 63; ideology and, 79–81, 169–70, 176, 196; legislative history and, 22, 32, 67, 77, 79, 84; legislative supremacy and, 55; public choice rejection of, 30–33; research on, 136–38, 143–45, 148–54; textualism *v.*, 12–13, 22, 25, 29–30, 43; votes and, 156–57
legislative, meaning of, 9
legislative pivot points, 77–78
legislative process: improving, 109; logrolling in, 71–72, 78; structural biases of, 107; textualism on, 32–33, 43–45, 55–56; votes in, 64. *See also* legislative drafting
legislative purpose, 46, 117; legislative history and, 60, 69; pragmatism and, 117–18, 125
legislative supremacy, 3, 12, 16, 18, 55
legislatures, national *v.* state, 19
lenity, rule of, 85, 88–89, 95, 97, 147, 163–64, 166
liabilities, 7–8, 28
liberal interpretation of remedial statutes, canon of, 95–96
liberalism: canons and, 96, 162; ideology and, 20, 47, 53, 54–56, 79, 81, 83, 158, 160, 163–77, 185–86, 194, 196
liberal statutory decisions and legislature, 105–6
libertarians, 87, 89
linguistic canons, 58, 85–88, 93, 98, 100–101, 190–91
Llewellyn, Karl: on canons, 91, 97, 99–100, 162; on pragmatism, 104
logrolling, 71–72, 78
Lopez-de-Silanes, Florencio, 126
lower federal courts, 180–200; future research on, 198–99; interpretive methods in, 181–82; legislative history and, 181–87, 189–91, 197–98; precedent and, 181–82, 191–98, 199; textualism and, 187–90, 192, 195–99. *See also* circuit courts

Madison, James, 6
Mahoney, Paul G., 126
Manning, John: on canons, 97; on congressional oversight committees, 39; on legislative history, 34, 35–36, 38–40; on rule of law statutory text, 11–12; on Stevens, 141; on textualism, 24, 50, 80, 109, 127, 137
Mansfield, Senator, 78
Marshall, John: on *Dellmuth v. Muth*, 98; on intentionalism, 59; on legislative history, 135–36, 142; on legislative intent, 10; on pluralism, 46
McCulloch, Representative, 78
mens rea, 95
Merrill, Thomas, 37, 104
Metaphysical Club, 102–3
Mikva, Abner, 44, 97
Minnesota, 19
Molot, Jonathan, 134
morality, pragmatism and, 121

National Environmental Protection Act, 198
negligence, 42
neutral law, 53, 77
Norris-LaGuardia Act, 7
noscitur a sociis ("known by its associates"), 87, 88, 166, 190

objectified intent, 29–30
Occupational Safety and Health Act, 62
O'Connor, Sandra Day: on canons, 147; ideology and, 165, 166, 168, 170, 173, 175, 177; on legislative history, 142
O'Halloran, Sharyn, 5
ordinary judging, 46, 104, 126, 131
ordinary meaning, 53, 156
originalism, 56, 164
overrides/overrulings, 19, 33; bankruptcy decisions, 82, 106; federal, of states, 90, 95–98; textualism and, 82–83, 106, 192

Peretti, Terri Jennings, 48–49
Pierce, Richard, 8
pivot points, legislative, 77–78
plain meaning, of statutory text, 25–29, 50, 52, 82, 104, 139; ideology and, 164–66, 169, 179; plain statement *v.*, 90; whole act rule and, 143, 144, 146

plain statement, 90
pluralism, 182; of circuit courts, 191; discretion and, 46–47; Easterbrook on, 81; indeterminacy and, 46, 104; interpretive, 17–19; legislative history and, 17–18, 19; legislative supremacy and, 18; pragmatism and, 104; research on, 136, 157–58, 177; as self-delegation, 17; textualism *v.*, 45–47, 81
polymorphic principle, unitary *v.*, 51
Posner, Richard: on canons, 88, 91, 92, 96, 100; on formalism, 104, 127; on future circumstances, 6; on ideological judicial decision making, 49, 55, 80; on jury selection statute, 61; on negligence, 42; on pragmatism, 14, 53, 103–4, 112–13, 115, 117–19, 121–22, 124
post-enactment legislative history, 66–67
practical reasoning, 103, 104, 121, 183
pragmatic canon, 88
pragmatism, 13–16, 102–33; absurdity doctrine, 108–10, 143–44, 174, 189; activism and, 115, 117–19, 125, 132; best policy and, 2, 13, 15, 120–21; case-by-case decisions and, 105, 109, 112; case for, 106–8; *Chevron* doctrine, 37–38, 110–12, 174–75, 177; in circuit courts, 189–90; common law and, 107, 123, 126–28, 130, 133, 135; delegation and, 9, 14–16, 107, 109–10; discretion and, 14–16, 102, 107, 118–19, 123; formalism and, 104, 124, 127, 128, 130–31; ideology and, 115, 118, 124, 158, 173–74, 176; judicial power and, 112–19, 132; legal, 103–5; morality and, 121; nautical metaphor for, 14–15; partnership and, 14–15; Posner on, 14, 53, 103–4, 112–13, 115, 117–19, 121–22, 124; of pragmatism, 119–26; precedent and, 119, 122–25, 130, 133; public choice and, 33; purposivism and, 115, 117–18; research on, 143–44, 147–49, 151–54, 156–58; societal outcomes/consequences and, 106–7, 116, 121–22; statutory text and, 13, 15; textualism and, 107, 109–11, 129–31, 132, 195–97
precedent, 21; common law, 126–27; costs *v.* benefits of, 74; lower federal

courts and, 181–82, 191–98, 199; pragmatism and, 119, 122–25, 130, 133;
Supreme Court, effect of, 191–98, 199
preemption canon, 95–96
preference elicitation, 16–17
preferences: ideological, 48, 54, 83, 106;
pivotal voters', 78; public choice and,
31–32
presentment/bicameralism argument, 12,
33, 37–38, 63
president: delegation to legislative committee disempowers, 37; ideological
preferences of, 48; presentment and,
33; signing statements by, 37; veto by,
37
Priest/Klein hypothesis, 52
principal/agent relationship, 3, 11–12,
14, 16, 19, 76
prison reform litigation, 123–24
Pritchard, A. C., 44
Private Securities Litigation Reform Act,
7–8
public choice, 30–33, 44
public interest, 8
punctuation rules, 86
purposivism, 18, 29, 47, 56; intentionalism v., 60–63; legislative history and,
62–64, 68; pragmatism and, 115,
117–18; research on, 136

Radin, Max, 33, 92
Raz, Joseph, 59
Redish, Martin, 15, 114
regulatory capture theory, 39
Rehnquist Court: decisions by, 23, 134,
138, 146, 158; on legislative history,
182, 185, 187
Rehnquist, William: as conservative, 158;
ideology and, 161, 165, 168, 169, 170,
173–75, 177; views of, 142
rent-seeking, 124–25, 132
restraint, judicial, 47
Richerson, Peter J., 129
Rorty, Richard, 104
Rosenkranz, Nicholas, 18
ruleness, 40, 42
rule of law: canons and, 89; common law
v., 42; ideological judicial decision
making and, 21, 48, 49; statutory text,
11–13; textualism, argument for, 40–43

rules: clear statement, 98; of grammar,
35, 85, 86–87, 88, 93; of last
antecedent, 87; of lenity, 85, 88–89,
95, 97, 147, 163–64, 166; of punctuation, 86; top-down determination,
case-by-case decisions v., 5, 6, 112,
130; top-down v. bottom up, 129;
whole act, 51, 143, 144, 146, 162

Sacks, A.: on language as social institution, 26; Legal Process school and,
136; on purposivism, 60
SARA (Superfund Amendments and
Reauthorization Act), 7
Scalia, Antonin: on activism, 119, 140;
on canons, 86, 94–96; on common law,
42, 126–28; on consent by silence,
74–75; as conservative, 56, 158; ideology and, 165, 168, 169, 170, 173–75,
177; on legislative history, 68, 75, 77,
91, 135, 138, 140, 142, 149, 182–83,
185, 187, 197–98; on pluralism, 17–18,
47; on textualism, 26–27, 29, 32–33,
34, 36, 52, 55–56, 137, 140, 148–50,
158, 189
Schacter, Jane S., 137, 142
scienter, 8, 31
search and seizure decisions, 182
Securities Exchange Act, 192
securities law opinions, 80, 192
Segal, Jeff: on dynamic statutory interpretation, 105–6; on ideological judicial decision making, 20–21, 160
selection effect, 83
self-delegation: congressional committees and, 36, 71; legislative history
and, 35–36, 40, 65, 67–68, 71; pluralism as, 17
Senate: committee chairman in, 78; pivotal voters in, 78
Shepsle, Kenneth, 30
Sherman Antitrust Act, 15, 27, 107–8,
122
Shleifer, Andrei, 126
signing statements, 37
silence: consent by, 74–75; statutory, 28
Slawson, W. David, 109
"social choice" critique, 10
societal changes: factual settings, litigation and, 8; statutes and, 6, 123

societal outcomes/consequences: of different interpretations, 13; pragmatism and, 106–7, 116, 121–22; precedent and, 191–92

Souter, David, 158; on canons, 147; ideology and, 165, 168, 170, 173, 175; views of, expressed, 141–42

Spaeth, Harold, 20–21, 160

special interests, 39

Specter, Senator, 75

Speedy Trial Act, 73

sponsor statements, 66, 72, 171, 172

stare decisis, 74

states: legislatures, national *v.*, 19; sovereign immunity, federal overrides of, 90, 95–98; statutes, legislative history and, 68

statutes: canon of liberal interpretation of remedial, 95–96; changing over time, 41; constitutionality of, 89–90, 113; domains of, limiting, 54–55, 87, 163, 169; enactment process, intentionalism and, 61; errors in, 37; extraterritorial effect of, 89; findings and purposes section of, 63; indefinite duration of, 122; invalidation of, 90; jury selection, 61; preambles of, 63; purpose of, textualism on, 27; retroactive effect of new, 89; societal changes and, 6, 123; state, legislative history and, 68; Superfund, 7; superstatutes, 17. *See also* bills

statutory interpretation: as delegated power, 3–5; dynamic, 66, 83, 103, 105–6, 111–13, 115, 117–18, 132, 139; empirical examination of, 142–48; federal judicial hierarchy and, 181–83; goal/purpose of, 1–2, 10, 18; hypothetical law banning vehicles with, 26. *See also* interpretive methods

statutory lacuna, 6

statutory law, 32

statutory silence, 28

statutory text: compromise and, 43–44; extrinsic sources in, as source of law, 36; manipulation of meaning and, 28, 34, 42, 54; meanings changing over time, 41; plain meaning of, 25–29, 50, 52, 82, 90, 104, 139, 143, 144, 146, 164–66, 169, 179; pragmatism and, 13, 15; rule of law, 11–13. *See also* ambiguous language

Stephenson, Matthew, 4, 5, 111

Stevens, John Paul, 141, 158; on *Dellmuth v. Muth*, 98; ideology and, 165, 168, 170, 173–75; interpretive theories and, 149–52; on purposivism, 60; on self-delegation, 35; views of, expressed, 141, 142

straw man, 40, 56, 58

strict constructionism, 26–27

subsequent legislative action, 66–67

substantive canons, 85–86, 88–90, 100; ambiguous language and, 88, 97; critiquing, 94–96, 98

Sunstein, Cass, 92, 105, 110–11

Superfund Amendments and Reauthorization Act (SARA), 7

Superfund statute, 7

supermajority vote, 33, 107

superstatutes, 17

Supremacy Clause, 95

Supreme Court: ideological differences between House of Representatives and, 83; ideology and, 20–21; lower federal courts and, 180–83, 185, 187, 189, 191–99; precedent, effect of, 191–98, 199. *See also specific cases/justices*

surplusage, 51, 65, 88

textualism, 2, 9, 24–57; agency and, 33, 38–39; on ambiguous language, 12, 26, 28–29, 36, 43–45, 47, 50–51, 54, 57, 81–82; canons and, 29, 85, 90; in circuit courts, 187–89; conservatism and, 32, 67, 151, 161; constitutional argument for, 33–40; on context, 26–28, 51, 74; delegation and, 24; dictionaries and, 27–28, 34–36, 41, 54, 57, 136–37; Eskridge on, 38, 82, 163–64; on extrinsic sources, 36; ideology and, 47–56, 79–83, 159, 164–68, 176, 178–79; indeterminacy within, 50–53; intentionalism and, 28, 42, 63; on legislative compromise, 62; legislative history *v.*, 25, 27, 30, 33–36, 38–43, 54–57, 58–59, 67, 69, 73–74, 134; legislative intent *v.*, 12–13, 22, 25, 29–30, 43; on legislative process, 32–33, 43–45, 55–56; lower federal courts and, 187–90, 192, 195–99; Manning on, 24, 50, 80, 109, 127,

137; meaning of, 25–30; overrides and, 82–83, 106, 192; pluralism *v.*, 45–47, 81; pragmatism and, 107, 109–11, 129–31, 132, 195–97; public choice and, 30–33, 44; research on, 135–37, 139, 143–46, 148–54, 156; rule of law argument for, 40–43; rule of law statutory text and, 11–12; Scalia on, 26–27, 29, 32–33, 34, 36, 52, 55–56, 137, 140, 148–50, 158, 189; strict constructionism *v.*, 26–27; Vermeule on, 38, 56–57, 82–83, 84. *See also* statutory text
Thomas, Clarence: on activism and pragmatism, 119; as conservative, 56, 158; ideology and, 165, 168, 170, 173–75, 177; on legislative history, 138, 142; on whole act rule, 51
Three Mile Island, 124

unitary principle, polymorphic *v.*, 51

Vermeule, Adrian, 155; on common law, 128; on empirics, 23; on legislative history, 73, 77; on pragmatism, 15, 110–11, 121, 124, 130; on textualism, 38, 56–57, 82–83, 84

veto: by president, 37; supermajority vote overriding, 33
Vishny, Robert, 126
Vocabula manent, res fugiunt ("the words remain after the thing has vanished"), 41
votes: closed rule voting, 70; legislative intent and, 156–57; supermajority, 33, 107; trading, 71–72, 78

Wagner Act, 7
Wald, Patricia: on canons, 97; on legislative history, 72, 137
Waldron, Jeremy, 67, 69
Warren Court, 136
Warren, Earl, 63–64, 81
Westlaw Keynumber system, 184, 187–89, 192–93
White, Byron: on canons, 142; on legislative history, 135; on pluralism, 46, 47
whole act rule, 51, 143, 144, 146, 162
workplace law decisions, 146

Young, Ernie, 95

Zeppos, Nicholas, 138–39, 153

The authorized representative in the EU for product safety and compliance is:
Mare Nostrum Group
B.V Doelen 72
4831 GR Breda
The Netherlands

www.ingramcontent.com/pod-product-compliance
Lightning Source LLC
Chambersburg PA
CBHW021554210326
41599CB00010B/442